AVA'S MEN

The Private Life of Ava Gardner

JANE ELLEN WAYNE

SPHERE BOOKS LIMITED

A *Sphere* Book

First published in Great Britain by Robson Books Ltd 1990
This edition published by Sphere Books Ltd 1991
Reprinted 1991

Photoset in North Wales by
Derek Doyle & Associates, Mold, Clwyd
Printed and bound in Great Britain by
BPCC Hazell Books
Aylesbury, Bucks, England
Member of BPCC Ltd.

ISBN 0 7474 0876 9

Sphere Books Ltd
A Division of
Macdonald & Co (Publishers) Ltd
165 Great Dover Street
London SE1 4YA

A member of Maxwell Macmillan Publishing Corporation

Jane Ellen Wayne is the bestselling author of four star biographies, including *Robert Taylor*, *Stanwyck* and *Crawford's Men*. She lives in New York City.

To my daughter

Elizabeth Jo Wayne

Contents

Author's Note

No writer has focused on the men Ava Gardner knew, loved, and sometimes hated. To understand her complexity is to seek out the men who were responsible for Ava's life style and her escape to Spain in 1954.

She was married to Mickey Rooney, Artie Shaw, and Frank Sinatra. Among her many loves were Howard Hughes, George C. Scott, and Luis Miguel Dominguin, one of the world's greatest matadors.

The theme of this book is based on Ava's philosophic search for identity and contentment – beyond the temple of sex referred to as 'the movies.'

Introduction

She was married to Frank Sinatra, filming *Mogambo* in Africa. The crooner was in a slump and heavily in debt. Ava was fed up with him, the unbearable heat, and the movie's director, John Ford, who was host at a dinner party for the British Governor of Uganda, and his wife.

Ford, trying to be funny, asked Ava, 'Why don't you tell the Governor what you see in that hundred twenty pound runt you're married to?'

'Well,' she replied casually, 'There's ten pounds of Frank and there's one hundred and ten pounds of cock!'

Everybody, including the Governor and his wife, thought it was hilarious, but the usually raucous John Ford was in shock. His joke had backfired and he took it out on Ava the next day on the set by working her unmercifully. Ava collapsed and demanded to fly to London for medical treatment. The truth came out on her way back to Africa, when she told a traveling companion she had just aborted Frank's baby.

When Sinatra gave her a mink coat for Christmas, she opened the box and dropped the fur on the floor.

Her *Mogambo* co-star Clark Gable remarked, 'I'd never let a woman treat me like that.'

'You'd have to if she paid for it!' Ava exclaimed.

Gable and Gardner had been more than just friends in years past, but on the Dark Continent, he was involved with newcomer Grace Kelly. At first she disliked Ava, who screamed obscenities at Sinatra during the torrid nights and ran through camp nude after a shower in broad daylight. But the two women who were poles apart would become friends for life.

During the filming of *Mogambo*, they were walking past a group of Watusi warriors. Ava turned to Grace and said, 'I wonder if their cocks are as big as they say.' Grace blushed and kept going, but Ava pulled up one of the Watusi's loincloths and a magnificent penis gleamed in the sunlight. Grace stared despite herself, but Ava laughed. 'Frank has a bigger one!'

Ava Gardner was one of the few Hollywood stars who was invited to Monaco for the royal wedding of Grace Patricia Kelly to Prince Rainier.

Monte Carlo is a long way from the tobacco fields of North Carolina where Ava roamed in her bare feet as a little girl. The seventh child of Mollie and Jonas Gardner, Ava was born on Christmas Eve, 1922, in Brogden. Her parents rented a rooming house in Newport News, Virginia, and took in boarders. Breakfast consisted of hominy grits, fried chicken, and hot biscuits.

Her oldest sister, Bappie, married photographer Larry Tarr and moved to New York City. When Ava was eighteen, she was allowed to visit them there. This was a mighty sacrifice for the overly protective Mollie, who had chaperoned her youngest daughter on her dates.

Bappie's husband took photos of Ava and displayed one in the window of his studio in Manhattan. A talent scout for Metro-Goldwyn-Mayer Studios wanted to meet the girl in the picture. MGM officials were not disappointed. She had sunny brown hair, green eyes, and stood five feet seven with a perfect figure, 36-20-36, weighing in at one hundred twenty pounds.

Despite Ava's drowsy Southern drawl and lazy temperament, she was summoned to Hollywood in 1941 and put under contract for fifty dollars a week. Bappie went along as chaperone. Louis B. Mayer, head of MGM, viewed her screen test and said, 'She can't act. She can't talk. She's terrific! Give her diction lessons and make another test next year.'

Four months after her arrival in Hollywood, Ava was visiting a friend on the set of *Babes on Broadway* and was introduced to Mickey Rooney, who was dressed up like Carmen Miranda. The five-foot-three King of the Box Office was wearing a headdress of fruit, false eyelashes, a bra, a slit skirt, and platform sandals. He might have looked like a woman, but Mickey reacted like a man when he laid eyes on Ava.

Rooney pursued her, but she turned him down until MGM decided it would benefit her career to be seen around town with a famous movie star. Ava finally agreed to have dinner with Mickey, provided Bappie went along, too. He doesn't remember how many times he proposed marriage. Hundreds. On Christmas Eve, 1941 (her birthday), he tried again and she accepted. A month later they became man and wife. An MGM publicity man accompanied them on their brief honeymoon. Ava said she saw more of him than she did of Mickey, who preferred playing golf. 'I was too young to accept the responsibilities of marriage,' he said. Ava, who preferred a vine-covered cottage with a white picket fence to the glamorous life of a movie star, was a virgin when she married Rooney. Her famous husband, however, was not home long enough to appreciate the immaculate apartment decorated and cleaned by Ava, who also cooked dinner every night hoping for a cozy evening with Mickey once in awhile. They were divorced in May 1943.

Her dream shattered, Ava began making the rounds of nightclubs with Fernando Lamas, Billy Daniels, attorney Greg Bautzer, and Peter Lawford. Her most steady beau was millionaire Howard Hughes, who had Ava followed when he was out of town. When he was informed she had been out all night dancing at the Mocambo, he slapped her so hard her jaw was dislocated. She grabbed a heavy brass object and knocked him out cold. Despite their fights, they reconciled time and time again.

Ava's career progressed slowly. Her first major role was opposite George Raft, whom she kissed with her mouth open in *Whistle Stop*. Bored with Howard Hughes and the studio system, she became the fourth wife of bandleader Artie Shaw on October 15, 1945. He was undergoing psychoanalysis and insisted she have therapy, too. 'It really fucked me up,' Ava said. A year later they were divorced, but remained good friends.

Clark Gable, with whom she had an intimate relationship, convinced her to co-star with him in *The Hucksters*. The film was a mild success. She turned down a marriage proposal from Howard Hughes, who refused to give up. She also dated David Niven and John Huston. During *One Touch of Venus*, Ava became involved with her leading man, Robert Walker, whom she gave up for actor Howard Duff. During *The Bribe*, she went out with Robert Taylor, who was separated from Barbara Stanwyck.

Filming *My Forbidden Past*, she was attracted to Robert Mitchum, who was under contract to Howard Hughes. Mitchum called up his boss and asked, 'Do you mind if I go to bed with Ava?'

'If you don't,' Hughes replied, 'they'll think you're a pansy.'

About Frank Sinatra, she said, 'I disliked him intensely. I found him conceited and arrogant.' But in 1950 Ava ran into him again in Palm Springs and they fell in love. There were several drawbacks, however. Frank had a wife, Nancy, three children, and his career was on the decline. When Ava attended his opening night at the Copacabana, he sang, 'Nancy with the Laughing Face,' and Ava fumed. 'Did you have to sing that fucking song?' she asked him. 'I felt like a damn fool.'

'It brings me good luck,' he said.

'Either that song goes or I go,' she exclaimed.

'Nancy with the Laughing Face' was eliminated.

During their visit to New York, Artie Shaw invited them to a party. Frank declined. Ava went alone and received a phone call during dinner. Sinatra told her, 'I just wanted to say goodbye' and then fired two pistol shots. Ava ran into the street crying hysterically, trying to flag down a taxi. In the meantime, Frank's mattress containing the two bullets was switched to another room. When Ava arrived, Sinatra was sitting up in bed reading a book. Ava told her story to police. Frank laughed, 'What are you? Crazy or something?'

Had she not been so upset, Ava might have killed him with her bare hands. Instead she flew to Spain for *Pandora and the Flying Dutchman* and into the arms of bullfighter Mario Cabre. When she arrived back in Los Angeles for *Show Boat*, Sinatra was waiting. On November 7, 1951, they were married in Philadelphia. After a brief honeymoon in Cuba, Ava was scheduled for *The Snows of Kilimanjaro*. Frank told her to be back in New York for his opening at the Paramount. The film took one day longer than expected and Ava told a friend, 'That motherfucker is going to give me hell when I tell him!'

She was torn between her obligations to MGM and to her husband. The studio was flexible. Frank was not. They fought over his cronies, who were always around. They fought when he sang 'All of Me' to Marilyn Maxwell at the Riviera nightclub. They fought over Ava's friendship with her ex-husband, Artie Shaw. They fought when she had to make *Mogambo* in Africa.

When Frank claimed his Oscar for his role of Maggio in *From Here to Eternity*, Ava was not with him. She was in Spain with bullfighter Luis Miguel Dominguin. In June 1954 she established residence in Nevada to obtain a divorce. Howard Hughes flew to her side. Several weeks before the divorce was final, Ava left abruptly for South America with her matador. She returned to New York for the premier of *The Barefoot Contessa* and was seen in the company of Sammy Davis, Jr. *Confidential* magazine linked her with Sammy and accused her of being involved with several 'bronze boyfriends.'

Ava fled to Pakistan for *Bhowani Junction* and tried to seduce her co-star Stewart Granger, who said, 'I'm married to Jean [Simmons].'

'Fuck Jean!' Ava exclaimed.

'I'd love to, darling, but she's not here.'

Ava laughed it off and found someone else to keep her company.

On her way home from Pakistan, she stopped off in Rome and met Italian comedian Walter Chiari. When Sinatra began dating other women, Ava picked up her divorce, which would not become final for a year. They were still in love and talked on the telephone for hours, cooing or fighting.

In 1957, out of boredom, Ava took up bullfighting. Her right cheek was gored by a young bull. Though the scar was barely visible, she was never the same. She viewed herself in daily rushes looking for signs of a mutilated face, cursed her co-stars, and banned all visitors from the movie set.

Sinatra came to see her, but Ava threw her old wedding ring in his face when she found out he was seeing socialite Lady (Adele) Beatty.

After buying a house in Spain, she was seen in the company of bullfighters and officers from the United States Air Force at Torrejon. Though Ava had announced her engagement to Walter Chiari, she continued to go her own way. Maybe she accepted the part of a heavy-drinking party girl in *On the Beach* because it was a good role, but most likely the real reason was to see Sinatra, who would be in Australia at the same time she was filming. Their reunion was disrupted by swarms of reporters. Ava was so distressed she threw a champagne glass in a newsman's face. Headlines read: AVA BUBBLES OVER!

She was troubled over the scar on her face and her love for Sinatra. Writer and director Nunnally Johnson said, 'Ava was very unhappy. If she wasn't crying over Frank, she was crying over losing her fabulous looks. She thought her beauty was her fortune. I never noticed the damn scar.'

She gave parties that lasted for several days. No one could outlast Ava. She turned her car over twice and walked away. Sinatra sent her a new one. She drank heavily, but maintained her enormous appetite – and her fabulous figure. She was linked to Shelley Winters' husband, Anthony Franciosa, Omar Sharif, and screenwriter Peter Viertel.

Director John Huston convinced Ava to do *Night of the Iguana* in Mexico. Richard Burton, her co-star, was known to have affairs with his leading ladies, a fact that haunted Elizabeth Taylor, who followed him to Mexico after they finished *Cleopatra*. Whether Ava was really attracted to Burton or in the mood to tease Elizabeth, it didn't matter. She drank and flirted with Richard, and spent many evenings with Huston or amused herself with the young Mexican beach boys.

More important, she gave a magnificent performance as the hard-bitten Maxine in *Night of the Iguana*, thanks to Huston's patience and coaching.

Huston also coaxed her into *The Bible* in which she agreed to portray Sarah, the barren wife of Abraham, played by George C. Scott, who fell in love with Ava. She was smitten for a while, until his temper flared. Huston made sure she completed her scenes and Ava flew to London. Scott followed and broke into her hotel suite. She managed to get away and Scott spent the night in jail. John Huston said, 'He was crazy about her . . . mad about her. He followed her around the globe.'

She lived hard, drank hard, and loved hard. Of her childhood, Ava Gardner has said: 'I never had any ambitions to be anything but dead in those days.'

About Mickey Rooney: 'We were babies, just children. Our lives were run by a lot of other people. We didn't have a chance.'

About the movies: 'Apparently, I'm what is known as a "glamour girl." Now that's a phrase which means luxury, leisure, excitement, and all things lush. No one associates a six a.m. alarm, a thirteen-hour workday, several more hours of study, housework, and business appointments with glamour. That, however, is what glamour means in Hollywood. At least it does to me.'

About Frank Sinatra: 'When he was down he was sweet, but when he got back up he was hell.'

About moving to Europe: 'Being a movie star in America is the loneliest life in the world. In Europe they respect your privacy. No one believes me when I say I'm going to Europe to live, but I am, and I won't be back.'

About her fast life: 'I'm one Hollywood star who hasn't tried to slash her wrists, take sleeping pills, or kick a cop in the shins. That's something of an accomplishment these days.'

We remember Ava Gardner because she was always one step ahead of us, and it was a challenge to catch up. Whatever pranks, she had the courage to laugh or curse with her chin up. Toward the end of her life Ava Gardner claimed she was just 'an old broad,' but the memory of her vivacious energy and natural beauty is more effective than face-lifts or stage make-up.

She lived in London, but never tried to impress us with a phony British accent. Nor did she insist her romances and affairs were untrue. She hated the press, but didn't blame them for her sensuous history.

ONE

The Early Years

London, 1953

Lana Turner lounged on the couch sipping a cocktail. Clark Gable sat on the floor at her feet with his own bottle of cognac. Sue and Alan Ladd stood in a corner chatting with Robert Taylor about a winter storm expected to blitz London that night. John Huston said the aroma of fried chicken was making him ravenous. 'What the hell are we waiting for?' he asked director Tay Garnett, who was hosting the dinner.

'My wife forgot to make gravy,' was the reply. 'Can't have chicken without gravy.'

The doorbell rang and when Garnett answered it, there stood Ava Gardner in a beautiful gown. 'I don't give a shit what everyone else is wearing,' she said. 'I bought this gown today and I had to spring it!' Taylor winked, Gable whistled, and Mrs Garnett was ready to cry. 'I forgot the gravy,' she sighed.

'Stand aside, honey,' Ava said, 'I just happen to be the best country gravy maker on earth!'

The stunning actress in the clinging, shimmering gown went into the kitchen and began stirring. Someone handed her an apron. 'I'm not a sloppy cook,' Ava laughed. 'There's nothing to it. Jesus! I don't believe you really made Southern fried chicken, hot biscuits, corn bread, and apple pie! Let's eat.'

Bob Taylor tasted the gravy. 'Best I ever tasted,' he said.

'Of course!' Ava exclaimed, putting down the wooden spoon.

Everyone but Gable dug into the home-cooked dinner. They had been in Europe making films for a few months and were hungry for American food. Ava ate two portions and then joined Gable, who had almost finished his bottle of Courvoisier. 'Eat something,' she said, running her fingers through his gray hair.

'Don't *you* start complainin' about my drinking, babe.'

'I'm hardly the one to talk,' she said, throwing off her shoes. 'But I always eat, honey.'

'You eat and I get fat,' he grinned, patting her thigh.

'You drink and I worry.'

'I'll get back to the hotel just fine.'

'Let someone else drive.'

'Do I look drunk?'

'I'd hate to see you crack up that beautiful new custom Jaguar.'

'So would I,' Gable said. 'That's why I'll be okay.'

Garnett never forgot how Ava Gardner breezed into the kitchen looking like a royal duchess about to attend a coronation ball. 'Her hair was unmussed, her forehead dry, her gown without a spot of gravy,' he said. 'I don't know how she did it, but the gravy was sheer cordon bleu.'

If Ava was modest about her cooking, it wasn't an act. She came from a large family who suffered through the Great Depression. Before she was ten years old, Ava was preparing meals for twenty people and making it look easy.

⚥

Mary Baker Gardner named her daughter after her mother, Ava, who died giving birth to her nineteenth child, Lavinia. Mary, known as Mollie, had been ten days overdue in her seventh pregnancy. The doctor delivered the child by cesarean section on Christmas Eve, 1922, in Brogden (Ava nicknamed it Grabtown), about fifty miles from the state capital of Raleigh in North Carolina. Mollie was forty, robust, and barely over five feet. Her husband of twenty years, Jonas Bailey Gardner, was a tall lean Irishman with green eyes. His father came to the United States during the Irish famine and had settled in Boon Hill.

Mollie Baker's family were Scottish Baptists from Virginia who moved to the rich tobacco fields of North Carolina. Though Jonas was a Catholic, he allowed the children to attend the Baptist Church. The only book allowed in the Gardner house was the Bible.

A year after Mollie and Jonas were married, his father died. They moved into the white clapboard four-bedroom house on three hundred acres of rich tobacco land in Boon Hill. This was Ava's first home. Her oldest sister was Bappie, nineteen. Then came Elsie May, eighteen; Inez, sixteen; Melvin, fourteen; and Myra, seven. Another boy, Raymond, was killed at sixteen months when a rifle shell exploded. He would have been fifteen when Ava Lavinia was born.

Mollie was religious, an overly protective mother and a possessive wife. Her Victorian principles were strictly enforced in the family. If Jonas had a roving eye, he had little time to pursue temptation. With only

3

one son to help in the tobacco fields, he hired white transients. Had Jonas not been bigoted against blacks, he could have hired cheap laborers.

Ava's first recollection as a child was the aroma of tobacco, a scent that filled her nostrils at birth. The predominating color in her life was 'bright leaf' – yellowish red. Her playgrounds were the field of dark, tar-like sticky soil that oozed between her toes. For a few pennies to spend at the candy store, Ava picked larvae and worms off the tobacco leaves that grew five feet high. She knew when it was time to fertilize and when the harvesting was about to begin. The pink, white, and red flowers she wore in her hair were from the tobacco plants. Ava rolled her first cigarette when she was five, and experimented with cigarettes when she was eight.

As Ava grew, so did the number of settlers in North Carolina. There were almost 300,000 tenant farmers growing tobacco by the mid-twenties. Squatters lived in shacks and drained the soil of its potency. When the Great Depression hit in 1929, tobacco prices tumbled. While Jonas struggled to keep his farm, Ava watched her family break up. Her oldest sister Bappie married first, then Elsie May, who settled in nearby Smithfield. Inez was the next to leave home, and finally Melvin, who wanted to attend high school in Winston-Salem, where he lived with an uncle. The family gathering at the dinner table and in church on Sunday mornings dwindled.

Mollie and Jonas argued bitterly about their future. She went to work at a 'teacherage' in Brogden, where Ava attended grammar school. Jonas sold the Gardner home and property for what little he could get and took a job at a sawmill nearby. Myra went to live with her brother in Winston-Salem, and Mollie rented a boarding house in Newport News, Virginia.

With Ava's help, she cleaned the rooms and cooked

the meals. It was hard work, but they managed until Jonas became ill with a streptococcus infection of the chest. Mollie insisted he stay at the boarding house, where she could care for him. When Jonas became bedridden, Mollie worked upstairs while Ava, age ten, took over the kitchen duties. Mother and daughter managed until Jonas died two years later. Yearning to be closer to her family, Mollie got a job at another teacherage in Rock Ridge, North Carolina, where Ava attended high school.

She recalled, 'I wasn't allowed to go the movies in Boon Hill. I saw my first one in Newport News – *Red Dust* with Clark Gable and Jean Harlow.' Twenty years later Ava Gardner would co-star in the Harlow role with 'The King' of Hollywood in the remake of that film, *Mogambo*.

Mollie had become excessively possessive of her youngest. At the boarding house Ava was accosted by a man when she passed his room. Her screams brought Mollie on the run and the guilty party was thrown out. This unfortunate incident might have made Ava's high school years drab and lonely because afterward her mother had a reputation for being unfriendly to every young man who showed an interest in her. When one of them dared to kiss Ava on the front porch, Mollie dashed out of the house with such force that the boy ran for his life, and Ava was severely punished. On another occasion, Mrs Gardner followed a hunch and found her daughter sitting with a young man in his car by Holt Lake. Mollie literally dragged Ava off the front seat, told the boy a thing or two in no uncertain terms, and marched her 'baby' home.

'Nobody wanted to take me out,' Ava said years later. 'No boy looked at me.'

She loved her mother dearly, but at sixteen Ava craved some freedom. There was the urge to make a decent living and help Mollie financially. Ava decided to become a secretary and, with the help of her brother Melvin, attended the Atlantic Christian College in Wilson. She studied business education and secretarial science – which included Gregg shorthand, composition of business letters, office secretarial practice, and the rudiments of accounting. Ava was a good student, but she disliked school and soon lost interest. It might have been different if the other pupils had been more friendly. Her spoken name was 'Ahvuh Gahdnuh,' an example of Ava's thick Southern hillbilly accent that amused her classmates. It is no wonder she said, 'I never had any ambition to be anything but dead in those days.' But underneath the altered and faded hand-me-down dresses was a tall, beauteous woman with a tiny waist and full, uplifted breasts. All that Jonas had bequeathed Ava were his green eyes, lean figure, and heavy dimple in his chin. These characteristics would be valuable assets someday, but at the time she had no confidence in her appearance. Ava, who was not permitted to wear makeup, could not comprehend the reasons why men stared and whistled when she walked down the street. Mollie said they wanted only one thing, and sex was dirty. Her daughter was expected to come home for lunch and directly after school every day.

At seventeen, Ava was smothering from Mollie's overprotectiveness, but her one glimmer of hope was Bappie, who had married Larry Tarr, a photographer from New York. With mixed emotions the sisters said goodbye, smiling and crying at the same time. Bappie hugged Ava and said, 'You'll visit us.' Mollie overheard and flared, 'She's not old enough! No self-respecting young girl would go to a big city alone. Don't be fillin' her head with such nonsense.'

Bappie, however, was optimistic and determined. She told her baby sister not to worry. 'I'll think of something,' she said. Ava clung to those words. 'Bappie was the real star in the family,' she said in later years. 'She could do anything ten times better than I could.'

Bappie was childless and doted on her brothers and sisters, Ava in particular. The Gardner family, their friends and neighbors, were aware of Mollie's hold on Ava. It was taken for granted that the pretty, long-legged, and unsmiling girl would get a job, marry the first boy who kissed her good night, and insist Mollie live with them.

According to Ava, she was finally allowed to go attend a Bing Crosby matinee movie with a handsome football hero from Rock Ridge High School. Sitting next to him was a great thrill for her. 'My heart was beating so fast I thought it would burst,' she recalled.

Ava had no one to talk to about her natural instincts and curiosities. She was brought up to believe that these feelings were wicked, which explains the turmoil and confusion that plagued Ava throughout her tempestuous life. She would not defy her mother, remaining virtuous and trying to concentrate on school. 'I changed my mind about being a secretary,' she said. 'It was too dull, but I could take down a hundred and twenty words a minute in shorthand. I dreaded the thought of being tied down to a desk all day, but what else was I qualified for?'

When Ava became a movie star, the MGM publicity staff wrote that Miss Gardner had been voted the most attractive girl in college but was disqualified because she did not reside in the girls' dormitory. Mollie, of course, would not allow her daughter to live away from home, and the beauty award went to a runner-up. This was the least of Ava's problems, however.

The Gardner children faithfully contributed what monies they could to support Mollie who, approaching her sixtieth birthday, was tired and haggard.

In the summer of 1940, Bappie decided it was time for

Ava to get away from home for a few days. She discussed the possibility with her other sisters, who agreed to look after their mother. Mollie finally gave her consent but worried about the train ride from North Carolina to New York. 'Ava will be eighteen in December,' Bappie said. 'She'll be just fine, and when she gets to the city, Larry and I will look after her.'

It was a thrill of a lifetime for Ava. Even Tarr's tiny apartment over his photo studio at Forty-ninth Street and Fifth Avenue was heaven to the shy hillbilly girl from Boon Hill. Bappie took her to see *Gone With the Wind*. Ava was so enthralled with the movie that she used what few dollars she had to buy the novel by Margaret Mitchell. 'It was the first book I ever read,' she said, 'except for schoolbooks and the Bible.' Clark Gable would congratulate her years later: 'I never did get through the damn thing,' he told her.

Bappie made sure Ava saw New York. And Larry, who was very impressed with his sister-in-law's striking face, took photographs of her. She had no idea how to pose but, as Tarr said, she was a natural beauty. Her hair had a healthy chestnut glow; her skin was smooth, pale and clear; her teeth were straight and white, her smile was innocent.

Though Ava never hoped to see much of the world beyond Broadway, she was grateful for a few days surrounded by tall buildings and well-dressed New Yorkers. For a while, the bright lights that twinkled until dawn kept her mind off her ailing mother. When Ava boarded the train for home, she wasn't disappointed. What she treasured most was being with Bappie, who promised faithfully to spend the Christmas holidays in North Carolina.

Ava returned to Atlantic Christian College. Her brother Melvin owned a diner in nearby Smithfield and helped with expenses. Mollie was suffering from breast cancer. Only time would determine her fate. Either way, Ava would be expected to contribute to her mother's care.

TWO

Picture in the Window

'Is this the Tarr residence?'

'Yes. Who is this?'

'Name's Duhan. I'm from MGM.'

'MGM?'

'Metro-Goldwyn-Mayer. I'm calling about a picture in the window of your photo studio.'

'This is Mrs Tarr. What portrait are you referring to, Mr Duhan?'

'The young girl with her hair pulled up ... a brunette with a cleft in her chin.'

'What about her?' Bappie asked.

'I'd like to talk to the girl. As I said, I'm from MGM.'

'My sister has returned home. She lives in North Carolina, but I'll send for her.'

'That won't be necessary,' Duhan stammered. 'I'd appreciate your sending some pictures of your sister to my office and I'll be in touch.'

'Don't you want to know her name?'

'Sure!'

'Ava Gardner.'

Bappie jotted down MGM's New York address, hung up the phone, and ran downstairs to tell her husband the exciting news. 'Mr Duhan wants you to mail the photos right away.'

'I'll do better than that!' Larry Tarr exclaimed. 'I'll take them over to MGM this afternoon!'

'Perhaps we'd better not tell Ava anything about this. It could be a terrible disappointment to her if nothing comes of it.'

'Who is this Duhan?'

'A talent scout, I think. At least he gave me that impression,' Bappie replied.

Tarr delivered pictures of Ava to the MGM offices on Fifty-second Street and asked to speak to Duhan personally. The receptionist said he wasn't in his office. Tarr explained, 'The model in these photographs lives out of town. I'd appreciate Mr Duhan getting in touch with me or my wife.' The receptionist smirked. 'I'll be sure to give him the message, Mr Tarr.'

When Duhan returned, she handed him the envelope. 'Up to your old tricks again, Barney?'

He looked over the pictures and sighed. 'Sometimes it works out and sometimes it doesn't. This kid's a real looker, though.'

'How often do you pull it off?'

'Four out of ten isn't bad.'

'They really fall for the old routine about getting them into the movies?'

'What do they have to lose?' he laughed. 'I see a pretty girl, ask her to go out, and she's very congenial.'

'Have any of them ever found out you're a runner for the legal department?'

'Hell, no!'

'What do you have in mind for this one?' she asked, pointing to Ava's picture.

'Maybe I missed out on a hot date, but I'm going to

show them to Marvin Schenck. He's head of talent and if he wants to meet her, that's his business.'

The Tarrs went back to North Carolina for the Christmas holidays. At Ava's eighteenth birthday party on Christmas Eve, Larry told her about MGM. 'They're very interested in you,' he said proudly. 'One of their talent scouts saw your picture in the window of my studio and wanted to know who you were.'

'You put a picture of me in the window?' she gasped. 'Why did you do that?'

'Because you photograph so well,' he beamed.

'It's not right! Why did Bappie let you do it?'

He was taken aback by her outburst. 'People stopped and stared!' Larry exclaimed. 'You should be very happy about that.'

'Well, I'm not.'

Bappie told her sister about the telephone call. 'Mr Duhan was very pleasant,' she explained. 'I offered to send for you but – '

'It's an awful thing being on display,' Ava hissed. 'I think it's embarrassing. Don't tell Mother anything about it because she'll never let me visit you again.'

'We thought you'd be tickled to death, that's all,' Bappie said.

'Well, I'm not.'

Ava resented Larry's intrusion into her privacy. She was furious. It wasn't only her puritanical background, because she continued to express her annoyance long after the incident proved to be the turning point in her life.

Aside from her mortification, this reaction offers another insight into Ava's teenage personality. Becoming a movie star was as remote to her as flying to the moon. Beyond earning enough money for basic essentials, Ava had no dreams. Mollie's health was not improving, although it was too soon for doctors to tell if her condition was terminal. If Ava had a wish, it was for her mother's complete recovery.

Bappie, however, had an open mind. She saw in Ava a rare sensuality aside from the sculptured face and body. Barney Duhan's phone call would not be forgotten. He had taken time to stop and admire the picture of a girl who wore no makeup, who had not been trained to pose, and who knew nothing of hairdressers. Though Bappie did not know Duhan was a messenger boy, she probably would have forged ahead, anyway.

The subject of MGM was not brought up again during the Tarrs' holiday visit, but when Ava finished her year at Atlantic Christian College, Bappie again invited her to New York. Mollie gave her approval, but Ava was reluctant to leave her until the family insisted she take a brief vacation before their mother got any worse.

When Ava arrived in New York, Larry called MGM and was referred to a legitimate talent scout, Ben Jacobson, who had never heard of Tarr's photo studio or Ava Gardner. Larry related the story about Duhan.

'I'm sorry,' Jacobson said bluntly, 'but Barney picks up girls that way. He's a runner for our legal department. If your sister-in-law had been in town, he would have taken her out that night.'

'Not without a chaperone,' Tarr retorted, trying to conceal his disappointment.

'If it isn't too much trouble,' Jacobson said, 'could you drop off more pictures of . . . what's her name?'

'Ava. Ava Gardner. How about this afternoon? I don't know how long she'll be in New York.'

'Fine, Mr Tarr.'

Bappie was disillusioned to find out that Barney

Duhan had no influence at Metro, but Larry assured her Jacobson was indeed a talent scout. 'I'm going there myself with the photos,' he said.

Ava was nonchalant about posing again. 'This is silly,' she told Larry. 'Movie stars are beautiful and exotic. I'm not.'

'Your sister and I don't agree,' he said, adjusting the lighting on her face.

'I guess if Bappie's tickled pink, that's good enough for me,' she yawned.

Ben Jacobson was impressed with Ava's photos. He showed them to MGM's New York publicity chief, Howard Dietz, who said, 'The girl's pretty enough for a screen test. Set it up, Ben.'

Bappie was ecstatic when she heard the good news. She took Ava's hand and chirped. 'We're going to Saks Fifth Avenue and pick out a lovely dress for you!'

'What for?' Ava asked drowsily.

'A screen test, honey.'

'I can't act . . . '

'It's a chance, that's all. You have to do it.'

'Why?'

'Because you have nothing to lose.'

'All that money for a dress I'll never wear again?'

'You let me worry about that,' Bappie said gently, pushing her sister out the front door and in the direction of Saks.

Ava remembered the dress as 'off the shoulder' but in good taste. As the big day approached, she became increasingly nervous. Bappie and Larry told her to say she'd been on the stage in school. 'But I haven't,' she moped. 'You tried out for plays, didn't you?' Bappie asked. Ava nodded. 'Well, that was on the stage, wasn't it?' Lasrry smiled.

Ben Jacobson was not disappointed when he met Ava, but astonished when he asked her name. 'Ah-vuh Gahd-nuh.'

'Why do you want to be in movies?' he asked.

'Ah doan't.'

Jacobson winced when he handed her a script. 'I had no idea what she was saying,' he said. 'Her accent was so thick you could cut it with a knife. I did not have the slightest idea if she could act. I told her we would make a silent test. If I sent a soundtrack out to the Coast with nothing on it but spoonbread they'd have my head examined.'

Jacobson consulted Marvin Schenck, who was in charge of talent. They decided to give her the best lighting available and make the most out of this sultry brunette with the type of animal magnetism 'only the good Lord gives away at birth.'

The director of the screen test said, 'Ava, look up. Ava, look down. Ava, sit down. Cross your legs. Get up and stand next to the table. Pick up the flowers. That's it. Now place them in the vase.'

Jacobson held his head in his hands when she dumped the bouquet with a thud. The director told Ava to sit down again and 'emote expression.' She looked confused, bored, and restless.

'It was hopeless. Terrible,' Schenck said. 'But we viewed the test anyway and she took our breath away. She was clumsy and uneasy, but we all wanted to go to bed with her. What a woman!'

Jacobson sent the print to Hollywood with a note. 'If you don't sign this dame, you're nuts!'

Meanwhile, Ava Gardner packed her suitcase and went back to North Carolina.

A few days later, the silent screen test arrived in Hollywood. Director George Sidney viewed it and thought Ava was terrible. 'But there was something

15

about her,' he told author Charles Higham in a rare interview. 'I can remember going to one of my assistants and saying, "Tell New York to ship her out! She's a good piece of merchandise!"'

Bappie called her sister. 'Mr Jacobson said MGM will put you under contract for fifty dollars a week, but you'll have to leave for Hollywood right away.'

'I don't believe it.'

'It's true, Ava. I have a meeting with an MGM press agent, Milton Weiss, tomorrow. He's going with you to California.'

'Mother won't allow it.'

'Let me talk to her, Ava.'

Mollie was too ill to put up a good fight. She agreed to let her baby go to Hollywood if Bappie went along as chaperone. With the only obstacle out of the way, Ava should have cried for joy, but she didn't. How could she leave her sick mother? Why was she going into a profession she knew nothing about? It was Bappie who gave her the answers and the confidence. It was Bappie who bought Ava a new wardrobe. And it was Bappie who went to the preliminary meetings at MGM in New York.

Ben Jacobson was the first to congratulate Ava, who said, 'Okay, so I got through the test. So I'm going to Hollywood. If I really do get there I'm going to marry the biggest movie star in the world!'

'And who do you think that is?' he asked.

'Clark Gable,' she winked. 'Who else?'

'About the biggest movie star in the world today is Mickey Rooney.'

Ava slumped in a chair and shrugged.

She told Bappie on the train, 'I want to make good,

but if I don't, I can always be a secretary.'

'Aren't you excited about Hollywood?' her sister asked. 'I am!'

'The movie magazines say it's heaven. Otherwise I wouldn't be going there.'

Milton Weiss, who accompanied them to the Coast, said, 'I think Ava was more anxious to see Hollywood than the fact she was going to be in the movies.'

THREE

Hollywood

When Joan Crawford arrived in Hollywood, she thought it was another planet. Was it actually seventy degrees in January? 'I had never seen a palm tree before,' she said, 'except in motion pictures. Everything was so bright and cheerful.'

Myrna Loy said, 'Hollywood was fabulous! It always is when you come upon it.'

Lauren Bacall remembered, 'Hollywood was so clean. I had never known there were cities as pure-looking. Beautiful.'

Ava Gardner said, 'Hollywood was just a dreary, quiet suburb of Los Angeles, with droopy palm trees, washed-out buildings, cheap dime stores, and garish theaters, a far cry from the razzle-dazzle of New York, or even the rural beauty of North Carolina.'

Comparing the comments of the four actresses proves that beauty is in the eye of the beholder. One sees only what one wants to see. Ava came to Hollywood as a tourist, theoretically, not as an eager and ambitious hopeful. The majority of contract players who arrived in Movietown agreed that their living accommodations were tacky. After a luxurious drive in the studio limousine, they were dropped off at a dingy, inexpensive hotel.

Milton Weiss thought Ava was different from the other girls he had accompanied to California. His job was to make sure they made the right connection in Chicago from the Twentieth Century Limited to the Super Chief and to protect the young ladies from male travelers who were after a one-night stand. Not that press agents were immune to such things, but Weiss said that with or without Bappie along, he didn't stand a chance with Ava. She was oblivious and cold where men were concerned. She had an icy exterior indicating 'hands off.' Weiss said, 'The three of us played pinochle. And then we played more pinochle.' He tried to impress Ava with the fact that MGM was the most prestigious studio in the world 'with more stars than there are in the heavens.' Ava would deal another hand of cards.

She arrived in Hollywood on August 23, 1941, early in the morning. Instead of taking a limousine à la Crawford or going on foot à la Gary Cooper, who wanted to know 'Which way is Hollywood?', the disappointed Ava Gardner was taken by taxi to the MGM studio. Again she failed to notice the historical buildings or scan the grounds for famous people. Instead Ava noticed a cemetery nearby and remarked to Weiss, 'That's a good beginning.'

She was taken to the wardrobe department and fitted into a black strapless gown. From there she and Bappie were escorted to a tiny dressing room where Ava was groomed for the camera. Her hair was styled and makeup was applied to her face, arms, and shoulders. Weiss had prepared Ava for the second screen test. 'They'll ask you about your hometown, your family, school, things like that,' he explained. 'You'll be expected to walk around as you did in New York, sit, stand, smile, and pose.'

George Sidney directed the sound test. He had the same reaction as Ben Jacobson. Terrible. She spoke a foreign language, but Sidney and the others responsible for the test were aware of her shortcomings and winced through it by concentrating on her voluptuous cleavage and the almond eyes that told them what clung to the black dress wasn't available.

One of the technicians said, 'She had it all. Like most women, Ava did not have to flirt or tease or try to be seductive. She honestly tried not to stumble over anything during the test. I had the feeling she knew how bad she was, but didn't want to make a complete fool of herself. I found out later she really didn't give a damn whether she was a success or not. I've seen them all come and go and give all they had. Not Ava. She gave what was in her heart – a sincere effort, with no phony fringes.'

When Ava was finished, Milton Weiss drove her and Bappie to a run-down hotel, the Hollywood Wilcox, where MGM reserved a room. 'I was getting only thirty-five dollars a week,' Ava said. 'I thought I'd be making fifty. We stayed at a shabby hotel with only one little bed and a small kitchen. For the first three weeks I was there, I didn't get paid at all. Bappie had to go to work and I had to take two buses to the studio.'

The Hollywood Wilcox is still in business and famous for touting 'Ava Gardner slept here.'

While she and Bappie were trying to get settled in their two-by-four hotel room, Louis B. Mayer, head of MGM and the most powerful mogul in Hollywood, sat down in a projection room to view Ava's screen test. When it was over he said, 'That girl can't act and she can't talk. But she's terrific! Hand her over to the voice and diction coaches for a year, and give her another test.' Then he turned to Weiss and asked, 'What kind of name is Ahvuh Gahdnuh, for Christ's sake?'

'It's Ava Gardner.'

'Perfect. We'll change it!' Mayer barked.

'But you said . . . '

'That's why *we're* going to invent it, Milton. Make up some shit about her real name. You know, Mary Lou or Lucy Ann, the Southern belle crap. What's her background?'

'Secretarial school,' Weiss replied.

'We can't put that in our press releases. Even I don't believe it.'

'How about the Powers model routine?'

'That's good. I'll have the legal department draw up her contract. Meanwhile, get the usual stills of her in a bathing suit and so on.'

'Do you want to meet her, L.B.?'

'After she's signed the necessary papers, I'll be delighted to welcome her to my MGM family.'

❦

L.B. Mayer was the most important and influential person in Ava Gardner's life. He was fifty-five when she came to Hollywood. His wife, Mildred, was an invalid, so there were rumors about Mayer's dalliances with the actresses at MGM. Joan Crawford said he usually managed to brush against her right breast, but that was the extent of it. Jean Harlow's biographer Irving Shulman claims Mayer lured her to his Malibu beach house and offered Jean a mink coat if she'd go to bed with him. If this is true, the Blonde Bombshell was the exception. Mayer's enemies and friends agree he did not have a casting couch. He did, however, play with nonentities in a private room near his MGM office. He was seen at premieres and white tie dinner dances with his prize possessions – perhaps Jeanette MacDonald or Greer Garson, two of his favorite goddesses. In public, he was always in the company of another couple to avoid embarrassing his beloved wife.

Mayer considered himself a father to Lana Turner, Judy Garland, Hedy Lamarr, Elizabeth Taylor, Eleanor Powell, Esther Williams, and Joan Crawford. Ava Gardner became another of his pampered darlings, groomed by the best hairdressers, designers, makeup artists, and diction coaches in the world. But Mayer did not create these beauteous legends to be pawed. They were above that. And he was above that.

The former Jewish scrap-iron merchant had only the welfare of his MGM 'family' at heart. 'I'll go down on my knees and kiss the ground talent walks on,' he said. Mayer was also capable of destroying anyone who opposed his wishes. He was hated, loved, or tolerated. He punished his contract players with bad roles and praised them with good ones. He arranged their marriages, divorces, abortions, mortgages, and vacations. He arranged a 'cathouse' for his male stars for their protection against venereal disease and scandal.

Though Mayer was rarely seen on the movie sets, he knew about everything that was going on, who was having an affair with whom, and who was putting on too much weight. In the MGM commissary, he insisted on homemade apple pie. Chicken soup was prepared from his personal recipe. If a star was on a diet, Mayer gave strict orders to serve only consommé and unsalted crackers with black coffee. According to his instructions, amphetamines and sleeping pills were prescribed by studio doctors to overworked players. When Lionel Barrymore was crippled with arthritis and appearing on the screen in a wheelchair, Mayer supplied him with cocaine to dull the never-ending pain.

Mayer knew it took years to make a star 'overnight.' When he was told that Wallace Beery was stealing props from the movie set, Mayer replied, 'Yes, Beery is a son of a bitch, but he's *our* son of a bitch.'

Furious over Joan Crawford's affair with Clark Gable, Mayer told her, 'I made you and I can break you.' That meant neither she nor Gable would ever work again in Hollywood.

Though Ava Gardner would never have been discovered had it not been for Larry Tarr and Ben Jacobson, it was L.B. Mayer who made her a star. He had an instinct for what the public wanted. She had no conception, however, that he would have complete control over her life from the day she signed a contract with MGM. It was Mayer who decided how much time and effort would be spent on a new player. Each actress was molded into a unique attraction – her hair, eyebrows, and lips, her gowns, her dialogue and voice. Any deviations had to be given the stamp of approval by Mayer personally. He protected images and made certain there was only one Turner, Taylor, Allyson, Crawford, and Gardner.

They were MGM trademarks.

Milton Weiss explained to Ava that her seven-year contract contained options. Every six months she would be evaluated and either advanced or dropped according to her potential. 'Do you mean they can throw me out and get away with it?' she asked.

'Just like that!' Weiss replied, snapping his fingers.

'The hotel's a dump and they have the nerve to charge seventy-five dollars a week for a room no bigger than a closet! I have to take two buses to the studio before daylight. When do I get paid, anyway?'

'It takes a few weeks to process everything, Ava.'

'How am I supposed to live?'

'Are you trying to tell me you don't want to sign a contract? That you want to go home?'

'Bappie insists we stick it out. She's looking for a job.'

'There are moral clauses in the contract, too,' Weiss said. 'But I don't have to worry about you. Also, you can't leave Los Angeles without the studio's permission and you'll be obligated to accept all roles, agree to all the necessary photo sessions, interviews, and to be on time for your scheduled voice and diction lessons. In other words, you do what you're told to do, Ava, no matter how ridiculous or unimportant you may think it is.'

'The whole thing's disgusting. One of the girls told me I wouldn't recognize myself in a few weeks. Why do they like something and then want to change it?'

'Not necessarily. The makeup experts will emphasize the good and camouflage the bad. They'll study every freckle, cover up every little blemish, measure the space between your eyes, the length of your nose, and how far it points to the right or left to the millimeter. Your teeth will be capped and your eyelashes matched to false ones. Then a team of hairdressers will decide what color your hair should be and whether it looks better long or short or in-between. Then – '

'I've heard enough,' she sighed.

'Mayer strives for perfection. He doesn't have to settle for less.'

'When am I going to meet him?'

'He welcomes every new member of his family. After that, his door is always open to you, Ava.'

'I'm not so sure I like that.'

'You don't have to worry about L.B. as long as you abide by the rules.'

'I've heard stories.'

'Not about Mayer. There's a saying around town that he couldn't catch a piece of tail in a cathouse.'

Weiss suddenly felt embarrassed and smiled apologetically, but Ava threw her head back and laughed.

24

'What else should I know about the Great White Father?' she asked.

'Don't ever say anything bad about anyone's mother, especially your own.'

'I love my mother.'

'Tell him that. He'll be touched. Show him a picture if you have one. Mayer's devoted to motherhood, MGM, and his country. Corny, but true.'

'How does he feel about sisters? Maybe he can find Bappie a job.'

'I'll see what I can do,' Weiss said. Within days Bappie was selling women's handbags at I. Magnin, an exclusive department store in Beverly Hills.

Ava signed the contract and from that moment on she was the property of Metro-Goldwyn-Mayer. It amused Ava to find out her 'real' name was supposedly Lucy Ann Johnson, who had given up modeling to become a movie actress. Weiss explained to her how the studio had once sponsored a contest in a film magazine to find a new name for Lucille LeSueur. 'The winner came up with Joan Crawford,' he said. 'Joan thought it sounded like crawfish. She was the first star discovered and developed by MGM.'

They were walking to L.B. Mayer's office on the third floor of the Irving Thalberg Memorial Building, nicknamed by studio insiders as the Iron Lung. Thalberg was MGM's boy genius who died at the age of thirty-six. Married to actress Norma Shearer, Thalberg was in charge of production and responsible for many film classics, such as *Mutiny on the Bounty* and *Ben-Hur*. After his early death in the late thirties Mayer erected the stark white building that overlooked the cemetery Ava had noticed when she entered the imposing gates of MGM. Weiss said, 'L.B. controls everyone in this town – the newspapers, the fan magazines, and the police department, but he can't convince the undertaker to sell his property.'

The Thalberg Building was occupied by the living, however. Hundreds of clerks and secretaries scurried from room to room and floor to floor. There were private dining rooms, a commissary, conference rooms, kitchens, and bathrooms. Aside from the public elevator, there were private ones used by executives.

Mayer's office was surrounded by rows and rows of desks occupied by secretaries and their secretaries. It was hectic but well-organized. If Ava was impressed with her boss's staff, it was nothing compared to what she felt when she was ushered into his office. It was a large room with white leather walls. At the far end was Mayer's huge, horseshoe-shaped desk and behind it a big chair that had been custom-built to make the short, chunky mogul appear taller. Many MGM players said the walk from the office door across the room was the longest they had ever taken. Mayer, much like a king or pharaoh, had his reasons for arranging the large office in this manner. Those who paid homage to their master were ushered into a great room where the throne loomed at the far wall. In Mayer's case, he wanted a full-length view of those who entered. Perhaps it was a test of their endurance as well.

Though Ava had yet to be convinced she had done the right thing by signing her life away, the contract was binding and Louis Burt Mayer was her master. He was very businesslike with Ava, stressing the basic rules and warning her about staying out late at night, drinking too much, and dating indiscriminately. 'If you need an escort,' he said, 'we can arrange one for you. I prefer, however, that you concentrate on getting to the studio on time every morning. Practice your diction faithfully. Read the newspaper aloud every morning. It will pay off. You'll see. And remember, Ava, there is always someone here at MGM who can solve your problems, answer your questions, and assist you in every way to get settled in Hollywood. Think of me as your father. Anything we discuss in this office will go no further.' With pride, he mentioned that she was in the hands of the greatest designers and makeup artists in the world. Her diction and dramatic coaches were the best. Ultimately Mayer was telling Ava that if she failed it would be her fault and no one else's.

She was introduced to his secretarial assistant, Ida Koverman, who was Mayer's closest confidante. She was the only person who could handle him, and if he was out of town, she listened to the stars' complaints and heartbreaking stories. Occasionally, she was better equipped to placate them. 'Aunt Ida' was responsible for convincing her boss to audition Judy Garland. And when he was too busy, she changed Spangler Arlington Brugh's name to Robert Taylor.

Ava had no conception that day how influential Mayer and Koverman would be in her life. She was taken aback when Weiss told her, 'L.B. is the highest salaried person in the United States. He makes over three thousand a week and gets 6.77 percent of the studio's profits.' It never occurred to Ava that anyone earned more than the President of the United States.

Living in the dreary Hollywood Wilcox was Ava's reality. Every night she and Bappie tried to cook Southern fried chicken in the tiny kitchen. Night after night they stayed in the shabby room with its stained rugs and dirty walls. Before dawn, Bappie made breakfast and then Ava left for the studio. With two buses to catch she didn't want to take any chances on being late. According to what Ava said over the years it was Bappie who urged her on and had confidence that she would succeed. Though Tarr was patient and understanding for a long time, the separations from Bappie would end the marriage.

Ava's daily routine was unchanging. She reported to MGM's makeup supervisor, Jack Dawn, who was responsible for the many faces of Lon Chaney and the unique look of Joan Crawford. Dawn determined the color of Ava's mascara. He trimmed her eyebrows and turned up her eyelashes with hair wave set. Her cheekbones were emphasized and the dimple in her chin was toned down. The procedure was a bore to Ava. Dawn enjoyed her jokes and casual interest in his facial masks, pancake bases, rouge tints, and powder puffs. He'd been cursed by nobodies and legends. Ava didn't care.

But her temper flared at an MGM executive who made a pass. She told him off with a string of four-letter words that made his head spin. Dawn liked her spirit and tried to accentuate this side of Ava's personality by arching her eyebrows, and placing emphasis on her almond eyes.

Sidney Guilaroff was the best hairdresser in the movie industry. He did not change the color of Ava's hair other than highlighting. Like Jack Dawn, he appreciated her down-to-earth attitude. Guilaroff set her hair off the face and gave Ava the windblown look with a soft wave in the front. He trimmed her hair below the shoulders – long enough to sweep up for a more sophisticated effect. She hated the lacquer sprayed generously like a layer of starch, but Ava had yet to face the rigors of a day's work at MGM. As a newcomer she would not have a maid at her beck and call holding a silver tray with hairbrush, comb, cosmetics, and a makeup woman for touch-ups as Norma Shearer did. Ava Gardner, Kathryn Grayson, Donna Reed, and Esther Williams had to brave the wind, heat, hot lights, and humidity without wasting the studio's time on primping.

Ava's voice coach Gertrude Vogeler was responsible for ridding Ava of her thick Southern accent. 'You drop your *g*'s like magnolia blossoms,' Vogeler said, 'and we've got to teach you how to pronounce your *r*'s.' Vogeler, by chance, overheard Ava singing and detected no accent. Putting words to music played an important part in erasing her drawl.

Lillian Burns was MGM's best dramatic coach. She gave individual lessons four times a week, but on Fridays a group of new players read from popular plays. Burns was strict but patient. She could criticize without being insulting. Each newcomer was an individual to Burns. In Ava, she brought out the natural qualities that would enhance her acting. It was Lillian Burns who saw the animal magnetism in Ava's lackadaisical manner and carriage. Her voice was soft and low. Her husky laugh was sexy and elusive. The most difficult task Burns faced was convincing Ava that she possessed these qualities. In North Carolina this was considered lazy. In Hollywood, it was mysterious. At MGM it spelled . . . class.

Ava looked forward to her sessions with Lillian Burns, to whom she attributed her progress during those awkward months.

Modern and ballet dance lessons were required to give the young starlets poise and muscle coordination. Stretching, bending, and rhythmic body movements toned their legs and waistlines, too. Almost as important was for them to get through an evening at the Mocambo, whether it was a waltz, fox-trot, or tango.

Because Ava had a good figure, she was one of the first in her group to spend endless hours posing in a bathing suit on the beach and next to a swimming pool. Not only was this tiring, it could be embarrassing since the public was usually around to observe the 'cheesecake.' Then there were the long days spent under hot lights in the photographic department.

'Do I have to do this?' Ava asked Anne Strauss from

the publicity department. 'I find it disgusting.'

'Be patient,' was the advice. 'You won't regret it.'

What Ava failed to grasp in the beginning was that all she had to offer was a pretty face and good figure until she learned to act. In the meantime, her pictures were sent to the newspapers and fan magazines until her face and name became familiar.

She told *Photoplay* magazine years later, 'You could have carpeted Hollywood Boulevard with my pictures from curb to curb. I don't remember how many swimsuits I wore – without getting near the water. I shot enough sultry looks around the MGM photo gallery to melt the North Pole.'

Ava hated to be 'promoted' and would never change her mind about that. She did, however, find an ally in Howard Strickling, chief of MGM publicity, who was not only loyal to and trusted by Mayer, but a man who had a warm and understanding relationship with the MGM family. Clark Gable said, 'If it hadn't been for Howard, I'd probably be driving a truck.' When actress Jean Harlow's husband committed suicide, Mayer wanted to destroy a note left to Jean before the police arrived, but Strickling convinced him otherwise.

When he retired, Howard gallantly refused to divulge studio secrets. Nor would he discuss the personal lives of the stars he promoted and protected, dating back to Greta Garbo in the late twenties. Strickling was the one person who could be faithful to Mayer as well as the mogul's temperamental galaxy of stars without conflict. He was a rare breed. Despite his sincerity in a town of cutthroats, Howard was brilliant, sharp, and top-notch in a very competitive business.

In 1941 Ava was not in Strickling's league yet. He was responsible for the major stars, whose drinking bouts, fistfights, and auto accidents had to be covered up swiftly and skillfully. He often accompanied an actor or actress on a honeymoon to shield them from the press or intervened during a boisterous argument before neighbors summoned police.

Strickling's staff members, such as Anne Strauss, were assigned to look after potential stars during interviews because politics, swearing, gossip, and religion were taboo. The publicist made certain that cocktail glasses, liquor bottles, and cigarettes were removed from the table in a restaurant or nightclub before reporters took pictures. Stars were required to look well groomed at all times. For special occasions, they were allowed to borrow clothes from MGM's wardrobe department. Ava laughed, 'I looked like a million bucks and I was flat broke.'

She was never especially interested in getting rich and living in one of the luxurious mansions in Bel Air. Nor did she have illusions of becoming another Greta Garbo or Loretta Young. Ava wanted to make good at MGM and have enough money to be comfortable. She was, however, determined to make a name for herself.

Yet on the day she signed her MGM contract, Ava Gardner sensed a loneliness that dimmed the tinsel and glitter. As young and innocent as she was, Ava knew the only true happiness was having a man who could return all the love she had to give.

FOUR

Mickey

It was during her first week at Metro that Ava Gardner met Mickey Rooney. Milton Weiss was taking her on a tour of the studio and visited the set of *Babes on Broadway* where Mickey was rehearsing with Judy Garland. He was doing an impersonation of Carmen Miranda, the late dancer from Brazil. Mickey wore a basket of fruit on his head, a bodice blouse with falsies underneath, a long colorful samba skirt, high platform shoes, rouge, lipstick, and long false eyelashes.

'I did look good if I must say so myself!' he said later.

Babes on Broadway was a musical with splashy and gaudy sets clamoring with technicians, dancers, bongo drums, and maracas. Ava was dazzled, as any tourist might be. Rooney was dazzled by her. 'My heart and breathing stopped,' he said. 'It was all of five seconds later before I told myself I had seen the girl I was going to marry. She was sleek and proud and graceful and tender and infinitely, infinitely feminine. She was love.'

Milton Weiss described Mickey's reaction bluntly. 'He took one look at Ava and he was horny as hell. He had to have her.'

After the introductions and small talk, Mickey asked her to have dinner with him that night. She replied with a thick Southern accent, 'No, I'm busy tonight, Mr Rooney.'

Mickey wasn't the least bit discouraged. He was 'King of the Box Office' and one of the hottest properties in Hollywood. Though only five foot three, he had the confidence of a giant. Rooney had as much power at the studio as Gable and Garbo. He was not about to let a difference in height prevent him from pursuing a beautiful hick from North Carolina.

That same day Mickey was having lunch in the commissary with his entourage when Ava walked in alone. He sent a friend to ask if she'd like to join them. But when Rooney stood up to greet her, Ava was stunned. 'Jesus,' she commented later, 'I thought he must have shrunk since this morning. But then I remembered he was wearing those high platform shoes.'

During lunch she paid little attention to Mickey, who put on an act for her benefit. Ava was more interested in food. She barely smiled at him and wasn't impressed with his jokes, while the others roared with laughter. After she left the table, Mickey couldn't stop talking about her. The others hinted that she wasn't interested in him – to forget it. 'I'm gonna marry her if it kills me!' Rooney exclaimed.

Ava mentioned his invitation to dinner and was surprised to learn that the other starlets would have accepted without a second thought. The fact that he was a big star attracted most women. Weiss was impartial, but he agreed. 'Mickey doesn't have to beg for a date,' he said. 'Girls follow and seduce him.'

'I'm not a one-night stand,' Ava emphasized.

She received notes and flowers from Mickey. Every day he either sent a gift or telephoned. She kept her distance and the answer was always, 'No, thank you, Mr Rooney. I'm busy tonight.'

Mickey assumed she was dating other men, but Ava was in her dinky room with Bappie every evening. The girls were on a strict budget. They needed a car and, above all, another place to live. During these lean weeks it was Bappie who convinced her sister that the hard work and sacrifices were worth the effort.

Howard Strickling remembered specifics about Ava that set her apart from the other beginners. 'She approached the basic training with a reluctance, but no one could challenge her sheer determination. She was offended by the rigid schedule that she called "nonsense," but Ava poured her heart into everything. Within a month or so, she wanted to be a star, but didn't admit it. To me, anyway. What I recall in particular about her first few months at MGM was her enormous appetite. While our other actresses were allowed only cottage cheese and fruit, Ava had a big lunch with two glasses of milk and apple pie for dessert. In the afternoon she had a big banana split. Judy Garland and Greer Garson, meanwhile, were sipping plain tea with lemon. There were very few like Ava who could eat three big meals a day and not gain an ounce.'

On the weekends, she played tennis, golf, and other outdoor sports. 'I had a choice,' she said. 'It was either calisthenics at the studio or getting fresh air and exercise.' She was, however, on call seven days a week if Metro needed her for a crowd scene.

After three months in Hollywood, Ava and Bappie found an apartment on Franklin Avenue, not far from the studio. Though it was in a second-rate building in a second-rate neighborhood, the girls were glad to move out of the dreary Hollywood Wilcox Hotel. Their new place consisted of one room with two couches used as beds and a small kitchen.

It was one step forward, but they could barely afford a night out at a hash house for dinner. Why? Mickey Rooney wanted to know. When he found out Ava was not dating, he became more intrigued. The flowers and telephone calls increased, and notes were delivered by his cronies, who told Ava, 'You're nuts. Being seen with Rooney would do wonders for your career.' Precisely whom she spoke to in the MGM publicity department isn't known, but Ava casually strolled into the offices and talked to one of the agents. 'Mickey's not my type, but he won't give up. What should I do?'

'Go out with him,' was the reply. 'It'll do a lot for you.'

Still undecided, Ava remained aloof. There was nothing coy about her and she wasn't playing hard to get, as some observers insist. Although Rooney was only twenty-one, he'd been in show business most of his life and was aware of the games women played. 'Ava didn't give a damn who I was, or what I was, or what I could do for her, or how much money I was making,' he said.

When she saw Mickey at the studio, she usually nodded and continued on her way. Gradually he lured her into conversations. If Ava smiled, he clung to the opportunity and teased her about having dinner. It was quite an accomplishment when Ava said she 'might go out with him sometime.' Like a lovesick teenager he told his pals, 'I can't believe it!'

Ava's conception of what the man of her dreams would be like was typical. He would be tall, dark, and handsome. Mickey was short, blond, and cute. She preferred the quiet type. Mickey was 'on' all the time. She had visions of romance. Mickey came close. What he lacked in height, he made up for with charm and perseverance, both of which he amplified once Ava showed signs of giving in.

Finally one evening he asked her out – again. 'I'd like to,' she said, 'but I promised to have dinner with my sister.'

'Bring her along!' he exclaimed, trying to contain his excitement.

They went to Chasen's, a favorite restaurant of who's who in Hollywood. Mickey reserved one of the banquettes covered in red leather against a pine-paneled wall. He was greeted personally by owner Dave Chasen. The best champagne was on ice and the most expensive caviar served as an appetizer. Mickey, holding Ava's hand, went from table to table to show her off. 'I met more famous stars that night than during my four months in Hollywood,' she said.

Rooney ordered *crêpes suzette* for dessert. Ava had seconds. It became one of her favorite dishes. While she ate heartily, Mickey did his impersonations of Cary Grant, Lionel Barrymore, and James Cagney. 'That's interesting,' she said blandly, but through it all, Mickey was likeable and fun.

After dinner they went dancing. His head came to her shoulder, but Ava was beginning to enjoy the attention. So what if she was almost a head taller than Mickey? This was her first glimpse into the fantastic, exciting, diamond-studded world she had read about in fan magazines – glimmering gowns and luscious full-length furs skimming the floor, emeralds, pearls, and rubies sparkling on tanned bosoms. These elegantly attired ladies and their escorts in tuxedos greeted Mickey with hearty handshakes and kisses. But he made sure it was Ava's night by introducing her name loud and clear.

Photographers were anxious to take pictures. Reporters asked Rooney to spell her name. He obliged and held her hand possessively.

Feeling like Cinderella, she got into Mickey's red convertible. He took his time driving back to Franklin

Avenue. When they walked into the dimly lit hallway of her building, Ava headed for her apartment.

'Thank you for a lovely evening, Mickey. Good night.'

He followed her and blurted out, 'Will you marry me?'

She turned around and squinted, 'Are you nuts?'

'No, I'm serious, Ava.'

'Good night!' she exclaimed.

The next day he called. 'You don't have a car, do you?' he asked.

'I can't afford one.'

'It's gotta be a big drag getting to the studio.'

'Not too bad.'

'Can I drive you to work?'

'Oh, I suppose so,' she said, with very little enthusiasm.

Mickey picked her up every morning and dropped her off in the evening. These trips were not merely rides. They were vaudeville shows on wheels. Rooney entertained her with gossip and funny stories. Ava began to find him amusing. Mickey knew he was progressing when she laughed at the same joke twice. He began a major courtship – dinner at Romanoff's, dancing at the Mocambo, cocktails at Don the Beachcomber. At premieres, he gave Ava the spotlight, which was apparent when their pictures appeared in film magazines.

But she gave him neither her heart nor her body.

Mickey decided that being chauffeured in his Lincoln would free both his hands. Ava held him off and slammed the car door in his face. Afraid of losing her, Mickey sent a hundred roses after these back-seat tussles. For no reason, he gave her sprays of orchids. If he wasn't filming, he sent the car for her anyway. When Ava was finished at the studio, the chauffeur brought her to Mickey's house in Encino, where he lived with his mother and stepfather. This was all very proper, but their relationship was considered a romance by Hollywood.

Les Peterson, the MGM publicity man assigned to Mickey, suggested he take other girls out, too. Indirectly (or directly!) this was a warning from L.B. Mayer. Rooney's family liked Ava, but they thought he was too young for marriage. Mickey said everyone was against it, including the girl he loved. With every drawback and rejection, he became more energetic and determined. It was nothing for him to spend over a hundred dollars – a good deal of money in 1941 – in one evening. Sometimes he was the big man by picking up the tab after double dating with Errol Flynn or Peter Lawford. Mickey didn't care how long it took to capture Ava or how much he spent.

Mayer was growing uneasy. He told Howard Strickling, 'I know Rooney. All he wants is to get into her pants. Make sure he doesn't marry her to do it!'

'I can't threaten him.'

'That kid's got me by the balls. The Andy Hardy pictures are worth millions.'

'His teenage following might not be interested if he's married. We might stress that possibility.'

'We'll wait it out,' Mayer scowled. 'From what I hear, Gardner's not biting. If she gave him what he wants, we'd have nothing to worry about. Suppose . . . '

'Not on your life,' Strickling laughed. 'I get the impression she wouldn't go to bed with Mickey if you threatened not to renew her option.'

'That's what I said. They've *both* got me by the balls!'

By the middle of November 1941, Ava was not avoiding Mickey's persistent marriage proposals with, 'Don't be silly!' or 'Let's not talk about it anymore.' Instead she began taking him seriously. 'Marriage isn't something to joke about,' she said thoughtfully. 'I wouldn't consider marrying anyone unless I thought it would work out.'

Ava approached the subject in general, but not personally until she allowed herself to relax and enjoy the night life, drinking, staying up late, and mingling with celebrities she now called by their first names. She was approaching her nineteenth birthday, but Mickey was the only man she'd been alone with on a date. Whatever happened in the back seat of his Lincoln, though innocent, was a first for her. 'What would our marriage be like?' she asked him.

'We'd both act. You'll be a big star like me. We'd have fun.'

'Besides that, I mean. What about our home life?'

'That would be fun, too.'

He promised her luxuries – cars, furs, a house, vacations. 'I offered her the world,' Rooney said. 'I kept talking and making promises. I don't remember half of them because I'd have done anything, bought her anything, if she'd say yes.'

One evening in early December, he asked her again in the back seat of his car and she replied, 'All right, Mickey, I'll marry you.' He kissed her over and over again. 'When?' he asked with their lips still touching.

'Don't you have to work it out with the studio?'

'The hell with them. How about tomorrow?'

'Please, Mickey, let's be sensible about this.'

The following day he gave her an engagement ring and called Louella Parsons with the scoop for her column.

L.B. Mayer spoke to Ava first. 'All Mickey wants is one thing,' he said. 'When he gets it, he'll be satisfied. Bored. Out for another conquest. I know him better than you do.' She shivered and kept her mouth shut. Ida Koverman walked out of Mayer's office with Ava and tried to warn her. 'I hope you know what you're getting into,' she told Ava, who didn't respond.

39

Mayer told Mickey he was making a mistake marrying an unknown starlet.

'We're in love,' Rooney said.

'I'm only thinking of your happiness.'

'Good, because she's the only girl I want.'

'For the wrong reasons,' Mayer stressed. 'You're so hot for her you can't think straight.'

'She's the only girl I've ever loved and I've known a few, as you know.'

'You're breaking my heart, Mickey.'

The MGM players claim that L.B. Mayer was the greatest actor of them all. He cried that day to prove his deep concern. Tears rolled down his cheeks. 'Please, Mickey. Don't do this. It's all wrong. You have nothing in common with the girl.'

Rooney wasn't buying it. He knew Mayer was worried about his image as Andy Hardy. How could America's typical small town boy take a wife? He sipped Cokes with Judy Garland, put on high school plays, and held hands at the end of the picture. Andy Hardy married? To a 36-20-36 who was four inches taller?

Mayer wiped his eyes and blew his nose, slumped in his chair, and sadly related, 'I warned Judy Garland. She married David Rose anyway. It won't last, Mickey. I warned Lana, too, but she eloped with Artie Shaw. She's a divorcée at twenty-one. You kids don't think. You're not prepared for marriage. Please tell me that you'll wait awhile . . . think it over.'

'As a matter of fact,' Mickey said, 'I was going to ask for some time off for a honeymoon.'

Mayer's face turned crimson. 'I'm not paying you a thousand dollars a week and twenty-five thousand a picture to satisfy your fuckin' fantasies. If I can't prevent you from getting married, you'll do it my way – quietly and without fanfare. Peterson will handle everything.'

'When?'

'After the holidays,' Mayer scowled. 'I'll let you know.'

'*Right* after the holidays,' Mickey emphasized.

Despite the shock of Pearl Harbor on December 7, 1941, a roster of MGM's biggest male stars gathered in one of the studio's huge dining rooms for Rooney's bachelor party. Mayer played host to Robert Taylor, Clark Gable, Spencer Tracy, Lionel Barrymore, to name a few. They gave Mickey pointers on how to stay happily married and cheat, too. The booze flowed and so did the advice. Rooney remembered in particular the story about the pebbles in the sink. The first year, every time he made love to his wife, he should put a pebble in the sink. After that, whenever he made love to his wife, take one pebble out. The sink would never be empty.

'Lipstick on the collar? Another woman? Nonsense! That's red pencil marks!'

'Take it easy in bed. If you sprain your back, the columnists will want details.'

'Watch the knee in your groin during a fight.'

'Nibble gently on her ear, kid.'

Mickey thanked his buddies for the great party, the gifts, and their good wishes. 'I appreciate all your jokes, you horny bastards,' he said, 'and the first guy I see looking at Mrs Rooney gets a right hand to the teeth!'

Mickey Rooney was born Joe Yule, Jr. on September 23, 1920 in a Brooklyn rooming house. His mother, Nell Carter, was a chorus girl from Kansas City. Joe, Sr. was born in Edinburgh, Scotland, but grew up in New York, where he met Nell and married her. They became a vaudeville team, traveling from town to town.

Mickey's nursery was backstage in whatever theater the Yules were playing. When he was a year and a half, he followed the orchestra into the pit, climbed on a drum, and pretended to play. The audience ignored the comic on the stage. Nell made a tuxedo for her son and he played the drums in every show, but Mickey grew tired of the orchestra pit. One night he walked onstage and told the performer, 'I can sing "Pal o' My Cradle Days" better than you.' This was the beginning of Mickey Rooney's career in show business.

In the mid-twenties, the Yules separated. Nell headed for Hollywood with her son. She read that Hal Roach was looking for child actors. She never got to see Roach, but she did get Joe, Jr. an audition for the movie version of the Toonerville Trolley series by Fontaine Fox. Yule, cast in the Mickey McGuire films, had his hair dyed dark to make him more like the brash tough kid from the original cartoon. He played in fifty of the McGuire short subjects.

When Universal hired him for several features, Nell thought he could be billed as Mickey McGuire, but legalities prevented that, so he became known as Mickey Rooney. In 1933 Metrol-Goldwyn-Mayer signed him on a week-to-week basis. In 1934 Mickey played Clark Gable as a child in *Manhattan Melodrama*.

He was loaned to Warner Brothers to play Puck in the screen version of *A Midsummer Night's Dream*. MGM finally signed him to a contract calling for $500 a week with subsequent automatic raises. In *Ah, Wilderness*, he was acclaimed star material in 1935, but it wasn't until two years later, in *Family Affair*, that his awkward but wholesome Andy Hardy was a smash.

Mickey attended Ma Lawlor's school for professional children where he met Frances Gumm, who would bloom as Judy Garland. He met Lana Turner at Hollywood High, and dated her for several months. They were both seventeen.

In 1937 Nell remarried. Fred Pankey was an accountant, and though Mickey liked him as a stepfather, he did not heed his advice on financial matters. With a new MGM contract beginning at $750 a week, graduating to $2,500, Rooney bought a house in the San Fernando Valley. It cost $75,000, but wasn't lavish compared to the mansions in Beverly Hills. Mickey was proud of his first real home on five acres with a swimming pool, lemon trees, gardenia plants, and English walnut trees. In the house built of stone were twelve rooms, nine telephones, and sterling silver fixtures in the bathrooms. 'What Mom, Fred, and I wanted was a comfortable place,' he said. This house was perhaps the best investment Rooney ever made. He thought nothing about money and would eventually regret it. Fred Pankey did his best to control Mickey's spending, his gambling, and marriages. 'It won't always be this way,' he told his stepson. 'Save something for a rainy day.'

However, Mickey Rooney had no rainy days. He was always 'up' or 'on.' He was sure of himself, not conceited. He could act and sing and dance, and he had boundless energy. Women followed him. He had his choice. His dates were treated to dinner, dancing, and what usually follows in the young lady's bedroom, 'I'll call ya, honey.' Mickey went out with Judy, whom he considered his best friend. Nell hoped they would get married, but they weren't in love. It was good publicity that he and Lana be seen together and Mickey was crazy about her. When he bought his first car, it was Lana who sat in the front seat next to him.

Mickey kept in touch with his father, Joe Yule, Sr., and brought him to Hollywood for a visit. 'I was happy enough that we could at least become friends,' Rooney said.

At the peak of his career in 1940, he had it all. He was a top star making his first million, he loved to drink, gamble, and clown for the camera, and he had dined with the President of the United States and Henry

Ford. He wasn't looking for a wife and he didn't need love. But Mickey Rooney wanted more. He was restless, ambitious, curious, and rich. Often he has said it was never the money he was seeking at the racetracks or in the poker games. It was the win. Remarkably he had conquered the world and was not yet twenty-one. What else could he ask for?

On the set of *Babes on Broadway* he found it. Surrounded by beautiful girls, he rarely paid attention to any new one who had just signed a contract with MGM and was taking a tour of the studio – just another pretty dame.

One glance at Ava Gardner and no other woman existed. Nothing else mattered. She would crown his dream. No longer would he sit on top of the world all alone.

FIVE

Love Forever

If L.B. Mayer could not prevent Mickey Rooney from marrying Ava Gardner, he took control of their life from the day the couple became engaged. Press agent Les Peterson was summoned to the mogul's office and given specific instructions. 'I want no publicity until it's over,' Mayer dictated. 'Find a church out of town and see to it the local press gets an exclusive after the wedding. We don't want snoopers or reporters getting wind of it beforehand. Strickling will take care of the rest. Under no circumstances is anyone to know where they will be spending their honeymoon. Find a hotel nearby. Stay with them every minute they're not in the room. Mickey will be very busy filming in the meantime so I want you to get the wedding ring. Ask him about the inscription, but it's important no one knows who's buying it. Then there's the matter of a place for Mickey and Ava to live. Make sure it's off the beaten path. Bel Air and Beverly Hills are out! A two-bedroom apartment in a nice building. Not too expensive because Mickey's paying off the mortgage on his Encino home. When you think you've found a suitable place, get his approval and take care of the lease.'

'What about the marriage license?' Peterson asked.

'That's a delicate matter,' Mayer said. 'I'll take care of it. This operation must be a discreet one, Les.'

Ava wanted a big wedding. 'I always dreamed of wearing a white dress and walking down the aisle,' she said.

'That's for everybody else,' Mickey explained. 'It can't be that way for us, honey. You wouldn't want a circus of fans and reporters spoiling our day, would you?'

'I guess not . . . '

'We'll have a quiet wedding with just the family present. It's more romantic.'

'All right . . . '

Ava considered buying a white dress anyway, but couldn't afford one. She was too embarrassed to ask Mickey for the money. Her biggest disappointment was knowing her mother was too ill to attend the ceremony. Bappie tried to keep her sister busy looking for a trousseau, a sheer long white nightgown, matching slippers, a simple dark-blue tailored suit, and shoes. MGM gave her a small bonus that she spent on these few items of clothing. Aside from packing her suitcase, she had nothing to do with the wedding plans.

Les Peterson was on the search day and night for several weeks. He found a small white Presbyterian church in the town of Ballard, located between Los Angeles and San Francisco. He promised the local

46

newspapers exclusive wedding pictures if they kept it quiet. In nearby Carmel, he made arrangements for the four-day honeymoon with reservations under an assumed name at the Del Monte Hotel.

He found an apartment in a building on Wilshire Boulevard near Westwood which was owned by Red Skelton and director Frank Borzage. Though it was decorated with white walls and carpeting, the two-bedroom flat was a drab hideaway on the first floor.

The date for the wedding was set for Sunday, January 10, 1942.

Very early that morning, Ava, Mickey, and Les Peterson drove north towards Santa Barbara. Squeezed in the second car were Joe Jule, Sr., Nell and her second husband, Bappie, and an MGM photographer. They stopped in Carpenteria, on the outskirts of Santa Barbara, for the wedding license issued by County Clerk J.E. Lewis who, for added precaution, was waiting at his house for Mickey.

At eleven o'clock they arrived at the little Presbyterian church, tucked away in the foothills of the Santa Ynez Mountains. The fact that Ava was a Southern Baptist and Mickey was a Christian Scientist apparently didn't matter. The Reverend Glenn H. Lutz performed the brief ceremony. Mrs Lutz played 'I Love You Truly' and Mendelssohn's 'Wedding March' on an upright piano.

The bride wore an orchid corsage pinned to her dark blue suit. Mickey chose a dark gray suit with a polka dot tie, a white carnation in his buttonhole, and a white handkerchief peeking out of his top pocket. He was so nervous he almost dropped the wedding ring on the floor before slipping it on Ava's finger.

After the ceremony, Peterson rushed to a phone and called MGM. The local press, silenced by the studio, had stayed away. They were furnished with the first

47

photos of Mr and Mrs Mickey Rooney. Hedda Hopper made the announcement in time for the morning edition of her column, but only a few people knew the whereabouts of the famous couple.

The Yules and Bappie drove back to Los Angeles. Mickey, Ava, and Les went to Carmel and checked into the Del Monte Hotel. When the newlyweds were safely in their room, Peterson left them alone for the night.

It took Mickey twenty minutes to get into his pajamas. He put them on backwards anyway. 'I tried to put my legs through the sleeves,' he laughed, 'and couldn't get the bottoms over my head. I was shaking. I wanted to be with Ava so bad and there she was stretched out on the bed in a beautiful white gown like a Greek goddess.'

Ava was terrified. She was about to engage in the act that her mother scorned and ridiculed. Was it a consummation of love to be cherished? Or was it the duty of a bride on her wedding night to be endured?

Rooney, who was experienced with women, confessed to being awkward and clumsy that night, but when Ava lost her shyness, she was warm and receptive. If Mickey thought his crowning achievement was in the tiny white church earlier that day, he was wrong. For he was the first man to possess Ava Gardner. 'I was proud,' he said years later.

The following morning, she was cozy and warm in their bridal bed. How nice to have breakfast in the room and lie around in each other's arms . . . maybe take a swim if the water wasn't too cold, have a drink together, dinner alone, and back to bed for love talk and lovemaking.

'Beautiful day, darling,' she sighed.

'It sure is. Perfect for golf.'

'Golf?'

He kissed her and hopped out of bed. 'Have you

48

seen the golf course here?' he yawned, rushing into the shower.

'No,' she yawned.

'You'll love it!' he shouted from the bathroom.

Golf clubs were part of Mickey's trousseau. He was very proud of his woods and irons. 'I've been playing in the seventies,' he cheered as they headed for the green. Ava tagged along, most likely in shock. For the remainder of her honeymoon, she stayed at the hotel with Peterson, who was in the dining room when the newlyweds came in for breakfast, lunch, and dinner. Mickey liked people and, though not overly fond of Les, a threesome was more entertaining. Ava said, 'On my honeymoon I saw more of Peterson than I did of my husband.'

Mickey was having a wonderful time. He called his family and friends to tell them not only was he playing excellent golf, but his wife was a virgin when he married her.

Ava concealed her hurt and rage in Carmel. The only time she was alone with Mickey was in bed. She joked about Peterson joining them because he was their constant companion. Fans and reporters were prowling the hotel grounds, however, and without his help the four days might have been a worse disaster, if that was at all possible.

Though Rooney made a horrible mistake by ignoring his bride on their honeymoon, he firmly believed that man was the master. He did what he wanted to do and his wife did what he wanted to do. Ava believed in the old-fashioned concept of marriage also – that the husband was boss, the moneymaker, and the one who made decisions. Rooney took advantage of it, as he would admit later. 'I don't think Ava forgave me,' he said, 'and I wonder if I've forgiven myself.'

From Carmel the threesome drove to San Francisco where they began an MGM promotional tour for the

Andy Hardy films. They stayed at the Palace Hotel and did some sightseeing before boarding the Santa Fe Super Chief to New York. The sudden death of Carole Lombard in a plane crash on January 16 put a damper on their tedious trip. Mickey tried to call Gable to express his condolences, but Clark was in Las Vegas with a search party trying to find the plane wreckage.

At the New Yorker Hotel, the Rooneys held a press conference. Ava sat in a deep chair while Mickey sat on the arm so that the difference in their heights was not too apparent. Bappie joined them for President Roosevelt's birthday celebration in Washington. While Mickey entertained the troops at Fort Bragg, North Carolina, Ava went to Smithfield to visit her family. The highlight of the trip was a private luncheon with President Roosevelt, but the long journey from Carmel, the press conferences, parties, and celebrations before returning to California were exhausting. That Mickey was the center of attention didn't bother Ava. She was used to that, but her expectations of sharing his life had been shattered. Her mother was dying and, with the exception of Bappie, she had no one but Mickey, who had yet to sit down alone with her and have a normal conversation. Weeks of resentment, loneliness, and bitterness were brewing inside. Could she put them behind her and set up household in Westwood with any hope? Ava wasn't sure.

In Carmel she competed with the golf course and Mickey's endless telephone calls to his buddies in Los Angeles. Back in Hollywood there were the racetrack, poker games, and her husband's soaring career in movies. Ava was still posing for cheesecake and taking drama lessons. Only a trace of her Southern accent was left. She went through the motions, resumed her dancing lessons, and came home to kick off her shoes, cook dinner, and flop. Mickey was so highly charged that he came home raring to go. Sometimes he called to say, 'I'll be late, honey. Eat without me.' On other occasions he didn't bother to telephone. Ava sat alone and fumed.

She invited a friend for dinner one evening and Mickey was decent enough to come home. 'They were like two kids,' the guest said. 'The whole time I was there they giggled, romped around on the floor, and played tag. I sat there and watched until I couldn't take anymore. I left. When they were having fun, no one else existed, but it was a silly scene – two grown people tickling and teasing. Maybe that stuff led to the bedroom. I don't know. Ava said they were sexually compatible and that was about it.'

Finally Ava was chosen for a screen appearance in *We Were Dancing*. Wearing slacks and a silk blouse, her solo debut entailed walking across a hotel lobby while Melvyn Douglas observed with interest. Mickey coached Ava on the set. He showed her how to walk, how to hold her head, move her arms. She did the scene several times, until it was perfect. Bappie took the day off from Magnin's to lend support, but Ava wasn't nervous. After the final take, Mickey went back to his own set. The girls decided to wait for the star of *We Were Dancing*, the legendary Norma Shearer, who arrived with her maid, hairdresser, makeup man, agent, publicity man, and dresser. Everyone paid homage to the movie queen who would retire after one more film. If she hadn't rejected *Mrs Miniver*, perhaps her career might have been salvaged. But on that important day in Ava's life, Norma Shearer represented the epitome of movie star status in the golden era that was slowly fading.

'Someday I'm going to have a crowd of people waiting on me like that,' Ava told Bappie. They watched with awe while the great Shearer was pampered, powdered, and prompted for her first scene.

In February 1942, Ava was rushed to the hospital with an inflamed appendix. Mickey arrived as she was coming out of the anesthesia. He was frantic. 'Why did you wait so long?' he asked.

'I've had stomach pains since I was a kid,' she replied. 'When I get upset, I . . . '

'As long as you're okay now,' he said, squeezing her hand.

'When I'm unhappy I get pains in my stomach,' she repeated.

'Why would you get upset, darling?'

'Waiting for you to come home. Everything gets tied up in knots.'

He laughed, told some jokes, and she laughed. 'I'm gonna take care of you from now on,' Mickey said with a kiss.

Ava was home in a few days and Rooney was attentive to her for a while. He tried to come home from the studio with her, change into old clothes, and spend a quiet evening doing nothing. She played phonograph records and wrote letters to her family. Mickey paced the floor, called his cronies, and tried to make conversation with Ava. 'She didn't talk much,' he said. 'She was a good listener, and when I was finished, the room was deadly silent. She'd go back to her magazine or letter writing. I went nuts. I had to have people around. Action. I dreaded those long evenings at home.'

At parties, the situation was no different. Mickey was center stage, while Ava sat in the corner pouting. She'd seen his act a hundred times. She was bored with racing forms, golf chatter, and how much money he won or lost at a poker game. Amusingly, Mickey did not appreciate his wife's sulking alone at parties, but he became a madman when she mingled. One evening she danced with actor Tom Drake several times at a studio party. Mickey went into a rage, but this time Ava stood up to him. She called him a runt and a midget. Then she stormed out and went to Bappie's apartment on Franklin. He followed and they made up, but Mickey was aware a new Ava was surfacing. When she volunteered to help out at the Hollywood Canteen, he went along, too. There was no way he would allow her to be by herself with a bunch of lonely servicemen.

Mickey used his influence at the studio to get her better parts. He felt if she were busy, it would ease the tension. In *Two Girls and a Sailor* she was a canteen hostess who falls asleep as she dances. In *Reunion in France* with Joan Crawford and John Wayne, Ava was a fashion model. Regardless of what Mickey was doing, he found time to be with Ava if she was in a movie. 'I owe everything to him,' she said. 'If I ever become anybody . . . make something of myself, Mickey will be the one responsible.'

When she became a star Ava commented, 'Even though he didn't understand marriage, Mickey sure as hell understood show business.'

In the spring of 1942 she was given a speaking part in *Kid Glove Killer* with Marsha Hunt and Lee Bowman. Ava played a drive-in waitress. If she was elated, Mickey was ecstatic! A trouper, who never forgot how his eagerness to be noticed as a kid got him where he was, impressed on Ava that whether she was a waitress or a queen, she should do it well and do it right. Being discovered overnight was for a fortunate few. 'Presence is very important,' he said. While most young actresses were more interested in their face and

53

figures, Mickey went beyond that. It wasn't the fact that Ava had beautiful eyes, rather what she did with them. Focus here or focus there. The camera doesn't exist, but remember where it is. Chin up. Walk slower, but don't take your time. Keep the head up. Always chin level with the ground. Pause. Very important is that pause . . . that slight hesitation.

Ava did what she was told to do, but wasn't getting any public attention. 'I didn't think you would,' Rooney smiled. 'It takes time.'

Mayer, however, renewed Ava's options and raised her salary to $150 a week. This was not a result of Mickey's influence. Quite the opposite. L.B. did not have to ask his spies about the Rooney marriage. It was in trouble, as expected. Andy Hardy had made the transition, thanks to the discretion of MGM's publicity department, but divorce would have a devastating effect on the Hardy series, which were making millions. Mayer observed and waited.

Ava fled to Bappie's more than once when she was angry, lonely, or depressed. Sometimes she returned to Mickey the same night, but more often she refused. In the fall of 1942 the Rooneys officially separated. Ava could not bear the long nights by herself. The studio might have left the couple alone to sort out their problems, but Mickey's performance in *The Courtship of Andy Hardy* was dull and listless. The dark circles under his eyes were almost as prominent as those of his father, Judge Hardy. Rooney's appeal, aside from talent, was his bouncy enthusiasm. Viewing the rushes after a day's filming, Metro officials noted the drastic change in not only Mickey's appearance, but his acting, too. At Mayer's request, Carey Wilson, producer of the Andy Hardy films, had a long talk with the Rooneys. Bappie was present and urged her sister to reconcile with Mickey. Ava thought she might give it another try, but was tired of the Westwood apartment, tired of throwing dinner in the garbage every night. She demanded a housekeeper.

Rooney found a cozy cottage on Stone Canyon Drive in Bel Air, and Mayer, in the background, rewarded Ava with a part in *Ghosts on the Loose* with the Dead End Kids at Monogram Pictures, a subsidiary of Allied Artists. Monogram produced the B-pictures. It was the cheapest studio in Hollywood, one reason Allied Artists did not want their label on its movies. The Dead End Kids were popular, however, and Ava handled comedy nicely.

Metro made sure the Rooneys were seen together in nightclubs to prove their togetherness. Mickey enjoyed their nights on the town, but Ava was no longer putting up with his one-ring circus.

'Would you do me a favor?' she asked on the drive home from the Mocambo.

'Sure, darling. What is it?'

'Shut up.'

Mickey was not getting the worn-out message. He continued on his merry way, ignoring Ava at parties and staying out late with his cronies. He came home drunk one night. She threw an inkwell at his head.

Rooney thought a baby would salvage the marriage, but Ava was terrified of pregnancy. He never knew why. In his memoirs, written twenty years later, he still asked, 'Why, Ava? Why?'

She claimed that Mickey didn't want children, but he remembers her getting out of bed one night after making love, turning to him at the bathroom door, and hissing, 'Mickey, if I ever become pregnant, I'll kill you.'

Ava never discussed the basis of this fear. Possibly

Mollie had related her own horrors of childbirth and the lonely responsibility of motherhood. Or maybe Ava did not want to ruin her figure. Rooney wasn't sure, but he knew his wife was not the same girl who sipped chocolate soda on their honeymoon while he played golf. Instead of taking the time to discuss their problems, he continued to stay out late. It should have been no surprise to him when he came home one night and discovered Ava had slashed the furniture and drapes with a knife.

After that, she began accepting invitations from friends to go out. Lana Turner was back in circulation following her divorce from Artie Shaw. She and Ava consoled each other by going to nightclubs without dates.

When Mickey went into a rage of jealousy, she told him, 'Get the hell out!' He went to the house in Encino, and Ava moved to the Westwood apartment that the studio had maintained.

Mayer, who was concerned about bad publicity and Rooney's welfare, conveniently sent him off on location in Connecticut to film *A Yank at Eton*. While he was away, Mickey sent Ava a $10,000 mink coat and jewelry. Not knowing if he might return unexpectedly, Ava asked Leatrice Carney, daughter of silent screen star John Gilbert, to move in with her. They enjoyed having small dinner parties for Fran and Van Heflin, agent Minna Wallis, who was responsible for getting Clark Gable into movies, Ava's lawyer Jerry Rosenthal and his wife, and Donna Reed and her husband, Tony Owen.

On one such occasion, when Ava's Southern fried chicken was sizzling on the stove, Mickey pounded on the door and demanded to see her. She refused to let him in. He broke the door down and had to be restrained by the guests.

Ava warned Howard Strickling that if Mickey tried

to see her, she'd tell the press the whole sordid story. Though Rooney was responsible for the marriage not working (by his own admission), sadly he was still in love with Ava. Leatrice Carney thought he was crazy with frustration because he couldn't sleep with her.

Mickey did not disobey the studio's orders to leave his wife alone, because he needed Mayer more than ever now.

'I just got my draft notice, L.B. I can't go. Not now.'

Mayer began to cry. 'I know how you feel, son.'

'I'm all busted up inside.'

'Don't be ashamed to admit you're afraid.'

'Scared to death,' Mickey said, fighting back the tears.

'Maybe I can do something. After all, the Andy Hardy movies are good for public morale.'

'Could you do that?' Mickey asked.

'I'm glad you came to me, son,' Mayer sobbed. 'I'm proud we were able to talk it out – that you were man enough to admit your fear.'

Mickey broke down. 'If I have to leave now, I'll never get Ava back. Never!'

Rooney was no coward. He was willing to go into the service, but the timing was wrong. He wanted to fight for Ava first and *then* fight the enemy. Mayer wasn't concerned why. He appealed, but the draft board cared less about Andy Hardy.

This was the first time Metro tried to keep one of its stars out of the service. Mayer was thinking of the millions that would be lost at the box office, but he sincerely hated to see Mickey go into the army.

❦

On May 2, 1943, Ava filed for divorce in Los Angeles City Court. She accused Rooney of 'grievous mental suffering' and 'extreme mental cruelty.' Wearing her dark blue wedding suit, she appeared before Superior Court Judge Thurmond Clarke on May 21 and testified that her husband did not want a home life. When asked if she was left alone many times, Ava replied, 'Yes. He often stayed away from home. Twice he stayed away for long periods. He spent a month with his mother, and when I protested he told me simply that he didn't want to be with me.' Bappie substantiated Ava's testimony.

Judge Clarke granted her a divorce. Instead of demanding half of Mickey's holdings, Ava asked for $25,000, a car, and whatever furs and jewelry he had given her.

MGM had intervened when Rooney put an engagement ring on her hand, and they intervened when she took it off. Mayer convinced Ava to settle for less rather than drain Mickey. In return, he promised to further her career at MGM. If she refused, Mayer indicated her contract would be dropped. He did not have to remind Ava that if that happened, she would never work for any other studio in Hollywood.

The day after Ava appeared in court, she received the news that her mother had died. She flew home for the funeral. Mickey Rooney wasn't present at the cemetery to draw the crowds, but they were there anyway. The local folks wanted to get a glimpse of Mollie's daughter, whose visit to town was featured on the front page of the *Smithfield Journal*.

SIX

Fame and Freedom

Bappie moved into the Westwood apartment with Ava, who now concentrated on her career. She appeared in such forgettable films as *DuBarry Was a Lady*, *Young Ideas*, *Lost Angel*, *Spring Fever*, and *Music for Millions*. Ava was expected to be seen on the nightclub circuit, and she obliged with Peter Lawford, Fernando Lamas, and Turhan Bey.

Mayer gave her plenty of exposure on the screen before putting Ava in *Three Men in White*, one of the popular Dr Gillespie movies that were almost as popular as the Andy Hardy series. Lionel Barrymore, who portrayed the old doctor, was a household word in America.

In the picture Ava played the part of a girl who is used by Dr Gillespie to try to seduce Van Johnson, a young intern who wants to become Gillespie's assistant. His strength of character is put to the test. Ava got her first billing in *Three Men in White*, and though the director, Willis Goldbeck, was helpful and patient, Ava turned to Mickey before production began. He was more than willing to give her support and was on the set until the film was completed. The press caught up with them at a restaurant and asked about a possible reconciliation. Ava commented, 'I couldn't get along without Mickey and I guess he couldn't get along without me.'

Rooney, holding her hand, beamed, 'I'm still in love with Ava and I hope we can get back together again. We're both young and have a lot to learn.'

A mutual friend recalled, 'This was a very confusing time in Ava's life. The death of her mother was a terrible blow. They had been very close and Ava regretted not being with Mollie at the end. Losing her husband and mother at the same time was difficult. When she was given her first big break in the Gillespie picture, Ava needed Mickey. Simple as that. When she said, "I couldn't get along without Mickey," it was in reference to facing the camera. Perhaps she was kidding herself again – that maybe they could make a go of it this time. All I know is when the picture was over so was possibility of their reconciliation.'

The preview of *Three Men in White* was at the Village Theatre in Westwood and was an enormous success. *The Hollywood Reporter* said, 'Marilyn Maxwell and Ava Gardner, two of the smoothest young sirens to be found, are superb and should delight the studio with their histrionic conduct here.' Other critics applauded, too. Bosley Crowther of *The New York Times*, however, wrote that Ava was 'sultry but stupid.'

MGM was pleased with the response and rushed Ava into *Maisie Goes to Reno*. Ann Southern played the hard-boiled, gold-digging Maisie in ten MGM comedy-dramas. Ava was cast as the millionairess wife of Tom Drake. Her part required little more than a haughty manner, which brought out her true lofty elegance.

Despite her success, Ava saw Hollywood no

differently than the day she arrived – a boring town with ragged palm trees, pink and white dull buildings filled with phony people, and garish movie theaters that reeked of the past.

She considered her roles bland and tedious. Occasionally she talked about going back to North Carolina and becoming a secretary. How pleasant and uncomplicated it would be to meet a nice guy who worked nine to five, get married, and settle down with children. Bappie knew it was too late for anything like that to happen.

The night before Mickey boarded a train as a buck private for Fort Riley, Kansas, he had dinner with Ava. He wanted her to see him off in the morning. 'Will you, please?' he pleaded.

'I don't know,' she replied, 'but I'll be waiting for you, Mickey.'

'What?'

'When you get out of the army, I'll be waiting,' she repeated.

Ava wasn't at the station on June 15, 1944. Maybe it was just as well. Observers said it was funny watching Mickey lugging a five-foot duffel bag, almost the same size as himself, but Rooney was the happiest of five hundred recruits that day. Ava had promised to wait! How did he know she had borrowed the line from any of a hundred war movie scripts?

Mickey wrote to her every day and she answered each letter. Then as the weeks went by, he received an occasional reply and then nothing at all. 'I wrote and I wrote and I wrote,' he said.

Then came the phone call that broke his heart. 'I don't want you writing me anymore,' she began.

'Hi, Ava, darling. What did you say?'

'Don't write to me anymore. It's over. Goodbye, Mickey.'

'You said you'd wait!' he yelled. 'I love you. I – '

'Goodbye, Mickey.'

He cried. He dwelled on memories, the good and the bad. Then he turned to the bottle for the first time in his life.

❡

Ava Gardner said she was the loneliest girl in the world after her divorce from Rooney. She had few dates that were not strictly for the purpose of keeping her name in the gossip columns, which MGM expected. Attorney Greg Bautzer might have been an exception. He was a handsome bachelor and man-about-town. Lana Turner had fallen deeply in love with Greg, who gave her a small diamond friendship ring. She was only nineteen at the time and a virgin when she met the debonair attorney. Lana had wedding bells ringing in her ears until Joan Crawford turned them off. She, too, had been seeing Greg. Theirs was a hot adult romance that lasted for several years. He broke a leg falling from her rose trellis attempting to get into her bedroom. 'God, it was romantic,' Joan told a friend. Fifteen years older than Lana, Miss Crawford thought it was best they had a talk to avoid heartbreak. Turner married Artie Shaw on the rebound.

Ava was seen in the company of singer-dancer Billy Daniels and actor John Carroll. But these flings meant little to her. Her evenings at home with Bappie were satisfying, although sleeping became a problem. Insomnia would plague Ava, though in time she would cure it by not going to bed at all.

Friends at the studio wanted to arrange dates for her. Ava wasn't interested until one afternoon when she was feeling particularly lonely. 'Where and what time?' she asked her girlfriend.

'At my place. We'll go home together.'

As if by magic, the house was set up for a dinner party when they arrived. Ava's blind date was the direct opposite of Mickey Rooney. This fellow was dark, very tall and thin, quiet, and simply dressed. They carried on brief but interesting conversations and he left after dessert.

The next morning her girlfriend reported, 'Howard was quite taken with you.'

'Howard who?' Ava asked.

'Howard Hughes!'

'The millionaire?'

'When you agreed to have dinner at my place, I called Howard and he made all the arrangements because he was anxious to meet you.'

'Why didn't he just call for a date?' Ava asked.

'He has someone else ask the first time,' her friend replied.

Howard telephoned Ava for dinner a few days later. She chose a slinky evening gown for the occasion. He came to the door dressed casually. His old Chevy was parked at the curb. Hughes was a man who did not bother to explain that he preferred out-of-the-way steakhouses and hamburger joints. His idea of a pleasant evening was watching a movie in his private projection room and having a light supper.

Lana Turner, who was interwoven in and out of Ava's life, had set her sights for Howard. In an interview with reporter James Bacon, Hughes did not deny the story that Lana was so sure he would marry her, she had her silk sheets monogrammed *HH*. He said he had no intention of getting married. When she pouted over the monogramming, Hughes said, 'Why don't you marry Huntington Hartford?'

Howard, who was also born on Christmas Eve, was forty when he met Ava. She was attracted to him right away. Not only was he tall, dark, and handsome, his bashfulness brought out the motherly instinct in her.

That Hughes was a millionaire impressed her least of all, but his money bought Ava the freedom and privacy she craved. His possessiveness led to bitter arguments and separations, however.

Howard was 'associated' with many famous women in his lifetime – Billie Dove, Katharine Hepburn, Olivia De Havilland, Ginger Rogers, Ida Lupino, Carole Lombard, Constance Bennett, and Bette Davis, to name a few. He was intrigued with the aloofness of Hepburn and Gardner, both of whom turned down his marriage proposals, as opposed to a harem of girls who were his for the asking.

Hughes was obsessed with big breasts and Ava had them. Oddly, he was never intimate with his two busty movie discoveries, Jean Harlow and Jane Russell, because he wouldn't mix business with pleasure. After *Hell's Angels* Howard sold Jean to MGM for a mere $60,000, but he signed Russell for twenty years and $1000 a week whether she worked or not. She was a receptionist in his dentist's office when Howard first noticed her remarkable bustline and cast her in *The Outlaw*. He supervised her career and it was during *Macao* with Robert Mitchum that Hughes wrote the famous brassiere memo:

The fit of the dress around Jane Russell's breasts is not good and gives the impression, God forbid, that her breasts are padded or artificial. They just don't appear to be in natural contour. It looks as if she is wearing a brassiere of some very stiff material which does not take the contour of her breasts.

I am not recommending that she go without a brassiere, as I know this is a very necessary piece of equipment for Rusell. But I thought, if we could find a half-brassiere which will support her breasts upward and still not be noticeable under the dress or, alternatively, a very thin brassiere made of very thin material so that the natural contour of her breasts will show through the dress, it will be a great deal more effective.

In addition to the brassiere situation, it may be that the dress will have to be retailored around the breasts in order that it will more naturally form to the proper contour.

Now, it would be extremely valuable if the brassiere, or the dress, incorporated some kind of a point at the nipple because I know this does not ever occur naturally in the case of Jane Russell. Her breasts always appear to be round, or flat, at that point so something artificial here would be extremely desirable if it could be incorporated without destroying the contour of the rest of her breasts.

I want her wardrobe, wherever possible, to be low-necked so that the customers can get a look at the part of Russell which they pay to see and not covered by cloth, metallic or otherwise.

In the test, both Jane Russell and Joyce Mackenzie were chewing gum. I strongly object, as I do not see how any woman can be exciting while in the process.

Miss Russell commented, 'Howard decided it wouldn't be any harder to design a bra than an airplane. He tried, but I never wore his bra. He could design planes, but Mr Playtex he wasn't. I wore my own bra. He never knew the difference.'

Howard Hughes was born on December 24, 1905 in Houston, Texas. His father invented the oil bit that made the Hughes Tool Company a legend. Drillers came running, but Howard, Sr. would only lease the bits, a multimillion-dollar decision.

Little Howard, in preparation for Harvard, was sent off to the Fessenden School in West Newton, Massachusetts. Unhappy in such formal surroundings, he was enrolled at the Thatcher School in Ojai, California. His uncle Rupert Hughes, a novelist who had turned to writing for the movies, sent a limousine for Howard on weekends. This was quite a thrill for a seventeen-year-old boy who had never seen so many pretty girls before. His visits to the studio were fascinating, too, and on the sets Howard studied not only the scantily clad actresses but the intricacies of moviemaking.

In 1922 his mother died on the operating table while she was undergoing abdominal surgery. Two years later his father had a fatal heart attack.

Howard Hughes was only eighteen when he bought out the family's interest for a mere £325,000. He married Houston debutante Ella Rice in June 1925 'to prove I'm a responsible man.' He was nineteen. She was twenty-one.

Bored with the tool company, he and Ella moved to Hollywood and settled in the Ambassador Hotel. It took Howard three years to make *Hell's Angels*, which was originally a silent film. He reshot it with sound and released it in 1930. Hughes did not attend the premiere. Nor did Ella. She divorced him and received a $1.25 million settlement.

Monies for his film projects and alimony payments came from the salary and dividends paid by Hughes Tool. After Howard left Houston, he never again set foot in the company his father founded.

Hughes fell in love with actress Billie Dove, offered her husband $325,000 for a divorce, but never married her. After they drifted apart, he became deeply involved with Katharine Hepburn. He taught her to fly, and for a few years their relationship was widely publicized. On his record-breaking, ninety-one-hour flight around the world in 1938, Hughes took off from Floyd Bennett Field in Brooklyn, but swung west first to dip his wings over Hepburn's Connecticut home. He kept in touch with only her and the man in charge of his airfield headquarters.

The independent Katharine wasn't keen on marriage, but she brought Howard home to meet her parents. It was a curious match because she was not the voluptuous beauty he favored. Howard's romance with Katharine was one of the longest and most serious. He got tired of waiting, however, and began to date Olivia De Havilland, who said, 'I'm grateful we did not marry.'

Hughes's relationship with Bette Davis was, according to her, more therapeutic than romantic. His physical self-consciousness was so extreme that he suffered from recurrent impotence with women in 1938. Bette helped him overcome his problem at her house that had been bugged by her jealous husband, Ham Nelson, who blackmailed Howard for $75,000. Hughes hired a gangster to kill Nelson, who informed police that if he were murdered, Hughes was responsible. To avoid exposure, Howard paid the blackmail money. Bette took out a loan and repaid Hughes. Supposedly he sent her a flower every year on the anniversary of the payment. Hollywood insiders said, 'The bastard actually accepted the money from her. Who the hell needed a damn posy as a reminder of an ugly incident?'

In 1944 Hughes had controlling interest in Trans World Airlines, and four years later he bought RKO Pictures. To avoid eavesdroppers, he made business deals in cars or in bathrooms with the water running. Three plane crashes affected him mentally and physically, though the only apparent damage when he met Ava Gardner was partial deafness.

Hughes was interested in recently divorced women, 'wet decks,' as he referred to them. He ran after Ava when she left Rooney as he had pursued Lana Turner after Artie Shaw, and Susan Hayward following her parting from Jess Barker. Indeed, he was labeled a cocksman, but his abilities in bed have been disputed. Hughes was afraid if he put too much into lovemaking it might tire him out. With most of his girlfriends, it was hit and run. If he concentrated on one girl for any length of time, he was a magnificent lover. His faithfulness was always in question, but Howard was intent on possessing Ava and she did not resist. He had her watched by Mormon bodyguards twenty-four hours a day. Though Hughes leased a house for her in Hollywood, she stayed with Bappie in Westwood primarily, and reported to the studio every day.

Howard and Ava flew to Mexico frequently in his private Boeing Stratoliner, with a bedroom in the back, a cocktail bar, easy chairs and sofas. Since Howard did not drink, he never had liquor on board. Ava had never known anyone like Hughes. 'He makes it easy for you by pressing a button and there's a plane ready to take you anywhere,' she said. 'Another button and there's a hotel suite waiting for you. If you want to be quiet and left alone, he arranges it. He's just the ticket for a simple girl from North Carolina.'

Hughes gave her expensive presents, including a Cadillac. He called her every day, but their dates were private. The only picture of them together was at ringside during a Joe Louis heavyweight match. Their romance was no secret, however. It would last off and on for over a decade. They were both highly charged sexually and preferred quiet evenings at home, but Hughes was just as dedicated to business as he was to women, more so perhaps, and his long absences left

Ava as lonely as she was the day before they met. She was aware of the bodyguards and it took her a while to figure out a way to slip out of the house without being noticed. When he was in New York in December 1944, Ava went to the Mocambo with some friends, including a Mexican bullfighter. After a night of dancing and drinking, they returned to the house Hughes had leased for Ava. She put the toreador to bed upstairs and dozed on the couch. In the morning, the bullfighter shouted for Ava, who ran to the bedroom. He went into a rage that she hadn't slept with him. Calmly, Ava said, 'I'll make breakfast. You'll feel better.' He pushed her down the stairs. When she played dead, he panicked and ran through the front door, passing Hughes on his way out.

Howard was thoroughly disgusted. He ordered Ava out. 'How could you bring another man into this house? Get out of here!'

He accused her of drinking too much. She spat out a barrage of four-letter words. Hughes spun around and slapped Ava so hard, he dislocated her jaw. When he turned and walked away, she picked up a heavy brass object and knocked him out cold. His bodyguards carried Howard out to his car and the following day they packed Ava off to her Westwood apartment.

Howard sent hundreds of roses and gardenias. He offered her the world, and when she consented to see him, he flew Ava to Tijuana, where an entire restaurant had been reserved exclusively for them. Though Hughes drove old cars, he ordered another new Cadillac to give her as a Christmas present. For Ava's birthday, he said she could have anything she wanted. Knowing her request was impossible, but craving it anyway, she said, 'I want a big tub of orange ice cream!' Two hours later a huge limousine pulled up in front of the Westwood apartment and a chauffeur brought Ava an enormous tub of orange ice cream with a simple card, 'Love, Howard.'

When her Cadillac needed repairing, he told her to take it to Hughes Aircraft and he'd see to it personally. They argued again over something trivial. Before they made up, Ava received a call that her car was ready. She picked it up, drove two miles, and the engine fell out. 'I was told he had it wired, that son of a bitch!' Ava told friends. To get even with him, she insisted he take her to producer Sam Spiegel's New Year's Eve party.

The gala was jam-packed with celebrities, but no one was too busy or absorbed to note who was flirting with and seducing whom. Movies and gossip were the two prime occupations in Hollywood. Ava Gardner was seen arriving with Howard Hughes, but when she disappeared he became attentive to a new girl in town. Shelley Winters had eaten too much and asked him to undo the back of her dress. He tried to oblige, but the zipper got caught in her shawl. At midnight, she threw her arms around Hughes and kissed him Happy New Year.

Ava was in one of the bedrooms used as a ladies' lounge for the party. She and a bored Rita Hayworth, asleep under the mink and sable coats piled on the bed, were waiting for a limousine to take them home. Howard assumed Ava had gone to another party so he concentrated on Shelley.

To Ava, one Hollywood party was like another. Wives fought with mistresses while husbands made business deals and looked for a deeper cleavage. Eventually someone jumped into the swimming pool fully clothed. Love affairs bloomed while others exploded. After breakfast, the Spiegel party was over.

At Camp Seibert, near Birmingham, Alabama, Private Mickey Rooney tried to ignore the articles about his ex-wife and the millionaire. 'I was hurt and lonely, reached out and grabbed,' he said. On September 30, 1944, he married Betty Jane Rase. When

70

Mickey Junior was born, Rooney was overseas. He doesn't remember too much about the courtship, which lasted only seven days because he was drinking heavily. 'I was determined to marry someone,' Mickey said. He was discharged from the army in 1945, went home, and discovered that his seventeen-year-old bride had grown four inches! Rooney tried to make the marriage work, but he was still in love with Ava.

Mickey paid dearly for a divorce three years later: $12,500 annual alimony for ten years, a $25,000 down payment on a new house for Betty Jane, and $5,000 a year for child support.

For two years Ava dated Hughes almost exclusively. Four decades later, she said, 'Howard was not my cup of tea. I wasn't in love with him.' In retrospect she was probably right, but in 1945 Ava had known only two men intimately – Rooney and Hughes. Immature and unsophisticated, she had no conception of what love was all about. Was it dressing up as Howard's co-pilot, complete with goggles, and flying off to an unknown destination? Was it the tray filled with diamonds and pearls he carried with him occasionally? 'Take your pick,' he said. According to Noah Dietrich, vice-president of Hughes Tool Company, Ava was just a big pair of boobies and a good lay to his boss. But her indifference and hot temperament appealed to Howard. His brilliance and looks appealed to her.

They spent many evenings in his Bel Air home, where his houseboy served a simple dinner. She took a dip in his indoor swimming pool, retired early, and was up at dawn to leave for the studio. But their peculiar relationship took its toll on Ava. Although she needed someone like Hughes who was protective and generous, he was too possessive. Both needed their freedom. He was preoccupied with business, airplanes, and movies. Her only outlet was nightclubs, an impossibility while she was being followed by Howard's Mormon bodyguards.

Four years in Hollywood brought Ava little happiness. She was chained to MGM and shackled to a tycoon, but neither cared about her feelings. She was given minor roles at Metro. Her acting was improving but not enough for starring parts. As the months passed, Hughes became more and more engrossed in his XF-11 photo-reconnaissance plane for the air force. Ava wanted wings, too, and went to Ciro's or the Mocambo alone or with Lana Turner. At closing time, their group partied at someone's home until dawn. While the others fell asleep or crawled to work, Ava was wide awake and refreshed.

There was no hint of scandal or misbehavior. She drank, but did not get drunk. Nor did she run off into the night with men. Ava and her friends exchanged jokes, laughed, and danced. L.B. Mayer had little to complain about other than that she was 'doing the town' without an escort. Most likely Ava Gardner didn't give a damn. When she failed to get proper recognition from MGM, it didn't matter how they regarded her private life. She felt the same way about Hughes. If he stayed home, she was there, too. However, both the studio and Howard were annoyed by Ava's behavior. Metro put her on their loan-out list of contract players, meaning she was available to other studios for a price without her consent. The next step was not picking up her option.

Hughes wanted to support Ava. She refused. How many other girls did he have hidden away who waited for him to call? He paid their expenses, and his bodyguards were their escorts if Howard permitted them to go out for dinner. These girls took acting, dancing, and singing lessons, but never had an audition. Nor did Hughes put them under contract when he bought RKO. One of his victims was Gina Lollobrigida in the late forties. She was kept a virtual prisoner and allowed to see no one. Happily married to a dentist in Italy, Gina escaped and flew back home.

Ava's contract with MGM prevented Howard from going to extremes. Ironically, his publicized attention to the ex-Mrs Rooney pleased the studio and kept her name in the newspapers. To the public, their relationship was serious, glamorous, and exciting. Metro emphasized his proposals of marriage and her refusals. When she went to nightclubs alone, the studio managed to photograph Ava with one of their popular single male stars.

One evening at the Mocambo, she was approached by writer Philip Yordan who was doing the screenplay for United Artist's *Whistle Stop*. He asked Ava if she would be interested in playing the female lead opposite George Raft. Ava was not his first choice for the role, but everyone else had turned down the part, and MGM wanted only $5,000 to loan her out. She played Mary, a woman with a mysterious and shady background who returns to a tiny whistle-stop Illinois industrial town where her lover (George Raft) has become a loafer and a drunk. The owner of the local hotel and saloon becomes strongly attracted to Mary, while her downbeaten lover is almost forced into theft and murder by a bartender.

The film's director, Leonide Moguy, noticed immediately that Ava was a product of MGM's Lillian Burns, but he hoped to get a natural performance out of Ava by rehearsing patiently until she relaxed. It took Moguy longer than expected since his leading lady, unbeknownst to him, was consulting with Burns each morning before reporting on the set. He had the charm to pacify Ava into being herself. Burns was a great drama coach, he confessed, but an actress must take over and exude her natural qualities. This wasn't easy. For Ava it was mixing oil and water – what she had been combined with what she'd been taught. Moguy refused to give up. There were many retakes and though Ava began to 'feel' the part of Mary, she was tense and nervous. There were sleepless nights and doubts and fear of failure.

Yordan hinted that neither Ava Gardner nor George Raft knew how to act. It was so bad, he had to rewrite the opening scene with her standing on the station platform wearing a mink coat and diamond ring. 'They couldn't speak the lines, 'Yordan said, 'so it was done in monosyllables.'

Raft: What's that?
Ava: A ring.
Raft: Where did you get it?
Ava: Chicago.
Raft: From whom?
Ava: A man.
Raft: What man?

Whistle Stop was finished in six weeks. United Artists decided to preview the picture in Pomona with no fanfare. Ava slipped into the theater wearing a scarf and sunglasses. She was horrified. Her acting was stiff and bland, but when she kissed Raft with her mouth open, men in the audience reacted. 'What a dame!' or 'God, she's great!' Ava waited for the letdown, but throughout the picture she had the male viewers sitting up and craving what they saw on the screen. She realized it wasn't only her acting that sold tickets at the box office. Ava had what they wanted whether she talked or not. She finally understood Moguy and what he was trying to accomplish. She didn't want to be a sex object in movies, but Ava knew she would

74

have to accept this if she wanted to stay in Hollywood.

To everyone's amazement the reviews were good. *Motion Picture Herald* said, 'With the dynamics of Gardner and Raft in it, *Whistle Stop* is certainly not a dull place.' *Variety* wrote, 'Miss Gardner does her best work to date as the girl who must have her man.'

Ava went back to Metro with her head held high, but she remained on their loan-out list of players. 'They never took much interest in me,' she said. 'I can't say I blame them very much.'

SEVEN

Artie

David Arshawsky was born in the Bronx and grew up on New York City's Lower East Side. At twenty he was one of the most gifted bandleaders and swing clarinetists in America. this tall, dark, and suave, well-read intellectual was near genius in all his endeavors. Married and divorced seven times before his fiftieth birthday, Artie Shaw was also an irresistible Don Juan. He charmed and seduced some of the most beautiful women in Hollywood with ease. But he had an ego to match his sex appeal – an ego that was overbearing. Artie's opening line with women was always the same. 'You're perfect except for one thing.'

Before Judy Garland made *The Wizard of Oz*, she met and fell in love with him. While MGM's seventeen-year-old Dorothy was skipping down the yellow brick road with a tin man, a lion, and a scarecrow, Artie was 'beginning the beguine' with Betty Grable, who planned to marry him after her divorce from Jackie Coogan. Betty's misfortune (or was it?) stemmed from the fact she had to wait a year before getting her final decree. Meanwhile Betty appeared in *DuBarry Was a Lady* on Broadway, three thousand miles away from Judy, who was necking with Mickey Rooney in *Babes in Arms*.

On another set at MGM, Lana Turner was filming *Dancing Co-ed*, featuring Artie Shaw and his band. When he complained to reporters that Hollywood reeked to high heaven, the cast and crew agreed he was a pompous egotist. Lana hated him, too. Laughing it off, Shaw left for Mexico after *Dancing Co-ed*, returned and looked in on Lana while she was making another movie. At first glance, she considered giving him a piece of her mind, but Artie was gracious and considerate. Barely nineteen, Lana was taken in by this intelligent and sensitive man, who wanted nothing more than a home and children. Twice divorced, he was willing to try again.

Artie had one date with Lana. They took a drive along the ocean and held hands. A few hours later they were on a chartered plane for Las Vegas. He kissed her once. On February 9, 1940, newspaper headlines read: ARTIE SHAW MARRIES LANA TURNER.

Betty Grable screamed, 'That son of a bitch! Who does he think he is doing this to me?' The future pin-up girl had her first abortion not long after the announcement.

Judy Garland wept.

The Shaw marriage was over in less than a year. During the separation, Lana called Artie to tell him she was going to have a baby. He claimed it wasn't his. Lana, like Betty, had *her* first abortion.

After his divorce from Turner, Artie was stricken with granulocytophenia, a rare blood disease that weakens the white cells and is often fatal. He fought it and recovered just in time for World War II. Still weak, he joined the navy and toured military bases with his band in the South Seas and Australia. In 1944 Artie collapsed mentally and physically, and was given a medical discharge. 'I was in a state of dysfunction,' he said. 'I was nowhere.'

In desperation he turned to psychoanalyst May Romm, whom he visited three times a week. Shaw's impudence and conceit undoubtedly nourished his pride. He reorganized a band and began to get his life in order with Romm's help.

Artie's relationship with women was complex. He demanded perfection, but always managed to find one flaw. 'Green's not your color, either,' was a teaser to a girl wearing pink. Was it a comment or an insult? Any woman with an ounce of curiosity would want to find out. Aside from his dynamic good looks, Shaw had presence like Gable and Flynn. When he entered a room people were drawn to him but, unlike Gable and Flynn, Artie was able to back up his handsomeness with impeccable grammar and knowledge of current affairs and ancient history. While he talked or listened, one had the feeling he was thinking about something else far beyond the limited scope of most.

Whether his subconscious aim was to change all females because he had little regard for his widowed Jewish mother, only his analyst knows for sure. Once Mrs Arshawsky threatened to jump out the window during an argument. Artie said that he walked across the street so he could watch her do it. In jest he told Betty Grable to push her mother out of a hotel window. Mrs Grable, a true stage mother, did not approve of Shaw – obviously the reason for what he said. Betty, however, told a friend she had the strongest urge to kill her mother after Artie's suggestion.

When Shaw was introduced to Ava in 1945, he had not yet recuperated from his nervous disorder, though he was on the upswing mentally, financially, and professionally. The uncompromising Artie considered himself indestructible, and if he was in need of analysis, the rest of the world required therapy more than he did.

Ava was a fan of Shaw's. She had collected his unforgettable records of 'Dancing in the Dark,' 'Copenhagen,' 'The Back Bay Shuffle,' and 'Begin the Beguine.' She went to see him in person, listened and danced to his music – only one of thousands of girls who had a crush on the tall, dark bandleader.

Artie was introduced to Ava at the Mocambo. He was enamored of her beauty. She was enthralled by his presence. After several dates, Ava moved into Shaw's house on Bedford Drive near Sunset Boulevard. Her friends said she was completely under his spell. Bappie did all she could to discourage her sister's outrageous decision. The studio was disgusted, but the publicity department convinced gossip columnists not to print the truth because ' . . . this is only a phase with Ava.' L.B. Mayer might have dropped her option had she not been married to Mickey Rooney, a very good reason to keep her reputation unblemished. MGM offered nothing in the way of good or bad roles. Ava reported to the studio every day with less and less enthusiasm. She was devoting herself to Shaw, who considered the Hollywood studio system degrading anyway. He convinced Ava it was the basis of her insecurity, which, he emphasized, should be analyzed by his therapist May Romm. He set up appointments for Ava three times a week. 'It really fucked me up,' Ava said later. But at the time she believed that Artie was straightening out her life by cultivating her mind with good books and classical music. She seriously considered giving up acting, too.

Shaw was shocked to find out Ava had read only one book, *Gone With the Wind*. He gave her works by Sinclair Lewis and Aldous Huxley. She suffered through them. As a treat, Artie suggested books by Hemingway. It was Shaw's way of improving on perfection, since he considered Ava one of the most beautiful women he'd ever seen.

They entertained his intellectual friends, William Saroyan, S.J. Perelman, and John O'Hara. The group's conversations went over Ava's head. She was, however, impressed and honored to be included. While the others discussed literature and politics, she remained silent because Artie preferred she keep her mouth shut. In the beginning Ava told him this was embarrassing, but he said any woman as lovely as she had nothing to fret about.

Yet he urged her to take English literature and economics at UCLA. Though MGM did not want one of their contract players exposed to the public, Mayer did not protest. Instead he made sure her official biography mentioned Ava Gardner had been a student at UCLA. Despite Shaw's effort to create an intellectual beauty, she became bored with his choice of books, her therapy, and her college courses.

Unfortunately Artie had a short fuse. He insisted she not walk around in her bare feet when other people were around. With Ava it was a matter of instinct to shed her shoes in the house. This sent Artie to the boiling point. 'That's uncivilized! You're not in the tobacco fields now!' he bellowed while friends squirmed.

Ava did her best, but that wasn't good enough for Artie. She did not resist his teachings nor did the facts penetrate her mind. She couldn't sit long enough to read an entire page of a book. She enjoyed drinking, dancing, and laughter. With her feet propped up, Ava adored chatting about the latest movie gossip – who was sleeping with whom, who was a fag, and who was waiting for the proper time to announce their divorce. She enjoyed fan magazines, but kept them at the studio or anyplace where Artie wouldn't discover 'such trash.'

Though their relationship was strained, Ava did not move back to her Westwood apartment. MGM was concerned over pressure from powerful gossip columnists Louella Parsons and Hedda Hopper, who asked repeatedly, 'When are they setting the date?' Translation: 'We can't hide the truth much longer.'

Hollywood moguls were still stung by a *Photoplay* article in 1938 entitled 'Hollywood's Unmarried Husbands and Wives,' revolving around such famous couples as Barbara Stanwyck and Robert Taylor, Paulette Goddard and Charlie Chaplin, Constance Bennett and Gilbert Roland, and Carole Lombard and Clark Gable:

> ... just friends to the world at large – yet nowhere has domesticity taken on so unique a character as in this unconventional fold. Unwed couples they might be termed. No hostess would think of inviting them separately. They solve each other's problems, handle each other's business affairs, take up each other's hobbies – even correct each other's clothes. Yet to the world, their official status is 'just friends.' No more.
>
> Bob Taylor and Barbara Stanwyck could get married if they really wanted to. Carole Lombard and Clark Gable and the other steady couples might swing it if they tried a little harder.
>
> Nobody, not even Hollywood's miracle men, has ever improved on the good, old-fashioned, satisfying institution of holy matrimony. And, until something better comes along, the best way to hunt happiness when you're in love in Hollywood or anywhere else is with a preacher, a marriage license, and a bagful of rice.

Though this article shocked the public and Hollywood in 1938, the moral clauses in movie contracts were no different in 1945. Studios expected their stars to be living examples of truth and righteousness. If they were divorced, the publicity was laced with heartbreak and remorse. Actresses sobbed on the witness stand. 'My husband came home late. He paid no attention to me. He interfered with my career. He wanted to be free.'

Divorce was accepted, but celebrities 'living in sin' was not. L.B. Mayer, who after the article rushed Stanwyck and Taylor to the altar and negotiated Gable's divorce so the actor could marry Lombard before *Gone With the Wind*, never forgot it. This was the first time a fan magazine defied the all-powerful studio moguls – the first time Hollywood's finest were exposed rather than protected.

Taylor said he was rushed off the movie set to San Diego, where he married Stanwyck. 'All I had to say about the whole thing was "I do," ' he confided.

Though Gable was the first choice to play Rhett Butler, it was with the stipulation that Lombard was either his wife or the affair with her be ended. All the stars appearing in *Gone With the Wind* had to be free of scandal. Vivien Leigh was not allowed to be seen with her lover, Laurence Olivier. Both were married to others, their divorces pending in England. Their backgrounds were unknown to moviegoers in America.

The purity of the players was worth the millions spent on the production of *Gone With the Wind* (seven years later, *every* film was costly). Maybe the public was a bit more broad-minded, but studios were not taking any chances, since the average moviegoer was also a churchgoer. The liberal-minded in New York City, Chicago, and Los Angeles were the minority. It was Mr and Mrs Jones from middle class America who supported the box office.

Warner Brothers, Paramount, Columbia, and 20th Century-Fox were not as strict with their stars. Nor did they go to great lengths to create virgin goddesses and gallant heros like MGM, the purest studio of them all.

L.B. Mayer could have dropped Ava for breaking the moral clause, but he chose not to. He was not only protecting Mickey Rooney but also Lana Turner, whose brief marriage to Shaw enraged Mayer. She was America's 'Sweater Girl' and had far more promise as an actress than Gardner in 1945.

The consensus in Hollywood was that Ava's affair with the bandleader was coming to an end. Friends witnessed embarrassing fights at parties, though it was usually Shaw who verbally attacked his so-called mistress about not wearing shoes or curling up her feet on the couch. Ava cringed and often ran out of the room in tears. Why, observers asked, didn't she hit Artie over the head and knock him out cold as she'd done with Howard Hughes? The big difference was that she loved Shaw.

Her friends assumed she would go home to a concerned Bappie. Instead Ava announced to her sister, 'Artie and I are getting married on the evening of October seventeenth.' Bappie was stunned.

The ceremony was held at the house of Judge Stanley Mosk at 1112 South Peck Drive in Beverly Hills. Frances Heflin was bridesmaid and Hy Craft was the best man. Ava wore the same dark blue suit she wore at her wedding to Mickey Rooney.

That the wedding took place at all is amazing. For the bride and groom it had been a long day that consisted of phone calls to friends expressing their doubts. Artie said he knew marrying Ava was all wrong, but he didn't know what to do about it. She was in love with a man who was domineering and had no patience with her lack of social graces and book learning. Being molded by the studio should have been more than enough for Ava.

Howard Strickling would not admit that MGM was the instigator of the nuptials, but he hinted as much. 'It was the only thing they could do,' Strickling said. 'The live-in affair was public knowledge. If Ava had stayed with her sister, marriage might not have been the only solution.'

It was not a blissful wedding. Artie thought the whole idea was ridiculous, but like Mickey he was consumed by Ava's body and her extraordinary beauty. She hoped marriage would bring them closer together. 'Our interests were poles apart,' Ava said many years later, 'but I was mad about Artie, just as I was about Mickey. I thought love could cure anything.'

The Shaws spent their honeymoon in New York because Artie was appearing with his band at the Paramount Theater. With time on her hands, and to impress her husband, Ava browsed through bookstores with enthusiasm. She chose Kathleen Winsor's best-seller, *Forever Amber*. Artie went through the roof. 'If I ever catch you reading shit like that again,' he bellowed, 'I'll throw you out!'

Ironically, author Kathleen Winsor would be the next Mrs Artie Shaw.

When Ava returned to Hollywood she was approached by producer Mark Hellinger about a starring role in a film based on Ernest Hemingway's famous short story, 'The Killers.' Hellinger had seen *Whistle Stop* and thought Ava would be perfect as Kitty, a beautiful and treacherous gang moll. Newcomer Burt Lancaster was making his first screen appearance as the killer Swede, whom two men come to a small New Jersey town to shoot down.

Hellinger was reluctant to ask Ava if she'd consider doing a test with Lancaster. 'I'd love it,' she smiled. Script in hand she rushed home to tell Artie the good news.

'We'll read Hemingway's story together,' he said. 'Then I'll help you interpret the dialogue. Kitty is not just an ordinary dame. She's a very clever liar. Fortunately you have an excellent director.'

'How do you know?' she asked.

'Robert Siodmak is a good friend of mine,' Artie said, glancing over the script. 'How the hell do you think you got the part?'

'I thought Walter Wanger and his wife Joan Bennett asked Mr Hellinger to see me in *Whistle Stop*.'

Shaw laughed. 'I spoke to Robert about you because Universal wants new faces in *The Killers*.'

'I really don't have the part yet,' she said.

'Naturally you believe the Wangers were responsible.'

'Does it matter?' she asked.

'It matters to me. It matters very much!'

'I believe you,' she chirped.

The next day Ava and Burt Lancaster did a screen test together. Hellinger stopped them halfway through because he knew immediately she was perfect. When Universal gave their approval, Ava was so excited she hugged everyone on the set. 'Maybe my luck's changing,' she said. 'I got an A in my English Lit exam and now this!'

Metro, however, refused to loan her out. Ava went on a rampage, though it's doubtful she got as far as Mayer's office. She made sure he heard about her ranting and raving to anyone within hearing distance in the makeup room, wardrobe, under the hot lights posing for stills, and between lessons in her drama class. 'Bastards!' she hissed while tears welled in her eyes.

Hellinger knew it was only a matter of dollars. He convinced executives at Universal to offer a thousand a week to MGM for Ava, who was being paid only $350. The deal was made. This breakthrough was better than a hundred years of psychoanalysis for Ava. Her attitude toward acting changed overnight. She knew Hellinger chose her for the role of Kitty because he had faith in her acting. Siodmak respected Ava for what he thought she was capable of, not mediocre past performances. Both men ignored the sexpot image. Ava did not have to project the obvious for them as they tried to give her confidence with praise and patience. As the sly Kitty who could not afford to give herself away, Ava was told not to overdo her facial expressions. She was playing a woman who did not miss a trick, whose eyes were always open but told no tales. The rare exceptions were fear and terror. She remembered Mickey's coaching and what he said about using her eyes effectively.

Ava, Burt, and Edmund O'Brien were met every morning with enthusiasm by Siodmak, who treated them like stars, not neophytes. If they overacted, he explained calmly that the camera was a magnifying glass and there was no need to exaggerate emotions. Siodmak did not rush the players. He was kind even when he had to be tough. At the end of the film, Ava was having difficulty portraying a hysterical Kitty, in complete contrast to the character she had mastered. For five weeks, Siodmak teased Ava day after day about that devastating scene in which Albert Dekker is shot. Kitty begs him to swear she is innocent, but the dying thief cannot bring himself to lie to the police. Siodmak remarked, 'Kitty's breakdown was Ava's breakdown because she actually fell apart. She was worn out. Drained. She was magnificent.'

The Killers was applauded by critics, who praised Ava's portrayal of Kitty. She won the *Look* Award as the most promising newcomer of 1947 and Ernest Hemingway said it was the first film of any of his work that he genuinely admired. Ava would eventually appear in two more movie adaptations from his novels. She and the writer became very close friends, and though he had fantasies about her remarkable figure, they were never lovers.

Ava returned to MGM with a feeling of triumph, but Mayer considered *The Killers* a second-rate movie. Her fan mail, forwarded from Universal, could not be ignored, however. She was no longer a starlet, but not yet a star. She couldn't sing or dance and she wasn't the girl next door. If nothing else, Mayer decided to cash in on her recent popularity in *The Killers*. He let it be known she was available for a good role at MGM.

Ava, in the meantime, relaxed on her laurels. She attended classes at UCLA and yawned during therapy. Artie worked at night and she was committed to the studio during the day. They saw little of each other. By the summer of 1946, Ava no longer shared a bed with her husband.

When they were on the same schedule he was annoyed that she lacked the responsibilities of being a wife. Unlike Ava's noble attempts during her marriage to Mickey, she came skipping through the door at the end of the day with a cheerful, 'What's for dinner?' Artie put up with it for a few months until he sat her down and said, 'Look, I do certain things for you, do I not?'

'Darling!' she gushed. 'You do everything!'

'I pay the rent, the utilities, the gardener, the help, I buy the food, your clothes, take care of business . . . '

'Darling, I know you do . . . '

'Ava, what do you do for me?'

'I love you!' she said with a kiss.

'And I love you,' he said. 'What else do you do?'

'I love you,' she repeated.

'Can't you at least tell *me* what we're having for dinner?'

The marriage didn't last long enough for Artie to find out. Though Ava had been staying with Bappie off and on, she moved out of Shaw's house on July 8, 1946, the day after Howard Hughes was critically injured in a plane crash. Doctors did not expect him to live through the night. Ava, according to her close friends, had been seeing Hughes. When Howard came out of surgery and regained consciousness, he asked to see only a few friends, one of whom was Ava. Sometimes she sat at his bedside with Lana Turner, who probably had plenty to say about Artie. In her memoirs, she wrote about having no knowledge of his previous marriages. Wife number one had been June Carns of Ashtabula, Ohio. Because she was so young, her parents had the marriage annulled in 1932. Wife number two had been a New York nurse, Margaret Allen, who divorced Artie in 1937 for infidelity.

After Lana, he married Elizabeth Kern, daughter of famed composer Jerome Kern. That union lasted two-and-a-half years and they had a son. Elizabeth divorced Artie in 1944, demanded alimony and child support, and had him in and out of court many times. Supposedly, Shaw had two children in the course of his eight marriages, but little is known about them. 'I didn't get along with the mothers, so why should I get along with the kids?' he remarked. Thirty years after his divorce from Ava, he was asked about his wives. 'Listen,' Shaw replied. 'I started getting married at roughly twenty-one and I'm sixty-seven now. During all that time I found maybe ten women. Now, when you think about it, that's not so many. The only problem was that I married most of them.'

The next inquiry in the brief interview was how he succeeded in marrying such beautiful ladies. 'I asked them,' Artie replied. 'I was a good-looking young stud at the time and I asked them! They either said yes or no. There are very few in-betweens.'

As for how to go about getting a divorce, Shaw explained, 'First call a cab and then get the hell out of there!'

Though his other wives disliked him intensely at the end and demanded alimony, Ava did not. The marriage might never have taken place if she had not been under contract to the publicity-minded MGM. However, she never denied her deep love for Artie was real. His disappointment over Ava's inability to grasp the arts broadened the gap between them. If she talked about having a home and children, there was also the drive to succeed as an actress. Artie was encouraging, but he expected Ava to be a wife, too. Having lived with Lana, who was the typical pampered and petted Metro queen, Shaw had only disgust for this symbol of unreality. Ava never lost her humble qualities or longed for an MGM crown. But she was experiencing the thrill of being recognized on the street and began to don the usual dark glasses and scarf, the trademarks of a well-known Hollywood movie actress. Artie considered this attention demeaning. To warrant such admiration, a cultivated brain should be underneath the disguise, not just a pretty face.

Shaw was disgusted with Hollywood. After the war and his nervous breakdown he lost interest in the clarinet. He preferred classical music to swing and wanted to become a writer. He sought perfection in himself and others. 'Happiness,' he said, 'isn't a state you arrive in, like Rhode Island or Vermont.'

On August 16, 1946, Ava quietly filed for divorce in

Superior Court. She charged Artie with cruelty and 'grievous mental suffering,' and asked that her maiden name be restored. She made no demands for a property settlement. 'All I want are my possessions,' she said.

Artie put his house up for sale. The price was $95,000 furnished. When the purchaser's lawyers checked the inventory they noted a waffle iron was missing. 'Ava took it when she left,' Shaw said. 'You wouldn't call off a $95,000 deal over a waffle iron, would you?' The lawyers said they would and Artie sent them a check for fifteen dollars.

'Word got around town,' a friend laughed, 'that Ava's settlement from Shaw was a waffle iron. She joked about it later, but at the time Ava was very unhappy. She and Artie remained friends and she consulted him over business matters. I know Ava considered Artie one of the brightest persons she'd ever met. Their marriage was a mistake from the beginning and they knew it. Ava wanted a home and husband. She was satisfied that her acting was improving and MGM wanted to star her in a good film, but that wasn't enough. "Fame and money do not promise happiness," she told everyone. "They mean nothing without a happy home." These words were not written by a publicity agent. Ava meant it from the bottom of her heart. I don't think it occurred to her that having two famous husbands made her name a household word. One look at her on the screen left no doubt in anyone's mind why men fell head over heels in love with Ava. Though she didn't marry for anything but love, Mickey and Artie had a lot to do with putting her name in lights. It was so typical of Ava to resent this.'

On October 24, Mrs Artie Shaw V testified in court: 'After a month of marriage, my husband's attitude seemed to change. He became moody and temperamental and completely and utterly selfish. He disregarded my wishes for the smallest things – like what we would have for dinner, whom we should see, what time we should go out and what time we should return.

'Everything should be done his way, he told me many times. He refused to see my friends and expected me to be with his friends at all times. If I didn't feel well or didn't feel like going out, he went alone. If we had friends over, he would constantly humiliate and embarrass me by telling me to shut up, that I didn't know what I was talking about in case I entered into the conversation.

'I finally became so nervous and upset, I didn't talk. Then when I couldn't tallk, he said, "Why don't you talk? Don't you have anything to contribute to the conversation?" I became very embarrassed. It was very tense for everyone around.'

Fran Heflin supported Ava's charges in court.

Superior Judge Harry R. Archibald asked, 'What did Shaw say or do to embarrass her?'

Heflin replied, 'It had more to do with her entering into a conversation than anything else. I remember one night he said, "Oh, shut up! You don't know what you're talking about. I don't even know why you open your mouth!'

Judge Archibald granted the divorce.

Artie, meanwhile, was dating twenty-seven-year-old Kathleen Winsor, author of *Forever Amber*, the book Artie threw out because it was trash. The fact that Kathleen was Mrs Robert Herwig didn't matter, she said, ' . . . because I'm supporting him and he doesn't interfere with my personal affairs.' Artie met the author on October 7. He'd been separated from Ava for three months. After a few luncheon dates with Shaw, Kathleen told Herwig she wanted a divorce and him to leave 'her' house. She gave him a $10,000 property settlement. After Herwig's departure, Artie began to date Winsor regularly. Two weeks later the subject of marriage came up. While Ava was testifying in court, Artie and Kathleen drove to El Paso where they registered in a hotel as Mr and Mrs Arthur Sanders to avoid the press. On October 26, two days after his divorce was granted, Shaw drove Winsor to Juarez, where they signed depositions in a lawyer's office to obtain 'quickie' divorces from both their spouses (California law required a one-year waiting period).

Artie and Kathleen were then married.

She called her publisher, George Brett, hurriedly. Obviously the telephone connection was bad because he told his staff, 'That's wonderful news. It means we'll get him as our author, too. After all, Irwin Shaw is a fine writer!'

Ava heard the news and was upset over one thing. She never got to read *Forever Amber*. 'That son of a bitch!' she exclaimed.

Artie told his sixth bride the truth. He'd never read her bestseller. When she gave him a copy he said, 'It's too long.'

'So's *War and Peace*,' Kathleen retorted.

When the marriage ended in divorce two years later, Winsor said, 'Never by any stretch of my own imagination or by anything I could find by research in any library, could I gain the knowledge brought me by being the wife of Artie Shaw. He told me what books to read and I read them. He told me what clothes to wear and I wore them. He told me what I must think on every subject conceivable and would tolerate no difference of opinion.'

Lana commented sarcastically, 'Artie was my entire college education.'

Ava said, 'I left before he had a chance to flunk me.'

EIGHT

The Single Life

Resting uncomfortably at the Good Samaritan Hospital, Howard Hughes survived a crushed chest, nine broken ribs, a collapsed left lung that filled with blood, third-degree burns and abrasions on his body, and a fractured nose. His heart had been pushed to one side of his chest cavity and he was in severe shock. His recovery was miraculous, but Howard was never the same after that. This was the beginning of his addiction to codeine, which was prescribed after doctors took him off morphine.

He grew a mustache to cover scars on his upper lip.

Hughes refused to see his aunt, Annette Lummis, who flew from Houston after hearing about the plane crash. But he permitted Ava and Lana into his hospital room. It is interesting to note that when Hughes died in 1976 Mrs Lummis was his closest living relative. She died four years later and her heirs shared the bulk of Howard's estate.

That his relatives came last in his lifetime is no

secret. That Hughes collected women is no secret, also. Accounts differ as to the validity of his marriage proposals. He pleaded with actress Gene Tierney to divorce her husband, Oleg Cassini, in 1946 so they could be married. Howard offered Elizabeth Taylor $1 million to marry him in 1951 when she was estranged from her first husband, Nicky Hilton. Miss Taylor considered him a sloppy bore and she married Michael Wilding instead. Around the same time Hughes chased actress Terry Moore, who fell in love with him. True to form, he disappeared and she married West Point football star Glenn Davis. Hughes broke up that marriage and made Miss Moore a star at RKO. She claimed they became man and wife on board a yacht at sea in 1949, but the records were thrown overboard. Moore subsequently sued the Hughes estate and received an undisclosed six-figure settlement.

True or false, Howard was known to 'marry' beautiful girls on the beach or on Mulholland Drive's lover's lane in the Hollywood Hills. By exchanging vows alone in the moonlight, Hughes hoped to open a locked bedroom door. If the girl was gullible and he was in a bind, Howard went through the motions. Ava, however, was not taken in by Hughes or his persistent marriage proposals. Most likely this intrigued him as much as the woman herself.

Six weeks after Howard's near fatal plane crash, he walked out of the Good Samaritan Hospital without his doctor's consent. He and Ava resumed their torrid romance, but his mind was on the X-11 and making it up again for another test flight. While he conferred with the air force in Washington, Ava went her merry way. David Niven, recently widowed, was one of her more amusing interludes. Charming and debonair, the irresistible English actor had romantic affairs with many beautiful actresses in Hollywood, a town he referred to as 'The Playpen.' His delicious sense of humor and his discretion appealed to women. Ava was no exception.

Director John Huston was another intimate friend and escort. The son of Walter Huston and acclaimed for *The Maltese Falcon*, John had secretly written the script for *The Killers* while serving as a major in the army during the war. The tall, lanky, hunched-over forty-year-old director with pouches under his eyes took actress Evelyn Keyes to the premiere of *The Killers* after a few dates. She called him three days later at his home in the San Fernando Valley following a hectic filming schedule. 'I'll be finished shortly,' she said, hinting for an invitation.

'Swell!' he exclaimed over the phone. 'Come on out, but you'd better hurry. Ava Gardner's here!'

In her memoirs, Keyes said she had no intention of competing with Ava. She went to the movies instead, but thought a lot about what might be going on at John's. The next day, however, he invited her to dinner at Romanoff's. Both tell the same story so it must be true.

'Why don't we get married?' she asked.

'Hell, Evelyn, we hardly know each other.'

'Do you know a better way for us to get to know each other?'

They flew to Las Vagas that night and Huston took a third wife. The following morning he went to Warner Brothers and she went to Columbia Pictures. That evening Evelyn called him. 'I'm all through, John. Come pick me up.'

There was a long pause before he asked, 'Uh . . . who is this?'

Huston had had a great deal to drink on his wedding night and considered an annulment, ' . . . but what the hell,' he shrugged. 'What do I have to lose?' Four years later the answer to that question was – everything.

This brilliant director and unpredictable character

was a hard-drinking rebel who had no problem keeping up with Ava. Huston would be responsible for choosing and directing her in *Night of the Iguana* and *The Bible*. On one of his leaves, he had visited the set of *The Killers* and met Ava. They were close ever after. Huston was seen dining with her during his four-year marriage to Evelyn Keyes and, according to alert reporters, Ava was a guest at his home in the San Fernando Valley, where they played in the swimming pool and frolicked on his front lawn. Beyond her close relationship with the director, she trusted him – a rarity in Hollywood.

Ava was also linked with Fernando Lamas, the dark suave Latin type she found impossible to resist. Then there was Peter Lawford, who squired most of the MGM starlets. He was a gentleman glamour boy with a clipped British accent and was the darling of teenage America. If Mayer arranged his dates with Ava to establish their charming image, she and Peter did all right on their own.

Singer Mel Torme was seeing Ava in December 1946 but she could not go out with him on New Year's Eve because she had a date with Lawford. Mel caught a glimpse of them and melted at the sight of her: 'Ava's fine physical configuration was shown off to pulse-quickening advantage,' he wrote in his memoirs. She called at two-thirty in the morning and invited Mel to her apartment. Lawford let him in cordially and said, 'I'm just leaving.'

Ava's sexual glamour was irresistible to men. There was nothing phony about her. An MGM executive once walked into her dressing room without knocking. Ava was naked from the waist up and cursed a blue streak. He disappeared fast, but the memory of her lingered forever. 'I had never in my life seen anything as beautiful,' he said.

Then there were those fun excursions with Lana

Turner and the girls. They went to out-of-the-way places to dance and flirt without being recognized. They chattered about the latest dirt at MGM, compared dates with the same men, and mingled freely with the crowd. But as 1947 approached, Lana was becoming deeply involved with the love of her life, Tyrone Power. And Ava would be too busy making movies.

Clark Gable joined the air force after the untimely death of his wife, Carole Lombard, in a 1942 plane crash. Two years later, handsome and gray at the temples, he returned to Hollywood a lonely and troubled man. MGM covered up when Gable recklessly drove his Duesenberg up Sunset Boulevard the wrong way and swerved into a tree. Fortunately the accident occurred on the property belonging to Harry Friedman, vice-president of the Music Corporation of America. He called Howard Strickling, who was there in minutes. The story released to the newspapers described a helpless Clark doing his best to avoid a car coming in the wrong direction. Strickling put Gable in Cedars of Lebanon Hospital and took his clothes away so the star would not try to leave. MGM wanted the public's sympathy, but it was more important to prevent the press from finding out that Gable was drunk. This accident was long overdue. The only solution was to put him to work, but finding the right vehicle was not easy. Mayer took charge and cast him opposite Greer Garson in *Adventure*. Though Clark's fans were loyal, the film was a disaster and the studio's publicity even worse: 'Gable's Back and Garson's Got Him.' Critics added, ' . . . and they deserve each other.' Gable was angry, embarrassed, and crushed. Mayer suggested Clark read Frederic

Wakeman's hit novel *The Hucksters*, which MGM was making into a movie. There was no love lost between Gable and Mayer, who finally had a showdown about the project.

'The character you want me to play is a goddamn heel,' Clark hissed. 'And the book is filthy.'

'What else?' Mayer scowled.

'The female lead, for another thing. I won't tolerate acting an affair with a married woman.'

'Only in real life, eh? What else?'

'The guy I play is oversexed. He's a satyr.'

'You should be able to do the part without looking at the script.'

Gable ground his dentures together. 'Make her single and give my guy some character and you might have a deal.'

Mayer had the script revised and asked Clark to test with English actress Deborah Kerr, who would play the elegant widow, and Ava Gardner, for the role of the sensuous singer who loses her man to the wholesome Deborah.

If Gable disliked *The Hucksters*, Ava detested it. She resented being typecast as the good-natured girl who's never good enough for the hero, and was willing to go on suspension if it came to that.

Clark called Ava personally.

'I hope you'll reconsider,' he said.

'I'm fed up.'

'Baby, when you've been around as long as I have, *then* you can say that.'

'The only reason I have for doing the fuckin' movie is because you're in it.'

'Best reason in the world!' he exclaimed. 'We'll have a good time. You'll see.'

She laughed. 'I have to tell you this. When I first came to this dump of a town I saw you driving down Sunset and I almost crashed into the car ahead of me.'

'Then do the movie with me, Ava. You're young. Plenty of time to find a really good script. I'm not quite as fortunate, kid.'

Deep sigh. 'All right, you talked me into it.'

Clark and Ava were attracted to each other from the start. Though he preferred blondes and was quoted as saying, 'I don't like brunettes because they look dirty to me,' he made an exception with Ava, who used profanity like Carole Lombard, fought with Mayer, and wasn't sure she belonged in movies. Gable sensed her nervousness and remained by her side on the set of *The Hucksters*. Ava, in turn, saw tragedy in his eyes and assumed his hands and head shook because he suffered from hangovers. He told her it was the Dexedrine he was taking to lose the weight he had gained from too much drinking.

Both were unsure of themselves in *The Hucksters* and fluffed their lines often. She took the blame because the love scenes with Gable made her nervous. But he apologized. 'I'm sorry. I wasn't thinking straight because I was so damn concerned about you. I know you don't think you're an actress. Well, I'm not sure I'm an actor.'

A retired MGM press agent said, 'If anyone says Clark and Ava didn't have a fling, they're crazy. To deny it would be denying the birds and the bees. No big deal. Gable was a hell of a guy and had hundreds of women, but Lombard wasn't kidding when she said he was a bad lay. In fact Clark said so himself. Ava was a passionate lady. She could turn a guy on without trying. What most people would never understand is the fact that they were two lonely people who were drifting. No one was sadder than Gable at that time. Ava was better at covering up her problems, just like Lombard. No matter how bad things got, they were both telling jokes and making funny cracks. This turned Gable on. He loved it. He was also quite amazed that Ava, despite her inexperience, helped him over the rough spots because his head shook before a kiss. She had to steady him . . . sorta take over. For Ava it was a dream come true starring with Gable. They worked well together. They really clicked. She was a no-nonsense gal and he went for that.'

Ava admitted having a big crush on Gable. 'In *The Hucksters* I had to sing a song to him,' she recalled. 'Clark used to leave the set at five, but on this day he stayed on so I could sing to him instead of to some prop man. He straddled a chair and sat just off-camera. Every once in a while I'd think, "It's Clark Gable!" and I'd go to pieces.'

Maybe Gable left the set according to his contract, but he rarely went home. To 'The King' it was a matter of principle. When he was a nobody playing opposite Greta Garbo in *Susan Lennox*, she left promptly at six o'clock and Gable swore to have the same privilege someday. He got it and took advantage of the clause because he hated MGM and refused to work one minute longer than required. But he could be found in his dressing room with a bottle of booze and maybe his leading lady. Not one to brag about his many, many conquests, Gable glanced at a group picture of MGM actresses and smiled, 'Aren't they beautiful – and I've had every one of 'em!'

Near the completion of *The Hucksters* Universal made a frantic call to MGM. Their leading lady in *Singapore* had taken ill. Could they borrow Ava immediately? Metro agreed, for $5,000. Ava was rushed from Gable, who was wearing a dark blue Madison Avenue suit, to an Oriental setting where Fred MacMurray, in a white tropical suit, was waiting to be kissed! She changed costumes and was told by the director to walk in front of the camera and into Fred's arms. 'I didn't even know what the story was about,' she said. For several weeks Ava simultaneously played a sexy single singer in *The Hucksters* and a married woman with amnesia and two husbands in *Singapore*.

Aside from her discreet meetings with Gable, Ava was too busy for dating. Many of her scenes were shot at night and she was required to drive her own car from MGM to Universal and back. Bappie helped her sister during this hectic schedule. The stagehands claimed Ava didn't change her attitude toward Hollywood. A technician commented, 'I overheard her talking about a recipe she was anxious to try. She worked very hard, but never discussed the scene she'd just finished or the one coming up. Rather than look over the script, Ava was planning her grocery list. She was not your typical actress who primped or consulted the director or her co-star or argued about wardrobe. I got the feeling acting was just a job – not a career to her. It was refreshing, actually, but I got the impression she'd rather be home setting the table for two. Let's face it, MGM did not pride themselves in developing great acting ability in their players. They were all great to look at. They had style and talent in their own right. They were personalities. Their roles were custom-made, the dialogue written to suit their images. I think Ava Gardner was one actress who knew this from the beginning and she went along with it, but fell into the same pit as Gable, Turner, Tracy, and Garland. How else could they make a living? They were spoiled but not rich in those days. Ava said more than once she was mad as hell that her brother-in-law put her picture in his window. She was voted the most beautiful girl in the world at one point. That's great, but even Greta Garbo used to cry in front of the mirror. The same damn thing would happen to Ava, who was so natural and stunning, but she didn't have Garbo's money to fall back on. That makes all the difference – all the difference in the world!'

Singapore was a failure, but *The Hucksters* established Ava Gardner not only at MGM, but at the box office. Gable and Deborah Kerr, who was making her film debut in America, were heralded. Ava was praised for her sultry beauty and acting ability by the critics who predicted she was 'going places.'

❦

In the fall of 1947 Ava went to New York to promote *The Killers*. Producer Mark Hellinger introduced her to Howard Duff, the voice of Sam Spade in the radio series. He had appeared on the stage in *Brute Force* and made his movie debut in the film version. At the time Duff was deeply involved with actress Yvonne DeCarlo, but was hooked on Ava instantly. After a quiet dinner in Greenwich Village, they went from nightclub to nightclub drinking and dancing, the quiet Howard doing his best to keep up with the restless and insatiable Ava. He returned to Hollywood the following day and did not see her again for a while. But Duff was 'drunk with Ava' and he ended his romance with Miss DeCarlo. Busy with his second film, *Naked City*, and a new Universal contract, Howard spoke often with Ava on the telephone. She, too, was on a hectic schedule at MGM, posing for publicity photos and getting ready for her next movie, *One Touch of Venus*. In her spare time, she flew to Mexico for the bullfights or hid out with Howard Hughes, who had just acquired RKO.

One of Ava's girlfriends provided an interesting insight into Ava Gardner. The acquaintance said, 'I think Artie destroyed her. After Ava divorced him she changed completely. She no longer trusted men. It was as if she wanted to get back at them. Make love and run. She was wild. She preferred fast flings. This was so unlike the innocent Ava who came to Hollywood with a dream – to meet a nice guy and live happily ever after. She subconsciously put a stone wall between herself and the opposite sex after Artie. Sex and laughs. Come any further and the wall was there. If a man wanted to go out with Ava it was on her terms. Take it or leave it, and they took it wanting more.

'Maybe it was the analysis that Artie put her through or the way he put her down or perhaps it was the sad fact she had failed twice at marriage. I don't know. Does anyone? Ava was like a rocket that was all fired up and suddenly zoomed into space. But no one was at the controls. She was a night person and took advantage of each spare minute, but Ava was never late at the studio. As a matter of fact, she was usually in makeup or wardrobe before the others arrived. Ava was beginning to drink quite heavily but maintained her enormous Southern appetite, one reason she didn't fall down by the wayside like the rest of us. She was an incredible woman, but not a happy one.'

Incredible, indeed. In 1948 Ava dated Ciro's bandleader Jerry Wald, Peter Lawford, Mafia boss Mickey Cohen's righthand man Johnny Stompanato, and, of course, Howard Hughes. (Johnny Stompanato was accidentally killed by Lana Turner's thirteen-year-old daughter Cheryl, who tried to defend her mother during a bitter argument between Lana and the mobster who had threatened to disfigure her face.) Fan magazines emphasized a serious romance with Howard Duff. They were photographed in nightclubs and he confessed his love for Ava to reporters, though it wasn't necessary. His face said it all. Duff was no fool, however. Their quiet nights alone together were restless ones for Ava, whose moods fluctuated from contentment to impatience.

She was also seeing Frank Sinatra on the sly. Under contract to MGM he was a member of Mayer's 'family.'

103

The crooner was linked by the press to Lana Turner and Marilyn Maxwell, despite the fact that he was a married man with two children. In 1946 he separated from his wife, Nancy, briefly. Hollywood insiders blamed Lana. L.B. Mayer protected his players. The gossip was hearsay, according to careful cover-ups by Howard Strickling.

Sinatra told a friend he had seen Ava's picture on a magazine cover and exclaimed, 'I'm going to marry her someday.' She wasn't overly impressed with him in the beginning. She thought he was too arrogant. Howard Hughes had Sinatra followed and put Ava under surveillance again. 'Frankie' had her watched, too.

During production of *One Touch of Venus* at Universal, Ava had a brief affair with her co-star Robert Walker, who was carrying an alcoholic torch for his former wife, actress Jennifer Jones. His baby face and pain-filled soul endeared him to Ava, who was four years older than Bob. The tortured actor would be dead in 1951 after doctors tried to revive him from a drunken stupor with injections of sodium Amytal.

In *Venus*, Ava portrayed a department store statue of a goddess brought to life by floorwalker Robert Walker's kiss. She had posed topless for Italian sculptor Joseph Nicolosi who wanted a more lifelike effect. But director William Seiter was shocked. 'We can't get away with that!' he gasped. 'The statue comes to life! Add a sexy Grecian gown off one shoulder and we'll have it duplicated by wardrobe.'

This was Ava's only costume in the movie. The dress was made of flimsy material tied around the waist by a cord. Supposedly she wore nothing underneath. The big news at Universal were the times Seiter turned on the wind machines. Ava was allowed a good stiff drink to get her circulation going again after the chill. The technicians had a few to cool off.

Ava and Walker frequently saw each other after

hours. Their time together ultimately turned into all-night drinking binges. She held her own on the set the following day. He did not. If Walker was able to stand up, the cameraman shot the back of his head in love scenes. Ava looked as beautiful and refreshed as if she'd just stepped out of a clear lake. In her own way she tried to comfort Bob, an impossible task. He fell in love with her, became possessive and abusive if she refused to see him. The fact that Ava was dating Howard Duff was no secret, but Walker was in no condition to be understanding. Near the end of *Venus*, Ava asked Duff to visit the set whenever possible. 'When you're here I feel safe,' she said.

The Gardner-Walker affair ended when the Greek goddess turned back to stone. He called her. She changed her phone number. Deathly afraid of what Bob might do in a drunken rage, she moved from apartment to apartment. Sometimes she stayed with Bappie or the Heflins. When Ava stayed home, Duff remained with her, answering the door and telephone.

Friends asked each other why she didn't turn to Howard Hughes at this critical time. Obviously two Howards were too many.

Duff told writer Charles Higham, 'When Ava and I ran out of things to do one night she suggested we get a blender and put everything in the house into it, vodka, gin, Scotch, brandy, you name it. It was fantastic and then, wham! We were out on the carpet. I was obsessed with Ava as any red-blooded man would be. She was maddening one minute and adorable the next. She was never satisfied.'

♈

Though Ava Gardner was a vision in *One Touch of Venus*, it was roasted by the critics and failed at the box office. Yet there is no doubt that the film helped her career immensely. Her extraordinary beauty and sense of timing could not be overlooked. MGM welcomed her back with star status. She was assigned to Norma Shearer's old dressing room, the largest occupied by any Metro actress. The three-room suit consisted of a boudoir, bathroom, kitchen, and the actual dressing room, which was lined with mirrors, light bulbs, and closets. MGM was going all out. They were paying Ava $1,250 a week and publicizing her as 'Hollywood's Glamour Girl of 1948.' Mayer, however, did not recognize Ava as an actress and while she luxuriated in her apartment dressing room with a maid who also served her on the movie set, Ava waited for that one juicy part that would prove she had talent. Though *Venus* was a disappointment, she expected MGM to forget about the dreadful espionage film, *The Bribe*. Unfortunately for all concerned – Ava, Robert Taylor, Charles Laughton, and John Hodiak – they were told to report for work on one of Metro's worst projects.

Like Gable, Taylor had returned from the service hoping to resume his thriving career. Instead *Undercurrent* and *The High Wall* were dismal failures. The romantic leading man, whom the press labeled 'more beautiful than Hedy Lamarr,' was relegated to stern bad guy roles that were depressing to him and disappointing to his fans. In *The Bribe*, he played a federal agent who falls in love with a honky-tonk singer (Ava) while investigating a smuggling ring in the Caribbean.

The only reward for Bob Taylor and Ava was their brief romantic interlude. Though she reacted to him as she did to most men in her life, as casual fun, he regained his masculinity. After his stint in the navy air force, Taylor had realized his marriage to actress Barbara Stanwyck was over. Fearing impotency, he complained of a prostate problem that made it difficult for him to be an attentive husband until the condition was corrected.

Barbara didn't accept this. She intimated he was homosexual since Bob spent so much time with his buddies on hunting and fishing trips. When his best friend called the house Barbara yelled, 'Hey, Bob, your wife wants to talk to you!'

Most men might have left home or laughed, but Taylor never forgot his pretty boy image in the thirties, when he played a powdered-down Armand to Greta Garbo's Camille. Bob went to a psychologist friend. Convinced he was losing his manhood, Taylor poured his heart out. 'I want my marriage to work out,' he said. 'I like and admire Barbara.'

Bob was asked if he'd ever had the urge to be with a man.

'Never,' he replied. 'I look at a sexy girl walking down the street and get a goddamn hot sensation in my groin.'

The discussion continued, but the doctor realized the important factor was convincing Taylor he was not a homosexual. The advice he got was, 'Go out and get laid.'

During filming of *The Bribe*, Bob and Ava saw each other occasionally in the afternoons at his mother's house. It's doubtful Taylor mentioned his problem because he had none with Ava. Ralph Couser, Bob's close friend, recalled, 'Miss Gardner was a devilish flirt. I was on the set with Bob and she loved to tease the boys. One day we were all sitting at a round table and she was massaging Taylor's crotch with her bare toe. He tried to keep a straight face, but she had a crooked smile on her face. It was very funny. It wasn't only Bob. She loved toying with the guys. Clark Gable used to say she was a 'good Joe,' direct and sexy. A real woman who could be one of the boys. Bob never talked much. He never came right out and told me about seeing Ava. His mother, who was a religious fanatic, didn't like the idea he was bringing another woman to her house. Bob asked her, "Would you rather I go to a cheap motel and be photographed?" ' When *The Bribe* was over, so was the affair. But Taylor was a new man.

It is alleged that Ava became pregnant in 1948 and decided to have an abortion. The painful procedure was physically traumatizing, and saddened her for years.

Her good friend Lana Turner was facing a similar crisis at that time. She was forced to abort her baby by Tyrone Power. According to him, he broke off their engagement because she dated Frank Sinatra. The real reason was Tyrone's love for Linda Christian, whom he married a few months later. Lana never got over Tyrone Power. 'He was the love of my life,' she said.

If Ava's personal life was a merry-go-round of nightclubs, men, and alcohol, she remained loyal to Metro-Goldwyn-Mayer. Howard Hughes, now in control of RKO Studios, offered her a picture deal, but she turned it down. Many sources claim that Ava was determined to achieve absolute stardom at MGM – to make a successful movie that was proof once and for all that they had not made a mistake by signing her to a contract. This resolution was mistaken for ambition. If it hadn't been for Artie Shaw, who helped her negotiate the contract that landed her $1,250 a week, Ava would have been satisfied with less. Although she did not have a high overhead, she should have given serious thought to saving or investing money. Ava Gardner never did.

The Great Sinner with Gregory Peck was the first

bone thrown to Ava by MGM. She was cast as the daughter of a Russian general who saves Peck from gambling his life away. The movie, based on the novel *The Gambler* by Dostoyevski, had great promise, but the script's co-author, Christopher Isherwood, was flabbergasted that MGM would choose Ava and Peck. He quit. Director Robert Siodmak refused to discuss the disastrous project and often denied directing it and no wonder. Moviegoers ignored *The Great Sinner*, which was withdrawn from the circuit before critics had a chance to put it on the barbecue.

Ava's elaborate period costumes were magnificent in the picture. For one scene she wore an elegant black ball gown with a billowing skirt, and the technicians wondered if this new image would make her a great star. She glided over to them during the lunch break and pulled the front of the dress over her head. Those standing behind Ava came running.

But Ava just laughed hysterically. What they saw became Hollywood legend – underneath the expensive gown Ava was wearing old jeans! Then she piped up, 'Anyone around here got a hot dog?'

Great effort was put into *The Great Sinner*. No one was blamed for the disaster. Gregory Peck did his very best after such fine performances in *Spellbound*, *Duel in the Sun*, and *Gentleman's Agreement*, for which he received a nomination for Best Actor. There was depth to Ava's acting, but no depth in the dialogue. She was breathtaking, perhaps more so since she had learned a lesson while watching *Whistle Stop* in that neighborhood theater a few years before. Photographed properly, she could keep the male public in their seats. The new Ava chatted with the cameraman and the lighting director. One of the grips said, 'She had learned her trade at last! This was the first time Ava spoke up about the small key spotlight that is so important as well as other details pertaining to camera angles. She was very sweet about it. Instead of telling anyone what to do, Ava said, "Don't forget this or that." She was paying attention to details. To tell the truth, I wasn't sure if she'd get around to it, or care that much. The bored kid was becoming a pro.'

Ava's luck was changing, all right. Much of it had to do with the end of L.B. Mayer's reign. Metro faced deficits amounting to $6.5 million. The studio's contract stars, producers, and directors were not winning Oscars or making the prestigious 'Ten Best' lists. Mayer, not one to take the blame for anything, had been more interested in his stable of racehorses and courtship of a new young wife. When the decline of MGM became public knowledge, he began to search for another production chief with the insight of the late Irving Thalberg. Dore Schary, who had resigned as production head of RKO, was Mayer's choice. On July 1, 1948, Schary signed a contract with MGM for $6,000 a week. Though he put Metro in the black again, he was not popular with many of Mayer's family. Ava was not particularly fond of Schary, who lacked a sense of humor. He did, however, make her a household name.

The MGM stars who thrived on their four-letter-word battles with Mayer – win or lose – found life rather dull at the studio with Schary. Twenty years ago it had been transition to sound that put a hush over Hollywood. Now it was watching Father Mayer fighting to keep his chicken soup in the commissary and a sense of dignity in Leo the Lion. Maybe Schary was 'adopted' into the MGM family, but he fought for colorful spectaculars to compete with television and put Mayer's heavenly stars on the screen with exciting flair and sparkle – *Quo Vadis, Showboat, Ivanhoe, Father of the Bride*, and *Annie Get Your Gun*, among them. These great films were yet to come, however. In the meantime, Mayer and Schary ruled compatibly, the latter taking an interest in several players who had not been given a chance to show their full potential. Ava was one.

Howard Strickling and his staff saturated the fan magazines and gossip columns with Ava's cheesecake photos labeled 'Hollywood's Glamour girl of 1948.' One such press release stated:

The year has brought this beautiful and talented young actress signal honors by the score. As the climax, it brought her first starring roles at her home studio, Metro-Goldwyn-Mayer, opposite two of the screen's foremost leading men – Robert Taylor and Gregory Peck. She went from Taylor's arms in *The Bribe* to Peck's in *The Great Sinner*.

These developments were prefaced by the impressive manner in which the year opened for her. After a number of Hollywood's young actresses had been tested, she won the role of the glamorous nightclub singer in love with Clark Gable in *The Hucksters*. Her performance opposite the King placed her on the threshold of stardom, and had every studio in Hollywood asking for her services.

There was no mention of *The Killers* or *Whistle Stop*, released by United Artists and Universal. With very few exceptions, Metro would use Ava exclusively in the future. When at last she had security in her own right, Ava decided to buy a little yellow cottage in Nichols Canyon. In the company of her maid, Mearene, she occasionally enjoyed an evening listening to Artie Shaw and Frank Sinatra records or tending to her garden.

Mention of her 'engagement' to Howard Duff

persisted and the studio did not confirm or deny it. They could not publicize Ava's other dates and affairs, with the exception of Lawford. Her seeing Howard Hughes delighted gossip columnists.

In her memoirs Jane Russell referred to Ava as 'Howard's girl' in 1948. Though she rarely socialized with her boss, Hughes was anxious to show off his new house to her because Jane told him the last one was god-awful and unlivable. What was supposed to be an early evening ended up an all-night affair because Ava wanted to go dancing at the Mocambo. With dawn about to break, Jane suggested she stay at Ava's rather than drive home. Hughes did not want the two girls comparing notes and told Russell, 'No, you won't get any sleep at her place. I'll drive Ava home and you stay here.'

Jane related that she woke up to find Howard standing by her bed. He whined, 'I'm freezing. I must have caught a chill driving Ava home. Can I get in with you?' She touched his hand and it was ice cold. 'Okay. Get in. But no funny business.' He curled up next to her and put his arms around Jane's waist. 'All right, Howard, that's it. Get out!'

'Okay,' he replied like a little boy. 'I'll go. But let me get out when I decide. I don't like people telling me what to do. I won't touch you again. I promise.'

Russell fell asleep again and he left quietly. 'I often hollered at Howard,' she wrote, 'and I think in a funny kind of way I scared him.'

A pathetic insight into the man Russell considered lonely and super-thoughtful are his words, ' . . . let me get out when I decide.' Jane had remarkable patience with 'the boss.'

NINE

She Loves Me. She Loves Me Not.

The restless Ava wanted to do anything but sit still and think. If she was in one place, she wanted to be in another. Moody, changeable, and volatile, she was making up for the teenage years that had been taken away by her mother. Until Ava fell deeply in love, she was on a merry-go-round that slowed down, but never stopped.

Frank Sinatra, whose third child, Christina, was born in June 1948, was in hot pursuit of Ava. One of his later recordings, 'I've Got You Under My Skin,' appropriately describes his frustration over her. She wasn't seriously interested in him, but they had much in common. Both were nocturnal creatures, hearty drinkers, chain smokers, restless, and passionate.

During one of their drunken sprees in a town near Palm Springs, Frank gave Ava one of his guns, a loaded thirty-eight, and they drove through Indio, California, 'shooting up the town.' Streetlights and store windows were broken and a bullet grazed a man's stomach. Ava and Frank were arrested, but it was kept quiet until he could reach his press agent. The couple was bailed out and quickly flown back to Los Angeles in a private plane. The charges were dropped and damages paid.

Sinatra, who had not made a hit record in two years, concentrated on movies. As a priest in *The Miracle of the Bells*, his hollow chest and stringbean legs were concealed underneath a long robe. But in *Take Me Out to the Ballgame*, released in 1949, his sailor bellbottoms were padded in the back to give him a fanny. He was thirty-three years old and already wearing a hairpiece. One nasty critic wrote that Sinatra looked flea-bitten in his early films. Maturity would, however, give his voice magic and his face a haunting aura of reaching out for love. Ava had much to do with this transformation by merely being there. But when she was Annie Oakley to Frank's Buffalo Bill riding high in the desert with loaded guns, Ava was having a good time and little else. Only a few Hollywood insiders knew about the secret rendezvouses. Very close friends made their houses available – with much more compassion than Robert Taylor's mother had!

In *East Side*, *West Side* Ava was cast again as a sexy nightclub singer, who tries to lure James Mason away from his wife, Barbara Stanwyck. Ava duplicated her other-woman role from *The Hucksters*. Smooth, glossy, and meaningless, the MGM film, based on a novel by Marcia Davenport about well-heeled New Yorkers, required her to lean against a piano wearing a tight black satin dress with long sleeves. When Ava glanced through the script for the first time she cursed with venom, got it out of her system, and walked through the role with ease. Good riddance. Having her friend Van Heflin working in *East Side, West Side* was a consolation.

Whether Barbara Stanwyck had any inkling about her real-life husband's relationship with Ava isn't known. She didn't speak to Lana Turner after Robert Taylor's admission that he wanted to marry the 'Sweater Girl' when they co-starred in *Johnny Eager* in 1942. Actress Virginia Grey was also deliberately snubbed because she was seeing Bob following his legal separation from Barbara, who somehow kept track of his dating activities. As for Ava, she was immune to these matters.

Stanwyck was not under contract to any studio and, therefore, was off the MGM lot upon completion of *East Side, West Side*. Not so with Mickey Rooney, whose career was beginning to fade. He had remained a bachelor since his second divorce in 1947 and was dating actress Martha Vickers. Ava was friendly to him, but kept her distance because it was common knowledge he still carried a torch. But Ava was at her most sympathetic and loving when the men in her life were in a slump. With the demise of Andy Hardy, Rooney returned to civilian life in adult roles – *Killer McCoy*, *Words and Music*, and a turkey, *Summer Holiday*. He wasn't a top draw at the box office any longer, but his fans were faithful and willing to adjust to the kid-next-door being an ex-GI and twice divorced. Rooney complained bitterly about his roles and not getting top billing. When he was not included in the huge male cast in MGM's *Battleground*, he confronted L.B. Mayer about purchasing the rights to Andy Hardy. 'I want to do a radio series,' he announced. When Mayer refused, Mickey and MGM parted company in 1950. Had he stayed on for another four years, Mickey would not have lost a $49,000 yearly pension. After the damage was done, he approached

115

Dore Schary with the admission, 'I made a mistake and want to come back.' MGM's new boss was sympathetic but could only offer an occasional film without a contract.

Mickey married, divorced, had children, relied on pills and booze, and filed for bankruptcy before emerging a man. During these dark days in the early fifties, Ava was in contact with Rooney, offering to help him out financially. She always came to his defense if an unkind word was said about him. 'He stands taller than anyone in this goddamn room!' was a typical outburst.

Ava Gardner, like most of the MGM family, returned to her hometown a celebrated star and received the keys to the city from the mayor of Smithfield in January 1949. Reporters and gossip columnists were accompanied to North Carolina by Metro's press agents. Pictures were taken of Ava sitting on the porch of her Brogden birthplace (Ava nicknamed it 'Grabtown' in interviews), with her relatives and schoolmates. No one had to ask her to take off her shoes.

'I dislike the script as much as you do,' Robert Mitchum told her on the telephone. 'But I'd like you to reconsider *My Forbidden Past*.'

'It's the same old crap,' Ava sighed.

'Yeah, I told Hedda Hopper that,' the sleepy-eyed actor said, 'and Hughes chewed my ass off.'

'Why didn't you belt him one?'

'I owe him money. How about it, Ava? Will you do the picture with me?'

'Why not?'

'Take the money and run, kid. Take the money and run.'

Ava was aware that Mitchum's career was in jeopardy after he was arrested on September 1, 1948 for possession of marijuana. A married man with two children, Bob was taken into custody along with two actresses and one of his buddies. The police had been tipped off and rushed the house just as the foursome were preparing to get stoned.

'I'm ruined,' Bob said on the spot. When the $3,000-a-week movie star was booked at the Los Angeles Jail and asked what his occupation was, Mitchum replied, 'Former actor.'

Reporters flocked to the scene. Bob volunteered, 'Well, this is the bitter end of everything – my career, my home, my marriage.' But Jerry Giesler, one of the best lawyers in Hollywood, was hired by David Selznick and Howard Hughes, who owned Bob's contract. Mitchum was released on $1,000 bail pending trial and told to report for work at RKO the next day.

Two of his films were not released until the publicity subsided. Hughes, addicted to codeine, and Selznick, addicted to amphetamines, supported Mitchum throughout the ordeal though neither mogul was available for comment. On February 9, 1949, Bob was sentenced to a year in the county jail. Suspending the sentence, the judge placed him on probation for two years, the first sixty days to be spent in Los Angeles County Jail. When Mitchum was transferred to the Honor Farm, Howard Hughes was smuggled in to see him. Their conversation is still a secret, but when Bob was released, Hughes bought Selznick's share of the actor's contract for $400,000 and loaned Bob $50,000 to buy a house for the wife and kids.

Hughes took a chance by releasing *Rachel and the Stranger* with Mitchum and Loretta Young. The public lined up at the box office and applauded when Bob appeared on the screen. Newspapers around the country were outraged and told the public to boycott his films, but letters poured into RKO supporting the actor who once said, 'If you can't drink it, spend it, or kiss it, then to hell with it.' Maybe it was a picture of Mitchum mopping his jail cell that proved he was paying his dues like any other prisoner. The face that rarely frowned or smiled said it all: 'I'm taking my lumps. What's the big deal?' Six foot two inches tall, one hundred and eighty pounds, light brown hair, hazel eyes, and a broken nose imperfectly reset was Robert Mitchum – former hobo, coal miner, prizefighter, and veteran of seven Hopalong Cassidy films. 'I've been happy in jail because I've had privacy,' he said. 'Nobody envied me. Nobody wanted anything from me.'

Though the scandal had a happy ending, Bob needed money to pay off his legal fees, thus his call to Ava, who had not yet met Mitchum. 'I could have fallen for him,' she said in later years. The truth is she did and Bob was in a quandary. During production of *My Forbidden Past*, he was taken with Ava. She wasn't just acting in their love scenes. Her kisses were deliberately lasting, passionate, and seductive. When he drove her home after work, they discussed the 'situation.' Bob was losing his grip and wasn't sure what to do about the woman repeatedly linked with his boss.

'Suppose something happened between Ava and me?' he asked Hughes over the telephone.

'Like what?'

'Should I go to bed with her, is what I'm asking.'

'If you don't, everybody will think you're a pansy.'

'If you want to discuss your problems, I'll discuss mine,' Mitchum exclaimed.

'You're like a pay toilet,' Hughes laughed. 'You don't give a shit for nothing, do you?'

Though he made light of it, Bob was frustrated over Ava Gardner. They became very close friends and talked in his car in front of her house almost every night. Ava was determined to have him before the picture was finished. Her last opportunity was on a tour to promote *My Forbidden Past* in Chicago. A concerned Hughes hired a bodyguard to make sure Mitchum was not set up, and extra precautions were taken in crowds to make certain no drugs were slipped into his pocket.

Ava was furious that Mitchum did not pay more attention to her in Chicago even though his wife, Dorothy, accompanied him. It wasn't Ava's vanity as much as knowing Bob had been deliberately holding back. In 1986 she talked about her leading men and cited him in particular. 'I think every girl who ever worked with Bob Mitchum fell in love with him.'

In 1949 the Hollywood marriage-go-round spun John Huston and Robert Taylor into divorce courts. Clark Gable married Lady Sylvia Ashley on a drunken binge. David Niven took a second wife. Artie Shaw was going through a bitter separation from Kathleen Winsor. Mickey Rooney married Martha Vickers and was awaiting the birth of his third child. Even L.B. Mayer settled £3 million on his first wife to marry a younger woman.

Was there an affair between Ava and Bob? No one knows for sure. Though a hard drinking rebel and a ladies' man, Mitchum would not hurt innocent people. His wife did not have to stand by him during the scandal, but she did even when their children were not welcome back at a private school because the other students might be exposed to a man with a record.

Before Ava left Chicago she made the rounds of nightclubs without an escort. Her fans rather than the

Scotch caught up with her, however, and she was forced to call one of Hughes's bodyguards, who found her locked in the powder room while a mob waited outside to tear off pieces of her beautiful black evening gown for souvenirs.

Depressed and very frustrated over the Mitchum affair, Ava got on a plane without telling anyone and returned to Los Angeles where Howard Duff and Frank Sinatra were waiting. She was coming to the crossroads with both men, but she wanted to negotiate her next film with Dore Schary before getting involved any deeper in romantic entanglements she deemed hopeless.

MGM was planning *Quo Vadis* with a budget of $7 million, the most expensive picture ever produced to date in 1950. *Gone With the Wind* had carried a cost of $4 million ten years earlier. *Quo Vadis* was going to be filmed at the huge Cinecitta studios, eight miles outside Rome. Ava wanted to play the part of Lygia, the Christian slave girl, but Schary thought Deborah Kerr was more suited to the role. Clark Gable was chosen to play Marcus Vinicius but told Schary, 'I'm not going to be seen in Roman garb with my bloody knees sticking out!'

'You have a point,' Schary pondered. 'Bob Taylor would make a better appearance.'

'Can't you find anything suitable for me?' Gable growled.

'We're looking.'

'If you come across a decent script I'd like Ava Gardner for my leading lady.'

'I'll keep that in mind,' Schary said with little enthusiasm.

Gable grumbled to Spencer Tracy, 'At least with that bastard Mayer a guy knew where he stood. He either gave you his word or threw you out of his office.'

Ava was disappointed over not being part of the

spectacular *Quo Vadis,* but she soon forgot about the Roman epic when MGM director Albert Lewin informed her he was writing the script for *Pandora and the Flying Dutchman.* 'From the beginning,' he said, 'I've patterned the willful, flippant playgirl after you. We hope James Mason will be available to co-star as the Dutchman, and if all goes well, Ava, we'll do the picture on location in Spain.'

'Can I read it?' she asked.

He handed her the script and added, 'We won't be ready until early next year, however. You'll be home for the holidays.'

Ava was excited about *Pandora* and looked forward to Spain. Being cast in a European movie was another indication that she was a valuable MGM property. She quickly forgot about Robert Mitchum and, against the advice of friends, concentrated on having a good time with Frank Sinatra. Ava's hunger for adventure, intoxicating sex, and thrilling abandonment was fulfilled by the skinny crooner. Love was not a factor. She told her friend Ruth Rosenthal at the onset of the affair that Frank was conceited, arrogant, and overpowering. 'They had instant hostility,' Rosenthal said. 'I guess you could say this instant hostility was a precursor of a sudden romantic interest.'

Though Sinatra had seen many women during his four years in Hollywood, he could not get the elusive Ava out of his mind. Her beauty and sensuality mesmerized him totally. Her availability for only a night or two before disappearing convinced Frank that she was unobtainable – far above him. Her temper was a fair match for his, and she went about living her own life regardless of his feelings. In spite of his infidelities, Frank was a family man even if his wife Nancy saw little of him after they settled in Hollywood. Their two-week separation in 1946 wasn't taken seriously. Lana Turner, who was blamed, told Louella Parsons, 'I am not in love with Frank and he is not in love with me. I have never in my life broken up a home. I just can't take these accusations.' Nancy, a devoted housewife, explained to Hedda Hopper, 'Frank wants his freedom without a divorce.'

Frank came alone to Slapsie Maxie's where comedian Phil Silvers was appearing. Mutual friends brought Nancy, who sat at a separate table. During the course of the evening Frank was asked to sing. His choice was 'Goin' Home' and near the end of the song Silvers took his arm and led him over to Nancy. They kissed, cried, and embraced. The following night Frank moved back to their Toluca Lake home.

For the next three years Sinatra's popularity as a singer waned. The 1949 *Downbeat* poll showed he was on a decline as a vocalist for the first time since 1943. Billy Eckstine was the most popular singer, with Frankie Laine second. Bing Crosby and Mel Torme were tied for third place. Sinatra limped in fifth while Perry Como, Vic Damone, Nat King Cole, and the newest sensation, Johnnie Ray, edged toward the forefront.

Frank was confident, however, that he would be a hit in movies. His *On the Town* with Gene Kelly was fairly successful in 1949, but the rumor spreading around Hollywood was that MGM was going to drop Sinatra's contract because instead of first billing as planned, his name appeared second to Kelly's.

L.B. Mayer was still the power behind MGM, and he was appalled by Frank's personal life. There was a moral clause in every contract that stated, 'The artist agrees to conduct himself with due regard to public conventions and morals and agrees that he will not do or commit any act or thing that will degrade him in society, or bring him into public hatred, contempt, scorn, or ridicule, that will tend to shock, insult, or offend the community or ridicule public morals or decency, or prejudice the producer (MGM) or the motion picture industry in general.'

The Women's Press Club voted Frank their 'Least Cooperative Actor.' He reported late for work and demanded the impossible. Mayer gave Sinatra warning from the very beginning, but the young crooner had more confidence than the U.S. marine corps.

Though Mayer's family of stars complained about the studio system, the majority had achieved fame after being trained, coached, punished, and rewarded by their 'father.' They protected each other, but most important they did what they were told to do. Ava was, despite herself, a product of MGM. She had worked hard, obeyed the rules, and crept up the ladder of success step by step. She resented Sinatra's brassy attitude when he arrived at MGM. She admired the man's singing voice, but not the man. Throughout her career Ava never achieved the confidence that Frank flaunted. But she had the upper hand from the start. Regardless of his bragging and cocky front, Sinatra knew he was going into a professional and financial slump while a frightened Ava became one of the most sought-after actresses in Hollywood.

Why Ava went to New York with Frank in early December 1949 is 'their secret.' She was not about to risk her career for a married man, especially one who had recently bought an expensive house for his family in exclusive Holmby Hills and had another home under construction in Palm Springs. They hoped to get away with traveling together and staying at a friend's suite at the Hampshire House. But they showed up with another couple at the premiere of the hit Broadway show, *Gentlemen Prefer Blondes,* on December

8. Four days later, on Frank's birthday, Ava was his date for a celebration at the Copacabana.

There was speculation that Sinatra was in a panic that Ava was going to Spain after the New Year. He had to take a stand or at least prove he was sincere about divorcing Nancy. Introducing Ava to his parents was a bit unusual, but part of the master plan, apparently. Frank's friends and his press agent George Evans tried to prevent what was happening. But Frank was obsessed with Ava, and she was seriously thinking about a permanent relationship with the thirty-four-year-old Francis Albert Sinatra.

The only publicity existing on the New York trip concerns their 'running into each other' at the premiere of *Gentlemen Prefer Blondes*. All accounts claim this was the beginning of the Gardner-Sinatra romance. It was handled so discreetly that very few people realized they attended the show together.

Frank returned to California and asked Nancy for a divorce. Ava followed and told Howard Duff she couldn't see him anymore. 'I wasn't surprised,' Duff remarked. 'I knew it was over. Ava never seriously considered marrying me.'

After the holidays Frank left Nancy. Nancy was an Italian-American girl and a devout Catholic. She told Hedda Hopper that life with her husband had become unhappy and almost unbearable. 'But I do not see a divorce in the foreseeable future,' she said. 'Frank has left home before and I suppose he'll do it again. But I'm not calling this a marital breakup.'

Ava's trip to Spain was postponed until March. Skeptics said that if she had left on schedule her explosive involvement with Frank might have cooled down. The next two months were a mistake, he admitted. 'But I was so in love I didn't care.'

The death of George Evans might have triggered what followed. The press agent had been with Sinatra since the early days at the Paramount Theater. Evans was the one person who could handle Frank and their first major disagreement was over Ava Gardner. Evans was responsible for keeping the Sinatra marriage intact, encouraging Frank to wear his wedding ring on stage. His swooning teenage-girl fans loved him more for it and their mothers approved. Using reverse psychology, Evans was a genius, but he had a constant battle trying to keep Frank's sexual encounters a secret during the forties. Ava proved to be his Waterloo. Evans was upset over recent developments, and at forty-eight he dropped dead of a heart attack on January 26, 1950. Frank was shocked and broken-hearted. He attended the funeral in New York and then proceeded to do what George Evans fought so hard to prevent. He allowed his romance with Ava to become a public affair by taking her to the Shamrock Hotel in Houston for a two-week singing engagement. A reporter spotted them in a cozy restaurant and the following day the story appeared in newspapers all over the world.

Nancy locked out her husband on Valentine's Day but said flatly there would be no divorce. Ava returned to MGM and faced L.B. Mayer, who called her a whore. 'You were denied permission to leave Los Angeles,' he said, 'because I knew what was going on. Have you read the papers? Do you know what Hedda and Louella are saying about you? Have you read your fan mail? They're calling you Jezebel and a bitch. A home-wrecker.'

Ava was in a state of shock herself. The incident at Vincent's Sorrento restaurant in Houston had been horrid. While she and Frank were dining, reporter Edward Schisser from the *Houston Post* approached their table with his camera. Ava screamed and covered her face with her mink coat. Frank threw down his napkin and pushed back his chair. The owner of the restaurant, Tony Vallone, hurried over to the table and Schisser left, but the incident was reported in the *Houston Post*. The damage had been done. Sinatra explained, 'A photographer asked to take a picture. I refused very graciously and he left. The next day the story broke that I not only refused to allow the picture to be made but threatened to punch the photographer in the nose.'

L.B. Mayer did not punish Ava. He did, however, negotiate a settlement with Sinatra whose contract with MGM was terminated. Frank said he asked to be released because he was tired of sailor roles.

He looked forward to opening at the Copacabana in March, his first nightclub appearance in five years. As for his personal life Sinatra told the press, 'The fact that Ava and I have had a few dates means nothing.'

TEN

Frankie

It was snowing in Hoboken, New Jersey, on December 12, 1915 when twenty-year-old Natalie Sinatra, who everyone knew as 'Dolly,' gave birth to her first and only child, a boy weighing thirteen-and-a-half pounds. The baby's face was scarred on the left side of his head and neck by forceps during the breech delivery, and he almost lost an ear in the process.

The boy's father, Marty, an Italian from Catania, Sicily, could not read or write, was a boxer, boilermaker, bartender, and fireman. Dolly Garavante immigrated from Genoa with her parents and worked as a midwife until she went into business for herself giving abortions. Dolly's strawberry blonde hair and blue eyes made it easy to pass for Irish and she used this to good advantage by taking the name O'Brien. In those days doors were closed to Italians and though Dolly was proud of her heritage, she joined forces with the Irish, who were in control of politics and law enforcement in New Jersey. Her husband was known as Marty O'Brien in the boxing ring, and during Prohibition the Sinatras opened up a saloon by that name.

It was Dolly who borrowed money for the barroom and bought the bootleg booze. The meek and mild Marty never got involved in business negotiations or financial matters.

Son Francis Albert had no ambition or direction. At the age of sixteen he dropped out of school and worked for a local newspaper as a clerk. But he demanded respect even then and his violent temper started many brawls he couldn't win. People referred to him as a WOP (WithOut Papers), a label given to Italians in the early part of this century. He looked at the upper crust with admiration, not envy. Whether on the streets of Hoboken or Hollywood, Sinatra always said, 'That's real class.'

He was a mama's boy and liked to do anything Dolly enjoyed. One of her favorite pastimes was singing and he formed a quartet called the Hoboken Four. With his mother's help and encouragement, the group competed on radio's 'Major Bowes Amateur Hour' and won the contest. After several singing engagements, a cocky Frank wanted to go on his own, and in 1938 he got a job as a singer-waiter at the Rustic Cabin, a road-house on Route 9W near Alpine, New Jersey, for $15 a week.

The following year was an eventful one for Sinatra. He was discovered by bandleader Harry James, who offered the skinny kid with a greasy pompadour $75 a week. He also married Nancy Barbato in February, a union that Dolly pushed to save her son from getting into more serious trouble with girls. 'In Nancy,' Frank said, 'I found beauty, warmth, and understanding. Being with her was my only escape from what seemed a grim world. All I knew up to that time were tough kids on street corners, gang fights, and parents who were always busy trying to make money.' But he warned his bride that he was going to be famous and did not want anyone holding him back. Nancy promised, 'I won't stand in your way.'

The newlyweds spent a four-day honeymoon in North Carolina and settled down in a third-floor walkup apartment in Jersey City.

At the age of twenty-four Frank was sure of himself and willing to tell that to anyone who might have doubts. According to Harry James, in an interview for *Downbeat*, a reporter asked the bandleader, 'Who's that skinny little singer? He sings a great song.'

James replied, 'Not so loud. The kid's name is Sinatra. He considers himself the greatest vocalist in the business. Get that! No one ever heard of him. He's never had a hit record. He looks like a wet rag. But he says he's the greatest. If he hears you compliment him, he'll demand a raise.'

Tommy Dorsey came along with an offer of $125 a week and in 1940 he and Frank recorded 'I'll Never Smile Again.' It became number one on the Hit Parade.

'You find that there are just as many angles to figure in being honest as there are in being crooked,' Sinatra said. 'If what you do is honest and you make it, you're a hero. If what you do is crooked and you make it, you're a bum. Me? I grabbed a song.'

Also in 1940, the couple's first child, Little Nancy, was born, and Big Nancy decided to stay home instead of traveling with her husband. Frank didn't mind this arrangement one bit. He had already been playing around with other women and now he could have his freedom. Even if he were appearing only a few miles from home, Frank sometimes stayed out all night. His friends claim Dolly made sure the couple stayed together. It wasn't just fondness for her daughter-in-law, because the two women did not get along. Dolly believed in family unity and she laid down the law to Frank repeatedly.

In 1941 Sinatra replaced Bing Crosby on top of *Billboard's* popularity poll. He bought out his contract with Dorsey and opened at the Paramount in New York with Benny Goodman on New Year's Eve 1942. Frank was a sensation, but it was press agent George Evans who thought up the idea of planting a group of bobbysoxers in the audience to jump up and down and swoon, 'Oh, Frankie!' on cue. Evans hired an ambulance to park in front of the theater to accommodate hysterical fainting women of all ages who filled the Paramount.

The crooner with hollow cheeks and protruding Adam's apple packed them in every night for eight weeks. Clutching the microphone, he sang with a hungry pathetic look in his eyes and a sexy vulnerability in his voice. Sad and romantic, critics said. It was not Evans who came up with the gimmick that, 'Frank made you feel like he was singing for you and you alone.'

In January 1944 Nancy gave birth to Frank, Jr. Her famous husband was in Hollywood doing concerts and breaking into movies. He was in no rush to move his family out West where beautiful women were as plentiful as oranges and just as easy to pluck. Finally he bought Mary Astor's estate in Toluca Lake, a section of the San Fernando Valley, fifty miles outside of Hollywood.

Nancy was out of her element in an atmosphere of glamour and elegance. She still prepared large Italian-style meals, cared for the children, and shopped at bargain stores. Though she saw little of Frank, Nancy was relieved that he was classified 4-F and not eligible to join the services. A punctured eardrum, an injury at birth, kept him out. While the top Hollywood male stars, Clark Gable, Jimmy Stewart, Tyrone Power, Robert Taylor, and David Niven, to name a few, went into the services, studios needed replacements for their heartthrobs and Sinatra stepped in.

Nancy had been in California only a year and a half when Frank moved into his own apartment in their first official separation. Lana Turner and Marilyn Maxwell had been seen in Sinatra's company. He went back home, but did not change his lifestyle in Las Vegas, Palm Springs, Cuba, or New York. Frank's friends agreed that he paid little attention to Nancy, but he fawned over Dolly, leaving no doubt that his mother was the most important person in his life.

Sinatra's films were popular at the box office and praised by critics. The entertainment editor of the *New York Daily Mirror*, Lee Mortimer, was not a fan, however. Frank took the gibes and seethed inwardly until the critic panned his performance with Kathryn Grayson in MGM's *It Happened in Brooklyn*: 'This excellent and well-produced picture bogs down under the miscast Frank (Lucky) Sinatra, smirking and trying to play a leading man.'

'Lucky' was a dig whether it referred to the singer's success in films or his reported relationship with Charlie 'Lucky' Luciano.

One night in 1947 Mortimer was leaving Ciro's when he was jumped from behind by Frank's pals and roughed up. In Los Angeles District Court, Sinatra paid Mortimer $9,000 in damages. Dolly commented, 'My son is like me. You cross him and he never forgets.'

Frank continued to do as he pleased despite repeated warnings from MGM. Ava Gardner was an addiction he would not overcome. Her aloofness in the beginning elicited his favorite saying, 'That's real class.' He talked about her constantly. She was, he said, a woman who shared his enthusiasm, his insatiable urge for excitement, and his unbounded energies. Unlike the other beautiful actresses he'd known, Ava was casual about her looks. Without makeup she was lovelier, in fact. She didn't worry about her figure or how much she drank. She was as sober and exquisite at dawn as she had been at sunset. She was an honest friend, a happy-go-lucky companion, a passionate lover, and more hot-tempered than he.

Though Ava had been warned that Frank was a family man despite his infidelities and independence, she didn't care at first. After her two failed marriages she was not interested in a permanent relationship. Nancy was described as an understanding woman and faithful wife who was willing to wait for her husband to come back home. Aside from a cleaning woman who came in once a week, Nancy cared for the home and children herself.

It's possible George Evans might have prevented the Houston restaurant episode from exploding. He had defused previous bombshells. Controlling Ava, however, was equal to controlling a hurricane. Once she found herself in love with the dark-haired Italian who sang love songs to her beneath palm trees and driving down Wilshire Boulevard, Ava followed her emotions. 'Not MGM, not the press, not anyone can tell me what to do,' she said before boarding the plane for Texas. Even Bappie could not dissuade her sister from going.

Nervous and moody, Sinatra feared opening at the Copacabana in March 1950. Ava went with him to New York on her way to Spain. Although they checked into separate accommodations at the Hampshire House, the *Journal American*'s headline was: STARS STAYING AT SAME HOTEL. The article said that Mr Sinatra took a lavish suite overlooking Central Park, and Miss Gardner, recently voted the 'sexiest female in the world' by Hollywood extras, was staying on another floor. Reporters staked out the Hampshire House twenty-four hours a day.

The past three months had taken their toll on Frank. His career was slipping and his confidence with it. He arrived late for an American Red Cross fund-raising drive. Actress Faye Emerson called him a 'big shot' and refused to pose with him for publicity pictures. Frank snapped, 'I don't give a damn!' To add fuel to the fire he failed to show up for the ball. Reporters found him making the round of nightclubs with Ava. When asked about a romance, Frank exclaimed, 'I'm still married!'

Maybe he wasn't home for Nancy's birthday party, but he gave her a mink coat. This tidbit in a gossip column did not sit well with Ava, but it was Sinatra who was crumbling under the pressure, as his all-important opening at the Copacabana loomed. He was tense, visibly shaken, and in a sweat. His close friends gathered at ringside to cheer him on while Ava tried to calm him in his dressing room. In desperation Frank asked for a sedative. Then Ava took her seat out front to lend support.

Sinatra faced a noisy crowd that did not fall silent when he made his entrance. With a blend of the sweet-and-sour he said, 'Hey, this is my opening night. Give me a break.'

The *Herald Tribune* critic wrote: 'Whether temporarily or otherwise, the music that used to hypnotize the bobbysoxers – whatever happened to them, anyway, thank goodness? – is gone from the throat. Vocally, there isn't quite the same old black magic there used to be when Mr Sinatra wrenched "Night and Day" from his sapling frame and the thousands swooned. He relies on what vocal tones are operating effectively and uses carefully made musical arrangements during which the orchestra does the heavy work at crucial points.'

Relieved that he was able to perform at all, Frank sang his standard numbers including, 'Nancy with the Laughing Face.' Ava burned in her seat and could feel prying eyes and hear the snickers. Some patrons thought it was a joke and laughed out loud. Ava sat through the embarrassment but after the show confronted Frank: 'Did you have to sing that fucking song? It makes me feel like a damn fool.'

'It's been a good luck song for years,' he replied. 'I sing it in every show. It doesn't mean anything.'

'Well, don't expect me to sit out there every night and listen to it. Either the song goes or I go.'

Frank dropped 'Nancy with the Laughing Face' from his act and for the next ten nights Ava attended each performance, spurring him on from a ringside table. His voice was weak, however, and his nerves about to crack. Friends were pressuring him to reconcile with Nancy, and his phone calls to the family were depressing him. The children cried and Frank cried. Nancy had sent a congratulatory telegram to the Copa but did not beg or pressure him to consider coming back home. The tightening in his throat was getting progressively worse knowing Ava was leaving for Europe soon. At this juncture fear of losing her was deeper than losing his voice.

When Artie Shaw invited Frank and Ava to see him perform at Bop City and to a dinner party at his apartment after the show, Sinatra was enraged. He detested Shaw, who remarked, 'Yes, I think Frank hated me. He wanted to sing for me, but I told him I didn't use boy singers.' Sinatra had warned Artie in the past not to see or speak to Ava – or else. Shaw pointed to Frank's bodyguard and made a crack, 'If you're so tough, why do you need him?'

Ava was bored and restless after two weeks of coddling, consoling, and mothering Frank's anxieties. She was annoyed by reporters hovering asking questions. Yet she did the best she could for as long as she could because she knew how hurt he was trying to pacify his ten-year-old daughter, who was pleading with him to come home. When faced with the reality of divorce, Frank was the softie few people knew existed. While he mourned Ava's leaving him for several months, she doubted his ability to live alone, knowing he could go back to Nancy.

So Ava had turned to Artie Shaw, who was always available to counsel her. Knowing her problems with Frank, he extended the dinner invitation. When a violent argument erupted with Frank about it, she went with another couple to see Artie perform at Bop City and returned to his apartment for the dinner party. Frank went back to the Hampshire House, expecting to find Ava there. Incensed he called Shaw's apartment, got her on the phone, and exclaimed, 'I just wanted to say goodbye!'

'Where are you going, Frank?' she asked. 'Can't I come, too?'

'Not where I'm going, baby.'

Ava heard a pistol shot, a pause, and then another shot. She dropped the phone, screamed hysterically, and, accompanied by Artie and friends, rushed to the hotel.

The gunshots caused quite a commotion on the eighth floor of the Hampshire House. Actor Tom Drake and Columbia Records chief Manie Sachs hurried from their rooms. Producer David Selznick told them, 'I think the son of a bitch shot himself!' They ran into Frank's suite, found the bullet holes in his mattress and switched it with the mattress in Sachs's room before police arrived.

Ava pushed her way through the jammed hallway and found Sinatra calmly sitting up in bed wearing his pajamas and reading a book. In a state of shock she related her story to the police.

'Are you crazy?' Frank laughed. 'I called you to say good night and went to bed.'

The following day MGM demanded that Ava leave for Spain immediately. She had delayed the trip several times because Frank needed her. The studio was not only disgusted by the adverse publicity, but they were losing money every day. Ava wasn't on location with the rest of the cast of *Pandora and the Flying Dutchman*. She had requested an MGM press agent on her New York trip, but MGM refused, under the circumstances. Considering the rigid moral clauses in her contract, she could have been suspended without pay. Getting Ava out of the country and away from Frank was the logical solution. After playing the fool to Sinatra's fake suicide she wanted very much to busy herself with work and see Spain. Leaving Frank at the airport in early April was a sad and tender moment, but he promised to visit her when his stint at the Copa was over.

Sinatra desperately wanted to settle his marital affairs with Nancy and get a divorce commitment. In her separate maintenance agreement she was temporarily awarded custody of the children, all property, and most of his cash until a final settlement could be reached. Nancy told the press that they were both Catholics and neither wanted a divorce.

Frank's phone calls to Ava were not encouraging. Her moods varied from anger to relief to despair over their relationship. Her salvation was the role of Pandora. The Costa Brava, eighty miles north of Barcelona, was untouched by tourism at that time. Its long stretch of beach was clean and secluded, a sandy unrestricted playground for a chosen few. Ava fell in love with Spain. She was inspired by the lazy spirit of the people, dancing the flamenco, and drinking in the dark corners of cozy, unpretentious nightclubs.

She was also attracted to Mario Cabre, who played

the matador in *Pandora*. Cabre was not Spain's greatest bullfighter, but his showy style in the ring appealed to spectators. He kept his name in the social columns by dating celebrated beauties. His poetry, like his bullfighting, was only fair, but these second-rate talents made him a public figure.

To Ava, he was the ideal Latin type – tall, handsome, broad-shouldered, narrow-hipped. He dressed elegantly in dark suits, with slim elegant ties. His manners were impeccable and his charm irresistible. He carried on a highly cultured conversation in Spanish but spoke very little English. He would not be the first matador to communicate with Ava despite a language barrier.

Cabre, strumming a guitar, serenaded her and wrote verses of everlasting devotion and love. With his permission the personal poems were published. Aside from his hunger for Ava, the flamboyant Mario hoped the courtship would make him a movie star. Ava took a casual view of the romance. A fling with the dashing Cabre meant nothing to her. MGM took advantage of the situation by publicizing the twosome and planting photos of them in the newspapers. L.B. Mayer hoped it would offset the Sinatra scandal. Ava told Frank the rumors were nonsense. The pictures spoke for themselves, he said. MGM was responsible, she explained. He retaliated by going out with Marilyn Maxwell and accommodating photographers. Transatlantic phone calls sizzled between the Hampshire House in New York and a Spanish villa in Tossa Del Mar on the Mediterranean coast – teasing and threatening calls that sent Ava off with Cabre for a good time while Frank nursed a bad throat and a bruised ego.

Skitch Henderson, who was conducting the Copa band, said, 'The understatement of the year would be to say that Frank was difficult. He has always respected sidemen, so when the band played badly, he'd get hacked at me instead of them. He was bugged, too, because he couldn't get a hit record while a harmonica group had a million-copy seller in "Peg O' My Heart." One night when the band was especially horrible, it all boiled over and he turned around to me and muttered sarcastically, "If I'd tried a little harder, maybe I could have gotten the Harmonicats to back me." It cut me deeper than anything that has ever been said to me.'

When Sinatra's voice gave out he could not work for five nights. Columnist Lee Mortimer bet a hundred dollars he would not finish his Copa booking. To spite the columnist, Frank forced himself to appear. During the third show one evening he opened his mouth. Not a sound. 'It was tragic and terrifying,' Henderson said. 'Frank opened his mouth to sing after the band introduction and nothing came out. I thought for a fleeting moment that the unexpected pantomime was a joke. But then he caught my eye. I guess the color drained out of my face as I saw the panic in his. It became so quiet, so intensely quiet in the club. Frank gasped, "Good night," and raced off the stage leaving the audience stunned.'

Sinatra's physician reported he had suffered a submucosal hermorrhage of the throat and suggested he take a two-week vacation. Billy Eckstine replaced him at the Copacabana.

Against doctor's orders, Frank flew to Spain. Reporters plagued him at the airport in New York. 'I'm not supposed to talk,' he whispered. To avoid the British press, he chartered a private plane to Barcelona from London. Rumors came through customs that Frank was carrying a mysterious and expensive package, which turned out to be a $10,000 diamond and emerald necklace. He and songwriter Jimmy Van Heusen drove to the Sea Gull Inn, where Ava was waiting. After dinner they emerged for a drive along the Midi's coastal highway.

Mario Cabre was in Genoa, but he spoke freely to the press. 'Ava Gardner is the woman I love with all the strength in my soul. I believe this love and sympathy are both reciprocal and mutual. Twice I have been gored by bulls, both times in the thigh. But Ava, she has hit me harder than any bull, in the heart.' To prove his undying love, Cabre gave reporters poems – odes to Ava.

'I adore Mario,' she stated. 'We all adore Mario. He's a wonderful guy, but there is no question of love. The whole story is absurd.' As for Sinatra she said, 'Frank's a wonderful guy, too. The press and everybody is talking about marriage. It's too soon. Frankie hasn't even got a divorce.'

Sinatra, looking pale and thin, said, 'Ava and I have been chaperoned every minute we've been together. She's a terrific girl. All I can say is there is no change in the matrimonial situation.'

Though they stayed at separate villas and were accompanied by Van Heusen, it was a mistake for the ailing Sinatra to rush off to Spain with a $10,000 necklace while Nancy celebrated Mother's Day without a gift. Frank admitted it was bad judgment on his part. The perpetual rains in Barcelona aggravated his throat and his disposition. Virtually secluded by bad weather, Sinatra had a horrible trip. When he ventured out reporters asked about Mario Cabre repeatedly. Frank pointed to his raw throat, swallowed painfully, but managed, 'Never heard of him.'

MGM press agents discreetly arranged separate villas, 'chaperones,' sent Mario Cabre to Italy for filming, and helped Ava with her statements to reporters. She was anxious for the weather to clear up and to resume work on *Pandora*. Sinatra did not want to leave Spain until he'd had it out with Ava over the handsome bullfighter. 'If I hear that Spanish runt has been hanging around you again I'll kill him *and* you!' Frank warned at a crowded dinner table.

'We're making a fucking movie together!' she snapped. 'And he's supposed to be my lover – how can he avoid being near me? Besides, I haven't raised hell about Marilyn Maxwell, have I?'

'That's different. We're old friends, and you know it!'

'Well, Mario and I are new friends,' Ava spoke up.

Though Frank was to be pitied, he was still a married man flaunting an affair, and a sick performer who seemed more concerned about Ava than his vocal cords. Close friends worried that he was not taking his financial straits seriously. MGM had canceled his contract. His records weren't selling and few club dates were forthcoming. Yet, he bought Ava a gift far beyond his means.

Newspapers in the United States were roasting Sinatra, who decided to fly home earlier than expected. Mario Cabre was delighted. 'The rain has been terrible,' he told a reporter. 'It has kept me from my beloved. But perhaps by tomorrow I will be able to see her.'

When Frank landed in New York he referred to Ava as 'only a dear friend' and denied giving her an expensive gift. 'The only present I gave Ava was six bottles of Coke,' he said. 'Ask the Barcelona customs people.'

Sinatra arrived in Los Angeles just in time to read about the triumphant reunion Ava had with her bullfighter during the Festival of San Ysidro in Tossa del Mar. She spotted him riding a horse-drawn carriage in the street and, blowing kisses, shouted, 'Mario! Mario!' He ran to Ava and engulfed her in his arms. 'Hello, baby,' he said loud enough for everyone to hear. Then he bared his chest and exclaimed, 'This is

Ava as a child.

An innocent and demure Ava arrives in Hollywood, 1941.

PHOTOFEST

Ava at 16.

Wedding day, January 10, 1942, with Ava, Mickey Rooney, and his father, Joe Yule.

A rare photo of Ava and Mickey on the green. He preferred playing golf with his buddies while the lovely Ava stayed home and fumed.

AP/WIDE WORLD PHOTOS

Bandleader Artie Shaw with Ava Gardner on their wedding day,
October 17, 1945.

Ava and Robert Taylor in *The Bribe*, 1949.

Ava as Julie in _Showboat_, 1951.

After their breakup, Frank would say, "If I could only get her out of my plasma."

The perfect 36-20-36.

"If you ask Clark, 'Hi, how are ya?', he's stuck for an answer."

Ava and Clark Gable in *Mogambo*, 1953.

Ava doing her favorite dance, the flamenco, in
The Barefoot Contessa.

where a bull gored me yesterday. I was distracted by my feelings for Ava. I think of her day and night. She is sublime.' That evening they had a secluded dinner in her villa.

Frank reportedly said, 'I hadn't counted on that bullfighter. He was an added starter they ran in at the last minute. I never did meet him. I assume that what he said was a publicity stunt.'

Frank and Nancy agreed on a permanent property settlement. She kept the Holmby Hills home, stock in the Sinatra Music Corporation, their 1950 Cadillac, custody of the children, one third of his gross income up to $150,000, and 10 percent of the gross above that figure until her death or remarriage. Frank kept the house in Palm Springs and a 1949 Cadillac convertible.

Nancy's attorney commented, 'It doesn't look now that they will get a divorce.'

Ava flourished in Spain. She refused to use a double for the scene in which Pandora swims nude to the Dutchman's anchored schooner. Though she had to do it several times, Ava was refreshed by the chilly Mediterranean. In the moonlight the camera shot a rear view of Ava climbing aboard. The final editing showed only her dripping wet hair and naked shoulders. The Dutchman, played by James Mason, had the front view in the film, implying Pandora remained on deck without a stitch of clothing on. The implication was exciting for Ava, who assumed the role of Pandora around the clock by living her romance with Cabre. To the cast and crew, however, Ava and Mario were not inseparable. For him it was too intense to last. As for Ava, she was in love with a crooner from Hoboken, New Jersey.

ELEVEN

All or Nothing at All

In June 1950, location filming on *Pandora and the Flying Dutchman* ended and the cast and crew flew to London for studio work on the movie. Cabre made headlines by sharing his love poems with reporters. Ava was his rainbow, and the dawn and the air he breathed.

MGM thrived on Mario's old-fashioned courting of their movie goddess. The handsome toreador was in direct contrast to the skinny, washed-up singer. But Cabre finished his scenes with Ava and had bullfighting commitments in Spain. He kissed her goodbye at the airport, making a dramatic fuss about leaving the woman he loved behind. Showing no emotion, Ava faced newsmen and said flippantly, 'I kiss a lot of people goodbye.' A reporter asked her if she and Sinatra had been in touch. She snapped 'No!'

Ava moved into a handsome London flat in Park Lane. Frank flew in for an appearance at the London Palladium in July. He rented a luxurious apartment in Berkeley Square within walking distance from Ava.

On July 12, Sinatra made his British debut with Ava sitting in the front row. Reviews of his performance were excellent. The *Sunday Chronicle* wrote, 'Bless me, he's good!' The *Times* said, 'To a people whose idea of manhood is husky, full-blooded, and self-reliant, he has dared to suggest that under the crashing self-assertion, man is still a child, frightened and whimpering in the dark.'

For Ava and Frank, their brief stay in London was a chance for happiness at last. British reporters were considerate and scarce, offering the famous couple peace and a good deal of freedom. They attended parties hosted by aristocracy and royalty including Princess Margaret. One British clergyman cited the blatant affair and labeled backstreet women as 'painted trollops who worship the shrine of Saint Ava Gardner.' There was, however, very little publicity, good or bad.

After a movie benefit Ava, Frank, Stewart Granger and his then-girlfriend, Jean Simmons, were presented to Princess Elizabeth and Prince Philip. Ava wore a strapless ivory silk gown and curtsied nervously. It was a very special occasion for her and especially for Frank following his triumphant show at the Palladium.

George Sidney, who directed Ava's MGM screen test, made several successful films in the forties – *The Harvey Girls* with Judy Garland, *Cass Timberlane* with Lana Turner and Spencer Tracy, and *Annie Get Your Gun* with Howard Keel and Betty Hutton. Highly respected, Sidney was assigned to direct MGM's *Show Boat*, Jerome Kern and Oscar Hammerstein II's operetta. Kathryn Grayson and Howard Keel were logical choices, but Sidney wanted Ava to play Julie, the tragic half-caste. She tested for the part, mouthing to Lena Horne's voice. MGM reluctantly consented. 'Ava was a Southern girl,' Sidney said. 'She had a lilting accent that suited Julie perfectly. It's been said that Ava's voice wasn't good enough. That isn't true. She and Frank pleaded with me to let her do her own voice and it worked. She half-sang, half-spoke "Can't Help Loving That Man of Mine." It was deeply moving. But the studio insisted we use a professional singer. Ava was very disappointed. On the soundtrack album they used her voice, however. This pleased her.'

As the result of her plum role in *Show Boat*, Ava was second only to swimming star Esther Williams at MGM. But the studio warned her about Sinatra, who had been advised by lawyers not to antagonize Nancy during legal negotiations. It was frustrating for Ava to see Frank only in the company of others. She might have accepted it on a temporary basis, but Nancy was adamant about not getting a divorce. And Los Angeles was Nancy Sinatra's territory.

When Ava threatened not to see Frank again, he whisked her to New York in September 1950 for the Joe Louis-Ezzard Charles heavyweight championship bout at Yankee Stadium. When they returned to the West Coast a few days later Frank gave her two Welsh corgis, Rags and Cara. This simple gesture touched Ava so deeply, she decided to stick it out. The dogs would remain in bed with her longer than Sinatra.

She resumed work on *Show Boat*, enjoying the company of Howard Keel and Kathryn Grayson, who joined her for cocktails at the end of the working day in her dressing room. According to Keel, the threesome 'got sloshed on tequila' almost every evening. Unlike the other Hollywood studios, MGM forbade their players to have liquor on the premises. Sneaking it in was half the fun.

Show Boat was one of Ava's finest films. At her most beautiful, she handled the role of a deteriorating alcoholic skillfully. At the end of the movie, in a heartbreaking scene, Julie hides in the shadows of the wharf wearing a long drab cape and no makeup, appearing haggard as the colorful showboat sails away.

Producer Arthur Freed said, 'I knew we had it made when we got Ava. She was wonderful. I don't think any closeups were as breathtaking as those she did in the picture. Dore Schary wanted Dinah Shore to play Julie. She asked me point blank why I didn't give her the part and I said, 'Because you're not a whore. Ava is. When she sings "Bill," she's every streetwalker you ever saw.' Freed did not literally mean Ava was a prostitute at heart, but that she could play the 'heart of a prostitute' in a way that would rip everybody else's heart out watching her.

Newsweek said, 'Ava does surprisingly well as the mulatto, Julie.' The other critics gave her good reviews, emphasizing her beauty, unfortunately, because *Show Boat* was a breakthrough for her as a fine actress.

Sinatra managed to get his own TV and radio series in the fall of 1950, but both were canceled. Ava placed a confidential call to Howard Hughes for help, and Frank sang two songs in RKO's forgettable *Double Dynamite*.

Universal offered him a crumb, *Meet Danny Wilson*, a musical with Shelley Winters, who was rushed into the film because, according to the gossip mill, Frank needed the $25,000, his meager fee. Miss Winters said in her memoirs that the picture began in chaos and ended in disaster: 'Mr Sinatra was in the process of divorcing Nancy to marry Ava Gardner. I think he thought that's what he wanted. His children were

145

quite young and there were always psychiatrists and priests and his kids visiting him on the set. Everyone in Hollywood knew of his struggle to divorce or not to divorce.'

Shelley made a joke about Frank's losing a pound a week, making her look heavier. They worked well together, but he was ready to crack. What others in the cast didn't recognize was that he was on the edge. No one remembers what started the vicious argument between Winters and Sinatra. He called her a 'bowlegged bitch of a Brooklyn blonde' and she called him a 'skinny no-talent, stupid Hoboken bastard.' Tension mounted and the production was shut down. A studio executive spoke to Shelley about her co-star. 'Mr Sinatra is going through a terrible and troubled period of his life and career. He's going against his religion and he has periods when he loses his voice. Perhaps you could examine his own humanity and realize the terrible trouble that young man is in and understand the reasons that are making him behave the way he did.'

Winters prepared for the final scene. Frank's last line was supposed to be, 'I'll have a cup of coffee and leave you two lovebirds alone.' Fade out. Instead he came out with, 'I'll go have a cup of Jack Daniels, or I'm gonna pull that blonde broad's hair out by its black roots.' Shelley threw a bedpan at Frank and hit her mark. She went home and refused calls until Nancy Sinatra tried to get through. In tears she asked a favor of her friend. 'Shelley, Frank doesn't get the $25,000 for the picture until it's finished. The bank might foreclose the mortgage on the house. My children are going to be out on the street. Please complete the picture, or they won't give me the $25,000.'

Winters went back to work and told Sinatra he could say any damn thing he wanted. *Meet Danny Wilson* was finished in less than five minutes.

Time magazine said, '[Meet Danny Wilson] cribs so freely from the career and personality of Frank Sinatra that fans may expect Ava Gardner to pop up in the last reel.' The other critics agreed that Frank was very similar to the crooner character he portrayed, and that *Meet Danny Wilson* 'was satisfactory entertainment.' Unfortunately, Sinatra fans did not flock to the Paramount to see him on the screen or in person.

It was a trying time for all those involved with Frank. He accused Ava of sleeping with Artie Shaw, whom he still hated with a jealous passion. She was not amused by these insinuations. After all, Frank was spending a great deal of time with his family for the sake of the children, occasionally staying for dinner. Ava considered these get-togethers unnecessary and hypocritical. Her mood went from bad to worse when she couldn't get out of doing *Lone Star*, a low-grade Western. L.B. Mayer personally asked Ava to play the tempestuous Texas newspaperwoman in this story of Andrew Jackson's fight for independence against the Union.

She might have told MGM to go to hell and gone on suspension, but Ava needed the money. Besides, Clark Gable was her co-star and he hated the movie just as much. As in *The Hucksters* they enjoyed each other's company regardless of the terrible script. They had much to commiserate about. Gable had told his wife, Lady Sylvia Ashley, he wanted a divorce and had had the locks changed on the house he once shared happily with Carole Lombard. Sylvia left for Nassau hoping he would change his mind. Drinking heavily, Clark poured out his problems to Ava, who understood better than anyone because Nancy Sinatra was putting off the inevitable, too.

147

Gable had aged considerably. A rumor that he was in the first stages of Parkinson's disease persisted because his head shook uncontrollably. Ava's heart went out to him again. She spoke to Clark gently, used the raunchy language he appreciated, and guided him through love scenes to conceal his shaking. They lunched with Spencer Tracy, who was good for a laugh when he was sober. Ava told him about a scene in *Lone Star* in which she walked happily down the street after spending the night with Gable. 'Schary cut it out,' she complained.

'Yeah,' Spencer said. 'Since Dore took over, nobody gets laid at MGM.'

Tracy's visits to the *Lone Star* set were great fun for Ava and Clark. The trio shared obscene jokes and gossip, howling with laughter. Ava made Tracy's hair stand up more than once. In the commissary one day they ran into Loretta Young, who had dated both Spencer and Clark in the thirties. Photographers wanted to take a picture but she declined. Observers had chuckled over Young's famous 'swear box', which held fines levied against anyone who swore in her presence on a movie set. Proceeds went to a home for unwed mothers. 'Loretta could have made a fortune on *Lone Star*.' Spencer grinned. 'She charged Bob Mitchum five cents for every *damn*, ten cents for *hell*, and a quarter for *goddamn*. He wanted to know what she charged for *fuck* and Loretta replied, "That's free." '

For Ava and Clark, laughter and booze were their only salvation against such mundane dialogue as, 'You're a lot of woman . . . you're a strange woman, but a lot of woman.' She concentrated more on Clark than on her silly lines. He was bloated, overweight, and the wrinkles were pronounced. The makeup people said, 'Gable doesn't look like Gable anymore.' Ava resented any criticism of her dear friend. The camera was cruel, but the public was crueler. She saw Clark in a different light – the gray at his temples, the sheepish grin, and the twinkle in his eyes. She wanted to make him feel like the man she believed in and loved.

Sinatra visited her on the set frequently. Ava wasn't particularly thrilled to have him moping around while Gable and the others were enjoying themselves. Frank saw a gradual change in Ava – an I-don't-give-a-damn attitude. He panicked when she told him, 'I'm going to Mexico on vacation after this damn movie's finished.' She made it quite obvious she had every intention of going her own way. Sinatra went to Nancy and begged for his freedom. 'If I cannot get a divorce,' he said, 'where is there for me to go and what is there for me to do?'

On May 29 Hedda Hopper hinted in her column that Nancy was losing public sympathy and support from Hollywood insiders. It was time she considered the children after a year and a half of sizzling publicity and bitter arguments. She might have run into Sylvia Gable filing for divorce from Clark on May 31, but Nancy was in no rush.

On June 22, 1951, L.B. Mayer resigned. Dore Schary, who had been in charge of MGM for some time, approved a $20,000 bonus for Ava, and promised her better roles. She took the money and shrugged off his pledge. Regardless of her feelings for Mayer, he was one of Hollywood's founders and the father of MGM. 'At least with L.B.,' she said, 'I knew where I stood.' Mayer might have called her a 'whore,' but he could have fired her for violating the moral clauses in her contract and didn't. His departure from MGM was a sign of things to come – the demise of Hollywood and the studio system. Without a family, the majority of MGM stars were orphans who did not know how to make an airline or hotel reservation. For the time being Howard Strickling extended himself, trying to hold on to tradition.

❧

In August Ava and Frank started out for Acapulco. At Los Angeles International Airport the press was out in force. Sinatra refused to board the plane until all reporters were removed from the ramp and tarmac. The couple had so many pieces of luggage that rumors of a quickie Mexican divorce and marriage not only tipped off the local newsmen but those on all stops along the way to Acapulco. An impatient Ava made a dash for the plane. Within a few minutes Frank gritted his teeth and followed without responding to questions, pushing reporters aside. He was on the verge of a nervous breakdown – pale, thin, and tired. He had no future, no money, and no family. He could offer Ava only his love.

In El Paso during a forty-five-minute layover, they managed to escape newsmen, but by the time they landed in Mexico City, Frank's nerves were shattered. 'Why can't you leave us alone?' he shouted. 'This is silly. You can tell stateside for me that what we do is our own damn business! It's a fine thing when we can't go on vacation without being chased!' *Newsweek* reported Sinatra was losing control when he hissed, 'You miserable crumbs! You s.o.b's!'

Ava was distressed over Frank's lack of diplomacy with the press. Howard Strickling had discussed these unpleasant outbursts with her and emphasized the importance of good press relations. She, in turn, pleaded with Frank not to be on the defensive. 'Neither could afford unfavourable publicity,' an MGM press agent said, 'because Ava was on her way up and Frank was on his way down. It doesn't matter which way you're going, the press can make or break you. Ava was Metro-trained, taught to pause, smile and say a few words to reporters, smile again and continue walking regally ahead. Frank had relied completely on George Evans. He cared little about a good image off the stage.'

Ava and Frank spent their first evening at the Mirador's famous La Perle, a club located on a rocky cliff. The 'floor show' was (and still is) a diving act the natives stage after sundown, swan diving from La Quebrada cliff into a narrow channel 136 feet below.

Ted Stauffer, who owned the club, welcomed the couple warmly, but his wife, Hedy Lamarr, ignored Ava, whom Stauffer had been very attracted to a few years before. Frank was upset with Hedy's snub and threatened to get even one day. He soon forgot it when he and Ava slipped onto a balcony for a loving embrace and kiss. One patron said, 'They thought nobody could see them when they went out there to smooch in the dark. But they were wearing white clothes and it was better than the floor show.'

Later they showed up at the exclusive Beachcomber Club where a photographer took pictures. Frank's bodyguard reportedly said, 'If you don't give me that camera, I'll put a bullet through you.' The police arrived and allowed Frank to dispose of the film. Fearing the worst, Ava wept during the fracas while Sinatra cursed furiously at reporters. The episode was written up in US newspapers the next morning. Three days later their private plane landed in a quiet non-commercial area of the airport in Los Angeles where Sinatra's Cadillac was waiting. Ava and Frank ran to the car followed by reporters. As he took the wheel, newsreel cameramen blinded him with their floodlights. 'Kill that light! Kill that light!' Frank shouted. He stepped on the gas and pinned reporters against a fence, just missing them by a hair. The car's bumper grazed the leg of one newsman. Frank leaned out of the window and yelled, 'Next time I'll kill you!'

William Eccles, an airport photographer, described what happened to him: 'Sinatra turned the car into me to scare me away. I figured he'd swerve from me so I shot the picture and didn't move. He slammed on the brake, and at the last minute I jumped. I went up over the fender and rolled off on my stomach, dropping my camera. It was a hit-and-run case. I could have sued.' Eccles did file a criminal complaint against Sinatra but withdrew it after Frank wrote a letter of apology. Sinatra told Jim Bacon of the Associated Press, 'I slammed my foot on the gas pedal without realizing the wheels were turned. The car swerved before I could straighten it out. I'm sorry.'

MGM officials discussed the unfavourable publicity with Ava and warned that the Legion of Decency might ban her films unless she either married Sinatra or ended the affair once and for all. With the spectacular and all-important premiere of *Show Boat* approaching, the studio did not want to risk her chances for international stardom. Also, it was vital that Frank make peace with the fourth estate. MGM cited the motion picture editor of the *Hollywood Citizen News* who wrote, 'It takes a big man to fill the shoes of a big position. It takes a man of depth to keep his balance when constantly in the spotlight. On both counts, Sinatra doesn't measure up.'

Hedda Hopper sadly predicted, 'A year from now

when their romance is over, Frank will be as thin as your backbone, and Ava will be more beautiful than ever.'

In mid-August Sinatra flew to Reno for a singing engagement at the Riverside Hotel and established residency for a Nevada divorce. He also accepted an offer from the Desert Inn in Las Vegas. With a broad smile on his face and sporting a mustache, he shocked reporters by greeting them with, 'I hope I'm going to get along with you fellows.' At the hotel he was cooperative and hinted that the Mexico fiasco was grossly exaggerated. 'I got sore,' he said, 'because I got some pretty rough handling from a couple of guys. They were the exception, though, because the press has done a lot for me.'

When Ava arrived in Reno, she held Frank's hand while he told newsmen cheerfully, 'I think you can safely say that Miss Gardner and I will be married.' But he admitted not knowing what Nancy's plans were since she had not followed through with her divorce plans. A reporter asked Ava about a fan magazine article about her entitled, 'I'm Through with Romance.' She laughed and replied, 'Me? That must have been someone else you're thinking of. I've never been through with romance at all.'

Over the Labor Day weekend they went to Lake Tahoe with friends. On September 1, 1951, the *New York Daily Mirror*'s headline read: SINATRA FELLED BY SLEEPING PILLS. The story reported his attempted suicide after a violent quarrel with Ava.

'I've never heard of anything so ridiculous,' Frank responded. 'This would be a hell of a time to do away with myself. I've been trying to lick this thing [divorce] for two years and I've practically got it licked now. I did not try to commit suicide. I just had a bellyache. What will you guys think of next to write about me? Tuesday night, Miss Gardner, my manager Hank

Sanicole, and Mrs Sanicole dined at the Christmas Tree Inn on Lake Tahoe. Ava was returning to Hollywood that night. We came back to the Lake and I didn't feel so good. So I took two sleeping pills. Miss Gardner left by auto for Reno and the plane trip back to Hollywood. By now, it was early Wednesday morning. I guess I wasn't thinking because I'm very allergic to sleeping pills. Also I had drunk two or three brandies. I broke out in a rash. The pills felt kind of stuck in my chest. I got worried and called a friend. He sent a doctor who gave me a glass of warm water with salt in it. It made me throw up, and I was all right. That's all there was to it – honest.'

Ava flew back to Reno immediately. She was gracious and patient with newsmen. 'The whole thing is ridiculous,' she said, holding Frank's hand. But this was the last straw as far as MGM was concerned. They took matters into their own hands and decided the wedding would take place on September 19, the day after Sinatra's six-week Nevada residency ended. Two days before the proposed date Ava and Frank 'went public' in Hollywood at the premiere of *Show Boat* at the Egyptian Theater. Ava looked magnificent in an emerald-green satin and black lace gown and a diamond necklace. The crowd called out, 'Ava!' and 'Frankie!' Metro officials were relieved, to put it mildly. Ecstatic. Not only did the public cheer the couple, but *Show Boat* was a smashing success.

Assuming he would be a free man in forty-eight hours, Sinatra said in an interview that night, 'It gives me great pleasure and pride to be able to escort Ava publicly. I've cared for her a long time – almost a year now. I'm very much in love with her and it's wonderful to know we can be seen together without hurting anyone. There's no ill feelings about it anywhere – with anyone.'

But while Hollywood's glittering stars admired the

reproduction of the helm room of the great showboat *Cotton Blossom* and clapped to strumming banjos, Nancy Sinatra was contesting the Nevada decree. She insisted on a California divorce, revisions of the property settlement and back alimony of $40,000. She sued Frank for legal fees and secured a lien on his Palm Springs home for security.

Coming so very close to marrying and having to wait again for an indefinite length of time did not have the devastating effect on Frank that it did on Ava. He was prepared to give Nancy anything she wanted. Until now Ava had held up fairly well, but she found stardom and her obligations to the studio more demanding than the steep climb to fame. She would be forced to make a choice if Nancy changed her mind about divorce and left all concerned in limbo.

The years of waiting, the fights, Frank's reported suicide attempt, the running, hiding, and frustration caught up with Ava. On September 26 she was trying on costumes at MGM when she collapsed and was rushed to St John's Hospital in Santa Monica where doctors diagnosed a severe virus infection and extremely low blood pressure. She remained in the hospital for almost three weeks, most of it without Frank, who had a singing engagement in New York. Ava's doctor, William Webber Smith, said she was tired, exhausted, and had lost a lot of weight. There was gossip about Ava having an abortion.

On October 31, 1951, Nancy was granted an interlocutory decree of divorce in Santa Monica, charging her husband with mental cruelty. The next day Ava flew with Frank to Las Vegas for a four-minute private-hearing before Judge A.S. Henderson. They checked into the Sands Hotel, smiled for photographers, and had a champagne dinner in their suite.

Ava made it clear to MGM she did not want a

studio-arranged wedding and refused to discuss any plans. She was terrified that reporters would ruin her wedding, ignoring the fact that Howard Strickling had been responsible for her secret marriage to Mickey Rooney, which had gone off without incident. Strickling's staff had a remarkable record protecting their stars. That Frank had been dropped by MGM created resentment on Ava's part, regardless of her fondness for Strickling, who could have taken over with finesse and dignity.

Sinatra did not want MGM involved in any way. He trusted his friends in the record business and relied on them for assistance. Ava, who was still weak, and shaky from her recent illness, went along with plans to be married in Philadelphia at the Germantown mansion belonging to Isaac Levy, founder of CBS. Frank asked his close friend Manie Sachs to assist with arrangements and give the bride away. On Friday, November 2, the couple picked up their marriage license. Since Pennsylvania law required a three-day waiting period, they returned to the Hampshire House in New York. On Saturday night the James Masons joined them at the Sugar Hill Nightclub in Harlem. Ava became insanely jealous because Frank was supposedly flirting with an attractive woman sitting at another table. Ava looked at Pamela Mason and exclaimed, 'It looks like I'm through with him. I can't even trust him on the eve of our wedding!' She screamed at Frank and he yelled back.

'Let's just call off this fucking wedding,' Ava hissed, throwing her six-carat diamond engagement ring across the room. Before anyone could stop her, she disappeared. Sinatra rushed back to the Hampshire House, but Ava wasn't there.

Reporters, meanwhile, had done their homework and knew about the marriage license and the whereabouts of the celebrated couple. Stories circulated that Ava threw her engagement ring out of the window at the Hampshire House and it was never recovered. Actually it was a very expensive gold bracelet given to her by Howard Hughes that went flying out of the Hampshire House window during an argument with Frank over her 'friendship' with the millionaire. 'I hope whoever found the bracelet knew how valuable it was,' Ava mused.

On Sunday the wedding was still off. Bappie and James Mason finally convinced Ava to see Frank the next day. Dolly Sinatra intervened with an invitation to a homemade Italian dinner in Hoboken. Frank's mother was thrilled that her son was marrying a beautiful movie actress, but the close friendship between the two women went deeper. Dolly loved Ava's casual, unpretentious manner and considered it an omen of kinship that her birthday was Christmas Day and Ava's Christmas Eve. Most important, they both wanted, above all, Frank's happiness and renewed success. To them the world revolved around him. Ava seldom talked about her career except for funny stories and risqué gossip about Hollywood, which Dolly devoured. Ava had never tasted the special Italian goodies served at dinner. Her healthy appetite delighted Dolly, who was happy to see Frank so in love and cheerful again.

While Ava partied with the Sinatra clan, newsmen were busy in Philadelphia trying to find out the date, time, and place of the wedding. Frank was alerted and decided to have the ceremony at the home of Manie Sachs's brother, Lester. On Wednesday, November 7, the wedding party left the Hampshire House and were approached by reporters. Frank waved them off, but when the limousine pulled up in front of Lester's house, the press was waiting. 'How did those creeps know where we were?' Frank growled. 'I don't want no circus here! I'll knock the first guy who attempts to get inside on his can – and I mean it!'

The list of wedding guests was small. Arranger and conductor Axel Stordahl was best man, and his wife, June, was matron of honor. In attendance were Bappie, Dolly and Marty, Frank's music publishing partner Ben Barton, and Dick Jones, an ex-Dorsey arranger. Before the ceremony began, Frank stepped outside to tell reporters, 'My own photographer will provide you with all the pictures you need as soon as possible.' One newsman piped up, 'My editor wants *my* pictures!' Sinatra snapped, 'I'll bet you fifty bucks you don't get a picture and another fifty that if you even point your camera at me, I'll knock you on your ass!'

An hour later the bride, wearing a cocktail-length dress of mauve-toned marquisette with a strapless top of pink taffeta, started down the stairs leaning on the arm of Manie Sachs. Dick Jones played Mendelssohn's 'Wedding March' on the piano. 'I was so excited and nervous,' Ava confessed, 'that when we started down the stairs I slipped and we slid down three steps. I had a quick vision of the bride in a heap at the foot of the stairs. But we regained our footing and made it down the rest of the way. As soon as I saw Frank standing there, I wasn't so nervous any more. He looked so composed. But he told me he had a lump in his throat.'

The bride and groom exchanged thin platinum wedding bands. His present to her was a sapphire-blue mink cape stole. She gave him a large, heavy gold locket with a St Christopher medal on one side and a St Francis medal on the other. Inside was her photograph.

'Well,' Frank beamed, 'we made it!'

Ava hugged Dolly, who broke down and cried. During the champagne buffet supper, Ava sent a telegram to Howard Strickling and signed the wire 'Ava Sinatra'. Her going-away outfit was a brown Christian Dior creation and her new mink stole. Before the newlyweds departed, around eight-thirty, Manie

Sachs took Ava aside and whispered, 'Look after him. He's had some hard knocks and he's very fragile. It's not going to be easy living with a man whose career's in a slump.'

'I'll do everything to make him happy,' Ava promised.

'Then help him get back his self-confidence.'

The honeymooners left Philadelphia in such a rush that Ava forgot her suitcase. 'Oh, hell,' she told Frank, 'let's fly to Miami without it.' Their chartered Beechcraft landed in Florida at dawn. Reporters respected their privacy at the Green Heron Hotel, but took some informal photos of them strolling along the beach in the Sunny Isles district on a chilly day. Hand in hand, they walked barefoot, Frank's trousers rolled up and Ava wearing his jacket over a casual blouse and skirt.

When the trousseau suitcase arrived they flew to Havana for a few days at the plush Hotel Nacional. Returning to New York meant another confrontation with the press. 'Where do you plan to stay?' a newsman asked.

'None of your damn business!' Frank replied.

Ava took his hand and reluctantly he got into a waiting limousine.

TWELVE

The Battling Sinatras

They planned to live in Frank's Palm Springs house. 'We're going to redecorate,' Ava smiled. 'Mama Sinatra has promised to send me recipes for Frank's favorite dishes. Oh, it's so thrilling and wonderful. I'm not used to my new name and it takes a second before it clicks – Mrs Frank Sinatra is the happiest girl in the world!'

This sounded more like an MGM publicity release than the real Ava speaking. Fan magazines were filled with articles about the most famous couple in the world. 'New Name for Happiness' was one title. A few months later, however, reporters and gossip columnists were referring to them as 'The Battling Sinatras.' Two weeks after the wedding Ava phoned Artie and complained, 'I can't handle it – it's fucking impossible!'

'We all know that,' Shaw said. 'Give it two more months and it'll get worse.'

'It can't get worse.'

She said divorce would ruin them both. The truth is the Sinatras thrived on their stormy marriage. Their domestic tornados were thrilling, especially for Ava, who was bored in paradise. Frank fell deeper in love with her when they made up. One of her mating calls was the scent of her perfume, which brought him to her side after a fight. A close friend remembers, 'They had a terrible battle and Frank came into the kitchen to talk to me. He was so depressed and unhappy. Then I smelt a sweet aroma. Frank smiled and said that everything was going to be all right and he dashed upstairs. Later they both came down all lovey-dovey.'

In early December 1951 the Sinatras flew to London, where Frank was scheduled to sing at an Anglo-American charity sponsored by the Duke of Edinburgh. Ava had agreed to sing a duet with her husband but suffered from stage fright at the last minute. The New York *Daily News* wrote, 'The Voice falls flat at British yawn party.'

The Sinatras' stay in London was also marred by the removal of $16,000 worth of jewelry from their hotel room by a thief who climbed thirty feet from the ground to their window. Among the items stolen were Frank's cameo cufflinks and a sapphire ring, but the worst blow was the loss of the diamond and emerald necklace Sinatra had publicly denied giving Ava. It was her favorite piece of jewelry because she knew Frank could not afford it, and as far as Ava was concerned, there could never be a replacement for it.

Returning to the states, Frank faced sour reviews of his new recordings of 'London by Night' and 'April in Paris.' The New York *Post* said they were 'poorly sung.' *Downbeat* wrote, 'Frank sounds tired, bored, and in poor voice, to boot.' Though Sinatra moved up to second place in *Downbeat*'s popularity poll, he registered a mere 276 votes to Billy Eckstine's 1,354.

The year 1952 was Frank's worst . . . and Ava's best. Fox wanted her for *The Snows of Kilimanjaro*, the film version of a short story by Ernest Hemingway, who had suggested Ava for the part of Cynthia. She is the twenties girl whom the big game hunter (Gregory Peck) loves and loses and finds again as she's dying in a Spanish Civil War battle.

Ava was eager to do the film. Frank did not want her to work, however. He needed Ava at his Paramount opening, which was tied in with the premiere of *Meet Danny Wilson* in April. Ava was honest with director Henry King. 'If you can promise me I'll be finished with *Kilimanjaro* in time to go with Frank to New York, he says it's okay.'

'I'll try,' King said.

'You'll have to do better than that,' she said. 'Frank's not doing well. He needs me. I must be with him. He insists.'

King revised the filming schedule. Sinatra hated flying to New York alone, but Ava promised to be with him for the opening. This put her under a great deal of pressure. Frank phoned every day to make sure there were no delays. When he got to New York, his calls were nerve-wracking to Ava and others in the cast, who sensed not only her nervousness but fear as well. She was concerned about Frank's insecurity, but being a professional, Ava was determined to do her best in *The Snows of Kilimanjaro*. Although small, her role was the heart of the movie. King promised to film Cynthia's scenes in ten days, but the Civil War sequence took longer than expected. He told Ava, 'You'll have to stay on an extra day. I'm sorry.'

'You're sorry?' she exclaimed in tears. 'That motherfucker is going to give me hell when I tell him and I'm just going to sit there and take it.'

Sinatra *was* furious. He made her last day sheer torture by phoning repeatedly to make certain she would be finished. King considered Ava's performance superb under the circumstances. 'No one else could have given Cynthia the sensitivity and the bruised quality that Ava imparted,' he said. The *Los Angeles Examiner* wrote, 'The lovely Gardner, with the best part of the three women, takes over with warmth and tenderness.' *Variety* said, 'She makes the part of Cynthia a warm, appealing, alluring standout.'

Frank had good reason to be forlorn. Determined he would make friends with the press, he arrived in New York prepared for interviews and pictures, but newsmen ignored him completely and not one flash bulb popped in his face. He sent a note to the Press Photographers Association: 'I'll always be made up and ready in case you ever want to shoot any pictures of me.' *Variety* headlined: SINATRA CROONS SWEETLY TO PRESS – 'SO SORRY NOW.' The *New York World-Telegram* wrote: GONE ON FRANKIE '42; GONE IN '52 and WHAT A DIFFERENCE A DECADE MAKES – EMPTY BALCONY. Newspapers joked about an interview with a bobbysoxer at the Paramount. When asked how she liked Frankie the teenager sighed, 'I think Frankie Laine's wonderful!'

Sinatra's performance at the Paramount was lukewarm, and *Meet Danny Wilson* a failure at the box office. As a result, Universal did not pick up his option for another film. His talent agency MCA dropped him as a client, CBS canceled his TV show, and Columbia Records did not renew his contract.

Frank and Ava left New York without fanfare and

arrived in Chicago, where he was to appear at the Chez Paree nightclub, which seated 1,200. Only 120 people showed up. He told Ava, 'We need a vacation in Hawaii.'

'I can't,' she said. 'I'm scheduled to do *Sombrero* in Mexico.'

'And I said we're going to Hawaii!' he exclaimed.

MGM suspended Ava indefinitely. No roles were offered to her and no money came in. She hired super-agent Charles Feldman, who cleverly informed Metro he would not negotiate Ava's new contract while she was on suspension. The studio conceded, revoked suspension, and paid compensation for her layoff. A new ten-year contract called for twelve movies at $100,000 per picture. She would have gotten more if she hadn't insisted that MGM agree to co-star Frank in one of her movies. She demanded a pregnancy clause and monies for a traveling companion when filming in Europe, most likely referring to Bappie.

In May 1952 Ava planted her feet and hands in wet cement at a special ceremony in the front of Grauman's Chinese Theater on Hollywood Boulevard. It would take Frank thirteen more years to achieve this honor. He appeared at the Coconut Grove in Los Angeles to mild reviews. Though Ava hadn't been feeling well she wanted to be with him on opening night. A few days later she was rushed to Cedars of Lebanon Hospital and underwent surgery. Details of her illness were never made public but friends suspected a miscarriage.

The men in Ava's life were also news in 1951. Instead of the usual elopement, Artie Shaw was betrothed to actress Doris Dowling, best known for her role of Gloria in *The Lost Weekend*. Artie planned to be married for the seventh time, but said it was rather interesting to be engaged for a change of pace.

Ava's former boyfriend Howard Duff married actress Ida Lupino, whose previous husbands were actor Louis Hayward and writer-producer Collier Young.

Mickey Rooney divorced Martha Vickers in June 1951. In his autobiography he wrote, 'I needed a depth which she was unable to supply. A depth and a passion. (God, Ava. Why? Why?)'

Rooney doesn't remember his reasons for picking the Shamrock Hotel in Houston to go on a two-week binge of booze and sleeping pills with a close buddy. 'Suicide never entered my mind,' he said. 'I had to get away, get under that blanket of sleep where they couldn't hurt me. I had to get out of this world for a while.'

Mickey returned to Hollywood and set up bachelor quarters with Don 'Red' Barry, a popular star of Republic Westerns in the forties. He, too, was rather short in stature and had an inferiority complex about his height. Rooney remained single until November 1952 (the same month Ava married Sinatra) when he took wife number four, Elaine Mahnken, who seven years later was awarded two houses, a motorboat, car, racehorses, jewelry, all the furniture, and alimony of $21,000 annually for ten years.

Reflecting on his marriages, Rooney said, 'When I proposed to Ava I was almost unconscious with passion. When I proposed to Betty Jane I was almost unconscious with booze. When I proposed to Martha I was almost unconscious with despair, and when I proposed to Elaine I was almost unconscious – period.'

Howard Hughes was seeing actress Terry Moore, who claims she gave birth to his baby in Germany. The premature girl lived only twelve hours. Hughes was philandering, nonetheless, chasing Mona Freeman, Mitzi Gaynor, Linda Darnell, Yvonne DeCarlo, Janet Leigh, Elizabeth Taylor, and Jean Peters, whom he would eventually marry before going into seclusion. In the meantime, Hughes kept tabs on Ava and knew her whereabouts and the status of her marriage to Sinatra. He was available to her by phone twenty-four hours a day if she needed him. He knew it would be very soon.

Hughes envisioned teaming Jane Russell and Robert Mitchum in a series of films patterned after Bogart and Bacall. But aside from *His Kind of Woman* only *Macao* was made. Jane and Bob didn't click on the screen any more than he and Ava had in *My Forbidden Past*. The *Los Angeles Examiner* wrote, 'It seems to us that Robert Mitchum wasn't as enthusiastic about his love scenes with the lushly lovely Ava as some fellows might have been, given the opportunity.' Mitchum called her 'Honest Ave – because she doesn't have to pad her bust.'

They wanted to do another film together (and Hughes offered her huge sums of money), but MGM punished Ava, as was their policy if a contract player of any magnitude proved difficult. She got a good contract but hadn't paid her dues for running off to Hawaii with Frank. The price was a mediocre western, *Ride, Vaquero*, starring Robert Taylor and Howard Keel, was filmed in Kanab, Utah – a hot, dusty dead town with one seedy hotel called Perry's. Without air conditioning Ava found sleep impossible. 'I wish I were dead,' she told Taylor, who was unhappy and disgusted also. He and Ava were good pals and he tried convincing director John Farrow (Mia Farrow's father) to find Ava decent living quarters. Farrow, a hard-drinking womanizer, ignored the request. It was

Perry, owner of the hotel, who offered Ava his small house near town. This afforded her some relief, but working in the 120-degree temperature with dry red dust in her eyes, nose, and throat was intolerable. Taylor, who had his own plane, flew back and forth to Los Angeles to see his girlfriend, Ursula Theiss. Ava called Frank to join her on location.

In the film Taylor portrays the outlaw Rio whose gang terrorizes settlers Gardner and Keel (Mr and Mrs Cameron). A typical review: 'Nothing could have been as static as the dusty shenanigans of such urban buckaroos as Taylor, Gardner, and Keel. In short, it rated not Tiffany's window but the old cat bin!'

In *The Band Wagon* Ava appeared in an unbilled cameo as a Hollywood star arriving in New York on a train.

Sinatra's career was now limited to nightclubs. He was having recurrent problems with his voice. Friends referred to these throat infections as 'guilt germs.' He was spending too much time with his family as far as Ava was concerned. They argued about these frequent visits. She did not try to impress his children, with whom she had no relationship. Many years later when Nancy, Jr. was writing a book about her father she sent letters to the friends and acquaintances 'with whom he had close contact.' Ava was disgusted. 'Close contact?' she laughed. 'Doesn't she remember I married him?'

Ava's possessiveness of Frank extended to his children. In that sense he was equally possessive and jealous of Ava's close friendships. They were both insecure and complex people. Another grievance of hers was Sinatra's cronies, who were always hanging around. Ava put up with them until one night Frank ignored her for two hours over dinner in a restaurant while he carried on a lengthy conversation with a male friend. She left abruptly and wasn't missed until he was ready to go home. Two days later Ava called from Italy. She had gone to the airport directly from the restaurant and boarded the first plane for Rome.

In September 1952 Frank played the Riviera in Fort Lee, New Jersey. *Variety* said, 'Whatever Sinatra had for the bobbysoxers he now has for the cafe mob. It adds up to showmanship rather than any basic singing appeal. His performance is notable for self-assurance and a knowing way with a crowd, whatever the misadventures of his personal life and career.'

Ava attended the New York premiere of *The Snows of Kilimanjaro* alone. In between shows, Frank hopped in a car, raced across the George Washington Bridge, down the West Side Highway, and brought his wife back to the Riviera for the last show. When Ava spotted Frank's former girlfriend, Marilyn Maxwell, sitting up front, she froze. Sinatra sang 'All of Me' in Maxwell's direction – or so Ava assumed – and she stormed out of the club, flew back to Hollywood, and mailed her wedding band to Frank at the Riviera with a bitter note. As usual she refused to accept his phone calls. He wanted to cancel his booking at the Chase Hotel in St Louis, but was advised not to risk the bad publicity. 'I've got problems,' he told Sammy Davis, Jr. 'That's what happens when you get hung up on a chick.'

Sinatra read in the gossip columns that Ava was making the rounds of Hollywood parties. 'We have a career problem,' he told the press. 'I'm going to see my wife in about ten days. I think everything will work out all right. It's something that might happen between a man and his wife – just a mild rift.'

The waiting was torture for Frank regardless of his success in St Louis. He told Earl Wilson, 'I'm nuts about her and I don't think it's dead. But it certainly is all up in the air.'

Losing Ava's wedding band upset his romantic plan to put it back on her finger when they reconciled. He managed to have a duplicate made, and when he returned to Hollywood Ava was waiting. They drove to the bullfights in Tijuana and were photographed holding hands, happier than ever – the calm before the hurricane.

Within days they would be involved in a notorious incident that Hollywood insiders whisper about to this day. Tabloids, including *Confidential* magazine, were very explicit with their versions and shocked readers into believing the sordid story.

Ava thought the Palm Springs blowup was very amusing. According to her, Frank wanted to go away for a few days, but she had plans with Bappie. He got testy and teased, 'Since Lana is staying at the house in Palm Springs, if you want me I'll be there fucking her.'

Ava laughed it off, but knowing Frank and Lana were previously involved, she got in the car with Bappie and drove to Palm Springs. Ava spotted Frank driving back and forth in front of the house. When he finally left, she walked in the front door and found Lana getting ready for a dip in the pool with their business manager, Ben Cole. They were shocked to see Ava, who shrugged, 'Hell, there's room enough for all of us.' Five minutes later, according to her, Frank burst through the door and told everyone, 'Get the hell out!' Ava said it was her house, too, and began collecting her possessions. Frank's temper blazed and he began throwing her things outside on the lawn. Lana and Cole fled and returned later for their suitcases to find the place crawling with police.

Lana claimed that Frank had said it was all right if she and Cole spent the weekend at the house. She was surprised to see Ava, 'who was separated from Frank

169

at the time.' They were eating fried chicken in the kitchen when Frank rushed in the door and shouted, 'I bet you broads have really been cutting me up!' Then he pointed to Ava and said, 'You! Get in the bedroom. I want to talk to you!' Lana and Ben left the house when they heard furniture being smashed in the bedroom. They came back to find Ava still battling with Frank. Eventually she went with them to a rented house. Lana said in her memoirs that none of them referred to that night again, but many vile rumors persisted, among them that Frank found her and Ava in bed together.

The L.A. *Mirror*: BOUDOIR FIGHT HEADS FRANKIE AND AVA TO COURTS.

The L.A. *Times*: SINATRA-AVA BOUDOIR NOW BUZZES. TOO MUCH LEFT TO THE IMAGINATION.

In his book about Turner, her former secretary Taylor Pero wrote that Lana, divorced from Bob Topping, fled to Palm Springs on that October weekend to get away from her jealous boyfriend Fernando Lamas. Lana and Ava were comparing notes on Artie and Frank, who happened to stroll in while the girls were 'cutting him up.'

Pero said that after the big fight Lana and Ava went to Mexico for a vacation.

Sinatra's explanation seems to be the accepted version. The late Jackie Gleason confided, 'Frank could not forget what he heard. He'd call me in the middle of the night for a long time to talk about what happened in Palm Springs because he was so hurt.'

Ava changed her phone number to avoid Frank's calls. She was busy getting ready to leave for Africa to film *Mogambo* with Clark Gable and Grace Kelly. Though Frank could not afford the plane fare, Ava offered to pay his way so they could be together. But after the disastrous weekend in Palm Springs she was determined to go alone.

This breakup was more serious than the others. A friend of Ava's got the impression she was pregnant. A source close to Frank hinted the same because ' . . . he wanted the baby.' Sinatra's buddy admits, 'I'm not sure if Frank was referring to "a" baby or "the" baby and I didn't ask. Ava had a history of chronic anemia that supposedly made her prone to miscarriage. Frank was close to a breakdown for a week. He couldn't eat, and lost weight. Everything was lost – Ava, the baby, their trip to Africa – everything, he said.'

Finally Sinatra asked Earl Wilson to print his appeal for reconciliation, and on October 27 the columnist wrote, FRANKIE READY TO SURRENDER, WANTS AVA BACK, ANY TERMS. She called Frank and they attended a rally for Democratic presidential candidate Adlai Stevenson at the Palladium Ballroom. Ava walked on stage in a black satin strapless gown, stepped before the microphone, and said, 'I can't do anything myself, but I can introduce a wonderful, wonderful man. I'm a great fan of his myself. Ladies and gentlemen, my husband, Frank Sinatra.'

Ava was radiant and Frank sang beautifully. They announced plans to visit her family in North Carolina before leaving for Africa.

❦

Mogambo was the remake of the 1932 film *Red Dust* starring Clark Gable and Jean Harlow. The new picture revolved around Gable, a big white hunter in Africa, a married woman (Grace Kelly) on safari with her husband, and Ava, who portrayed chorus girl Honey Bear. Originally Stewart Granger was set to play the male lead until MGM decided Gable needed a good picture to boost his career. Ava was disappointed that Granger wasn't going to co-star. She was attracted to him as she had been to Bob Mitchum. Sinatra was jealous of her leading men, including the recently divorced Clark Gable who was dating a string of beautiful young ladies. But knowing Ava would be out of the country for five months tortured Frank more than anything else. After reading James Jones's novel *From Here to Eternity*, Frank spoke to his agents about the film version planned by Columbia. For the first time in his life Sinatra said, 'I was reading something I really had to do. I just felt it. I just knew I could do it and couldn't get the idea out of my head. I knew I was the only actor to play Private Angelo Maggio, the tough little Italian-American GI. I knew Maggio. I went to school with him in Hoboken. I was beaten up with him. I might have been Maggio.'

Before leaving for Africa, Sinatra made an appointment with the hard-bitten, blunt head of Columbia, Harry Cohn, who remarked, 'You're a singer, not an actor.'

'About the money,' Frank began.

'Who's talking money?' Cohen growled.

'I used to get $150,000 for a picture.'

'Used to.'

'Yeah. I'll do it for a thousand a week.'

'Jesus, you really want the part, don't you, Frank? Well, we'll see. I have to make some tests.'

Cohn wasn't buying, and Sinatra sensed this. He called his agents and said, 'I'll do it for nothing. Nothing!'

Cohn relished telling the story about Frank's pleading. 'He owes $110,000 in back taxes, but offered to pay me if he could play Maggio!'

Ava spoke to Cohn's wife, Joan, and explained the seriousness of the situation. 'I'm afraid Frank might kill himself,' she said. 'All I'm asking is that Harry give him a screen test. That's all.' Ava had done this on her own and didn't want Frank to know about it. Joan promised to do what she could, knowing Cohn considered Sinatra a washed-up song and dance man. Ava was indeed responsible for Frank's being considered for a screen test, but not only because she talked to the right people. Cohn, after thinking it over, realized he might want Ava Gardner for a picture someday and she would flatly refuse if Frank wasn't given a chance to test for the part of Maggio. Before leaving for Africa, she spoke to Harry again, who called Sinatra and said, 'I'll let you know.'

Frank was elated until news about other actors being tested reached him. As each day passed it got closer to the trip to Africa. He went to see Cohn, who wasn't available, but Frank was informed his test had not been scheduled yet. The fact that Eli Wallach, a very talented actor, was being tested for Maggio was a severe letdown.

On November 7 the Sinatras celebrated their first wedding anniversary on a stratocruiser bound for Nairobi. He gave her a diamond-studded dome ring. Ava's gift to him was a thin platinum wristwatch. Clark Gable was at the airport and drove them to the New Stanley Hotel. Ava decided to have an anniversary party. 'This is quite an occasion!' she exclaimed. 'I've been married twice before but never for a whole year.'

Twenty-four-year-old Grace Kelly was a newcomer to MGM. Aside from a small role in *High Noon*, she was relatively unknown. Her affair with co-star Gary Cooper was no secret in the industry. The director of *Mogambo*, the hardboiled John Ford, commented about Grace's performance in the Academy Award-winning Western: 'All she did was shoot a guy in the back. Cooper should have given her a boot in the pants and sent her back east.' But when Ford saw her screen test for *Mogambo* he said, 'I was looking for her type for the role of Linda. You know, the frigid dame that's really a pip between the sheets.'

173

Going to the Dark Continent alone was an exciting prospect for Grace, who told a friend, 'I'm doing a picture in Africa with *old* Clark Gable and *old* Ava Gardner and *old* John Ford.'

Fortunately, she wasn't quoted until years later. Clark was only fifty-one and Ava was approaching thirty. Ford didn't let flippant remarks bother him. He referred to the future Princess of Monaco as 'Kelly.'

Though Grace had managed love affairs despite the strictness of her family, she was not a woman of the world. The real Grace Kelly would surface in Africa under the tutelage of Clark Gable, Ava Gardner, and John Ford – a breed apart from the rest of humanity. Sinatra became close to Grace eventually, but in 1952 he belonged heart and soul to Ava. Gable, however, noticed the strong resemblance between Carole Lombard and Grace, who fell head over heels in love with 'The King.' John Ford viewed the battling Sinatras and the budding May-December romance of Kelly and Gable as dull as the Mau Mau guerilla campaign against the white settlers. He cared less about who slept with whom or who fought with whom as long as everyone reported for work on time and knew their lines. He was unsympathetic to Ava's morning sickness, Gable's palsied trembling, and Kelly's lack of experience. A man's director and veteran of John Wayne Westerns, Ford had little respect for beautiful actresses. He would, however, teach Grace Kelly how to act and get a fine performance out of Ava that was worthy of an Academy Award nomination.

❧

The New Stanley Hotel was a luxury to be enjoyed on an occasional weekend off. But MGM's budget for *Mogambo* provided a comfortable location settlement near Mount Kenya. The 1,800-yard landing strip was literally hacked out of the jungle. Tents were upholstered and lavish. Thirteen were dining rooms. There was a movie theater, an entertainment section with pool tables, and a hospital with an X-ray unit. Members of the cast and crew had hot and cold running water. Behind each tent were two large oil drums, one propped over a wood fire. Roaming around the unit were 75 whites and 350 natives.

Gable explained that the wood fire in back of each tent served two purposes. 'It heats the water and keeps the lions away at night.'

Ava wasn't impressed. Gable put his arm around her and said, 'My dear, we have Bunny Allen, a true and great white hunter in our group. He's takin' me on safari if you'd like to come along.'

'No, thanks,' she scowled. 'I hate killing of any kind.'

Grace accepted his offer, and on their days off they were up early, 'bouncing around in a tin wagon with nothing but mosquitos and heat,' as Gable described it.

When she wasn't working Ava slept until the cocktail hour, but Frank had great difficulty sleeping. Every day he hoped to hear from Columbia regarding his screen test. Had Cohn changed his mind? Would the telegram get through to MGM's jungle location? Who else was testing for the part of Maggio? The pressure mounted. He took his frustrations out on Ava, who was not bearing up well. The 120-degree temperature drained what strength she had had. On the first day before the camera John Ford criticized her unmercifully. When she had had enough, Ava tore into him, using her most vile language. Then she stormed off the set, but he followed and cornered her in a secluded spot away from everyone else. 'You're damned good,' Ford said sternly. 'Take it easy.' In his opinion, no other actress could play Honey Bear, the stranded American show girl who wanders into the white hunter's camp and bed. To get the fire and gaiety out of Ava, Ford wanted her to know she could handle the part without trying so hard to please him.

The tension was eased somewhat when Frank received a cable to report for a screen test as soon as possible. Since Columbia did not offer money for plane fare, Ava paid his expenses. Thirty-six hours after the cable arrived Frank was in Hollywood. Producer Buddy Adler and director Fred Zinnemann were speechless during the test. Sinatra *was* Maggio. But Harry Cohn had the final say and since he was out of town, Frank decided to go back to Africa and spend the holiday with his wife.

Several days after Sinatra left for California, Ava felt nauseated and collapsed on the set. She blamed it on the heat and humidity, the constant postponements due to bad weather, and her fear that Frank would lose the part he wanted in *From Here to Eternity*.

Concerned about Ava's declining health, Ford contacted MGM officials in Hollywood requesting permission for her to fly to London for a checkup. The reply read: 'Feel Gardner's trip unwise for many obvious reasons. Suggest you use your persuasiveness and have lady stay put.'

Ford wired back: 'Gardner giving superb performance . . . very charming and cooperative . . . however really quite ill since arrival Africa and deem it imperative London consultation otherwise tragic results . . . not affect schedule . . . weather here miserable but we are trying . . . repeat . . . believe trip imperative.'

On November 23, 1952 Ava flew to London with her publicist Morgan Hudgins and the wife of cameraman Robert Surtees. They checked in at the Savoy Hotel and that evening Ava was admitted to the Chelsea Hospital for Women where she stayed for several days. The press was told she was suffering from severe anemia. *Look* magazine reported it was dysentery. Robert Surtees told a different story: 'Ava hated Frank so intensely by this stage she couldn't stand the idea of having his baby. She went to London for an abortion. I know, because my wife went to England to be at her side at all times through the operation and afterward, and to bring her back on the plane. She told my wife, "I hated Frankie so much. I wanted that baby to go unborn." Ava also mentioned that she'd gotten a bill for the ring Frank gave her on their anniversary.'

But Ava told writer Joe Hyams that she suffered a miscarriage. 'All my life I've wanted a baby, and the news that I lost it was the cruelest blow I ever received. Even though my marriage to Frank was getting shakier by the day, I didn't care. I wanted a baby by him.'

Twelve pounds thinner, discouraged and weary, Ava returned to Nairobi and three more months' work in *Mogambo*. With mixed emotions, she received the news that Frank would be in Africa for the holidays, wanting to be with him and dreading it at the same time. He arrived laden with gifts paid for with borrowed money. Ava shrugged at her new mink stole and tossed it aside. Gable's false teeth almost fell out. He seldom gave expensive presents. 'I'd never let a woman treat me like that,' he grumbled. Ava wanted to say, 'Why don't you send her the bill?'

She remained a time bomb and John Ford knew it. When British officials put in a formal complaint about 'Miss Gardner walking around nude in front of the native boys who prepared her bath,' Ford tried to keep it from her. Ava found out and, according to Surtees, in defiance took off her clothes and ran through the camp in front of everyone.

Grace glanced at Clark, who lit a cigarette. 'Anything wrong?' he asked casually.

'No,' she replied formally.

'Let's get one thing straight, babe. Ava has a bigger heart than anyone I know. If you think I'm defending her, you're right! Do you remember that mama hippo charging our canoe in the river?'

'How can I forget?'

'Ava was alone in another boat. She might have been killed. And how about the rhinos charging the truck? She didn't scream or panic or complain. Right now she's a bewildered girl having some harmless fun. Ava's a proud and wonderful girl.'

As Christmas approached, the *Mogambo* company became a close-knit family. Frank brought noodles and all the ingredients for Dolly Sinatra's homemade spaghetti sauce that Ava had achieved to perfection. She and Grace borrowed evening gowns from the wardrobe tent for Christmas Eve. The generator broke down, but there was only laughter in the darkness. 'We ate by candlelight,' Gable said. 'I thought it was a very warm and romantic setting. Ava's spaghetti sauce was the cause of the breakdown, but worth it. On Christmas Day I found my sock hanging on the tent. Grace had stuffed it. We trimmed the tree, sang Christmas carols with the natives, and had a dinner flown in by MGM – turkey, Christmas puddings, champagne, and plenty of whiskey. John [Ford] recited "The Night Before Christmas" – something we never expected him to do. We were family and it was a very special feeling. I'll never forget it.'

Ava's recollection was how thoughtful Frank was during the holidays. He fixed a tiny tree in front of their tent and decorated it with little colored lights. In his spare time he rigged up a shower for Ava, too. 'It consisted of a pump that took the river water through a pipe and down over my head,' she explained. 'Then he had a little wooden hut built around his gadget and every evening at sundown Frank would pump water up from the river for me.'

The Sinatras had their spats over the holidays, but they were closer than they had been in a long time. When Ford had a party for the British Governor of Uganda, Sir Andrew Cohan, and his wife, the gruff director's joke on Ava backfired. 'Why don't you tell the Governor what you see in that hundred twenty pound runt you're married to?' he asked her.

'Well,' Ava replied, 'there's ten pounds of Frank and one hundred and ten pounds of cock!'

Everybody, including the governor and his wife, thought it was hilarious. Ford was the only one who was shocked. He paled, in fact. Gable cherished Ava at times like this. He laughed the loudest at her description of him. 'Clark?' she said. 'He's the sort of guy if you say, "Hiya, Clark, how are ya?" he's stuck for an answer.'

Sinatra was holding up as best he could while waiting for the results of his screen test. When he received word that the part of Maggio was his at $8,000, Frank paced back and forth like a panther in front of his tent waving the cable. 'Now I'll show those wiseguys!' he exclaimed over and over again. 'I'll show those mothers!'

Frank's victory, however, arrived at the end of his marriage. Ava liked him better down and out. 'When he was on top he was a sacred monster convinced there was nobody in the world except himself,' she said.

THIRTEEN

Point of No Return

When word got around Hollywood that Sinatra was joining the renowned cast of *From Here to Eternity* – Burt Lancaster, Deborah Kerr, Montgomery Clift, and Donna Reed – it was rumored that the Mafia put pressure on Harry Cohn. He was the first to deny it. 'Sinatra's screen test proved he was right for the part,' Cohn said. (Eli Wallach was too muscular for the fragile Maggio.)

If it hadn't been for Ava, however, Frank would not have been considered at all. At the time, he prided himself for a successful and determined campaign.

Ava celebrated her thirtieth birthday in a maze of confusion, happy for Frank but hating the 'sacred monster' that was surfacing – the egotist she detested in the mid-forties when he was riding the crest. Their brief interlude with a humble Christmas tree and makeshift shower was coming to an end. Romantic nights by the fire eating homemade spaghetti were over. These were all the little things Ava appreciated.

❦

Shortly after Christmas, Gable asked Grace and the Sinatras to spend a weekend at a beach resort on the Indian Ocean. 'It's cooler at Malindi,' he said, 'and we can swim without crocodiles. I'm told it's a beautiful spot.'

They were forced to take an old plane to get there. 'Old was a feeble word for it,' Gable said. 'The damn thing was held together by baling wire, but it was the only available transportation. The others didn't mind, but I had a long talk with the pilot, who assured me there was nothing to worry about. I kept thinking about the four of us – maybe the hottest properties in Hollywood – taking a chance like this. MGM would not have been happy.'

Frank and Ava took advantage of the peaceful setting and kept to themselves. The hotel was small, cozy, and peaceful. The view of the Indian Ocean was soothing and the cool breezes a refreshing change from the heat and humidity of Tanganyika.

Before the *Mogambo* company settled in the desolate Isoila desert country in Uganda, the Sinatras flew to Paris for a few days. It was there Frank received word to report for work in *From Here to Eternity*, which would be filmed in Hawaii. Frank said they would meet in London, where Ava was scheduled for *Knights of the Round Table* with Robert Taylor. Her remaining time in Africa was enjoyable because she and Grace Kelly had become very close. Though 'Gracie' was a most unlikely candidate, she remained Ava's true friend throughout her reign as Princess of Monaco. The only difference between the two women was Ava's openness, particularly regarding sex. Grace's

181

image was far more reserved. Gardner said what Kelly was thinking.

Walking past a group of Watusi warriors, Ava turned to Grace and said, 'I wonder if their cocks are as big as they say.' Grace blushed and kept going, but Ava pulled up one of the Watusi's loincloths and a magnificent penis gleamed in the sunlight. Grace stared despite herself but Ava laughed. 'Frank has a bigger one.'

When *Mogambo* was finished, Ava and Grace flew to Rome with the Surteeses. 'As soon as we got there,' Robert Surtees said, 'Ava wanted to see every whorehouse in the city one night. Grace wanted to go, too. At one dive we met a guy who became attracted to Grace and got in the back of the car to neck with her as we drove along. Ava laughed till I thought she'd burst. We went from one place to another. Ava loved to talk to the girls and exchange raw and ribald jokes with them, and it wasn't until three in the morning, after we'd tied one on, that we got back to the hotel.'

The girls flew to London to complete interior scenes for *Mogambo*. Grace, who was being groomed for stardom, stayed at the luxurious Savoy Hotel. British MGM publicists planned a schedule of public appearances and interviews for her. In contrast Gable chose the quaint Connaught Hotel to avoid the press while Ava rented a place in Hyde Park Gate and kept open house day and night for her Hollywood peers who were in London for tax purposes.

Grace sought refuge there and poured out her heart about the boring rigors of being an MGM starlet. 'I prefer the stage,' she said, 'and signed a contract with Metro to do *Mogambo* with Clark. Hemingway is right. He wrote that Africa changes people. Some grow up, some grow old, and some go mad. I grew up and hate going through the star buildup. I literally have no freedom. I dread to think what I'm facing in Hollywood.'

'Crap,' Ava said. 'But you have it made. Clark is helping Ford edit *Mogambo*. It's good. Real good. You're a star, honey.'

'Clark told me to enjoy every minute of it.'

'Yeah, that why he's hiding out at the Connaught.'

'He's leaving MGM?'

'They're not renewing his contract,' Ava said. 'He's quitting them first. After twenty years, that's tough, but he'll never admit it hurts.'

'I don't want to leave Clark here in London. He's drinking too much. A whole bottle of cognac before dinner . . .'

'Honey, in this business that's par for the course. I'll look after him. Bob Taylor's here. He and Clark are good buddies.'

'I love him,' Grace said with tears in her eyes.

'As I said, in this business that's par for the course. How about another drink, honey?'

Sinatra dreamt, slept, and ate the part of Maggio. Montgomery Clift idolized Frank and the two men became good friends and drinking buddies. In Hawaii they spent all their spare time together. Every night it was a ritual to settle down in Frank's room at ten to put a call through to Ava in Africa. If she wasn't available, Sinatra hit the bottle. He talked about his wife constantly. 'We gotta get things settled,' he said. Members of the cast listened to his tributes to Ava patiently. 'She isn't just beautiful,' he exclaimed. 'Ava is the most beautiful woman in the world.'

There was only one major disturbance involving Sinatra during *From Here to Eternity*. He wanted to do a scene with Monty sitting down, regardless of the script. Director Fred Zinnemann didn't like the idea and neither did Clift. Sinatra persisted. They argued. Frank slapped Monty hard across the face. They were such good friends Sinatra knew he could get away with it. He had slapped Clift out of drunken stupors more than once on the set to sober him up.

From Here to Eternity was produced at a cost of $2.5 million. Within one year it grossed almost £20 million. Critics were unanimous about Sinatra – he was superb. The picture and all five leading players were nominated for Academy Awards – Montgomery Clift, Burt Lancaster, Deborah Kerr, Frank Sinatra, and Donna Reed. (Because Clift and Lancaster were nominated in the Best Actor category, Sinatra was classified as a Supporting Actor. This was to his advantage since William Holden won an Oscar for Best Actor in *Stalag 17*).

Ava Gardner was nominated for Best Actress for her portrayal of Honey Bear in *Mogambo*. Bosley Crowther of the *New York Times*, who was known to treat Ava harshly, said in his review, '. . . Miss Gardner really steals the show. She has received the advantage of shooting position and priority from the start. And she is nothing loath to take it with both barrels. As we say, Miss Gardner is as enticing as any calculated vampire could be.'

♈

In May 1953 Frank was booked on a three-month singing tour through Europe and asked Ava to accompany him. That he *asked* and not *insisted* was the new Sinatra. Before he left for England Louella Parsons wrote, 'The nervous unhappy Frank Sinatra, who declared war on newspaper people and let his hot Italian temper get him into trouble, is a character of the past. The new Frankie has put on weight. His eyes are clear and better still, he's happy. This is the new Frankie.'

He seemed to have no apprehension about the tour and did not press Ava, who was in the middle of having her costumes fitted for *Knights*. She was suspicious about Frank's nonchalant attitude and suspected another woman might be involved. They hadn't seen each other in four months and the reunion was more romantic than either suspected. Frank seemed more enthusiastic about having her along. 'It will be a second honeymoon,' he said. 'I feel great and my voice is better than ever.'

Ava told MGM officials she wanted a few weeks off. They refused. She told them to go to hell. The trip got off to a bad start when the Sinatras' car broke down and they missed the flight to Milan. They were forced to fly to Rome where, ironically, several Ava Gardner films were playing. Her fans and the press ignored Frank, who was booed midway through his concert in Naples because the crowd wanted, 'Ava! Ava!' The police were summoned and it was agreed that she should make an appearance to appease the angry crowd. She walked onstage, waved, and walked off. The audience went wild – 'Ava! Ava!' When they booed Frank again, she boarded a train for Milan. A Neapolitan paper read, FRANK SINATRA BOOED AS AVA SKIPS TOWN.

In Denmark and Sweden, Sinatra sang to half-filled theatres. One Scandinavian newspaper said, MR. SINATRA, GO HOME! Frank canceled the rest of the tour and returned to London with Ava. Basking in his wife's glory did not amuse Frank. Their bitter spats on the concert tour were building up to a major explosion.

In London they rented a flat in St. Johns Wood while Ava was working in *Knights of the Round Table* with Robert Taylor. Ava hated costume epics and rising at five A.M. to get into tight bodices and heavy skirts. She was playing Guinevere to Taylor's Lancelot – in her opinion a ridiculous followup to her role as Honey Bear. *Knights* was not one of Ava's better films. Her performance was wooden and her lifeless facial expressions detracted from her beauty. 'What the hell am I doing in a costume film, anyway?' she grumbled.

She and Frank spent quiet evenings in their rented apartment. 'We wanted a home, not a hotel suite,' Ava said.

One evening they invited Stewart Granger and Jean Simmons to the Ambassadors nightclub where Frank was singing. The Grangers arrived at the St. Johns Wood apartment during a violent argument that ended in total silence. Frank said he was going ahead and told the Grangers to drive Ava to the club. 'He's impossible to live with,' she complained bitterly on the way. At the Ambassadors, Sinatra sang his love songs to her and Ava cried, 'Look at the goddamn son of a bitch! How can you resist him?' The rest of the evening went smoothly.

Ava had almost completed *Knights* and planned to attend the New York premiere of *From Here to Eternity* and Frank's opening at the 500 Club in Atlantic City. He refused to wait for her. 'Finish your movie. I have to rehearse,' he said. 'I have a career, too!' Their fight was so violent the other tenants called the landlord, who threatened to evict the Sinatras.

Frank left for New York alone and checked into the Waldorf Astoria on August 12. Ava went to Madrid for a week's rest. She kept her whereabouts a secret. While on vacation, Ava was introduced to Spain's most famous bullfighter, Luis Miguel Dominguin, whom Hemingway described as a 'combination Don Juan and Hamlet.' When Ava met the toreador he was recovering from a bad goring in the stomach. The tall, lean, handsome playboy attracted Ava, who wasn't ready or interested in an extramarital affair just yet. Yet temptation almost got the best of her she flew to New York on September 2 and stayed at the Hampshire House. Frank read about his wife's arrival in the morning newspaper. He was crushed that she hadn't called him. Ava, in turn, was upset that he failed to telephone her. Reporters spoke to Frank, who said he saw a picture of Ava at the airport in New York. 'I didn't know she was in town. I don't understand it. I can't make a statement because I don't know what's going on.'

Ava wouldn't comment. 'It's my marriage and my life!' she exclaimed. When Frank opened at the Riviera, Ava attended a Broadway show.

Dolly Sinatra invited Ava to dinner at the house in New Jersey the following night. She also called Frank, who said he'd come in between shows. 'Who's gonna be there?' he asked.

'Never mind!' Dolly spoke up. 'Just come!'

When Frank walked in and saw Ava, he tried to conceal his happiness. A determined Dolly got them together in the kitchen and Ava returned with him to the second show at the Riviera. Earl Wilson reported, 'With Ava in the audience Frank changed one of the gestures in his act that had been getting a good laugh during his battle with her. Singing "I get a Kick Out of You," Frankie had illustrated it as though he were getting booted in the derriere by love, represented by Ava. He dropped that.'

The next day Frank moved to the Hampshire House. But when he came in at four in the morning, Ava complained bitterly.

'Don't cut the corners too close on me, baby,' he said.

On October 2 they attended the New York premiere of *Mogambo* at Radio City Music Hall and flew to Hollywood the next day. Almost immediately Frank went to Las Vegas for an appearance at the Sands

Hotel. Ava attended the Los Angeles premiere of *Mogambo* without him. Newspapers described her as ravishing in a very low-cut clinging pastel satin gown with a slit in the skirt and a long white fox stole. The next day she was in Palm Springs and once again the Sinatra's weren't speaking to each other because he felt her place was with him in Las Vegas.

Everybody tried to effect a reconciliation – Dolly, Earl Wilson, Hedda Hopper, Louella Parsons, and Bappie. They knew it was only a matter of getting Ava or Frank to pick up the telephone. Before either gave in, a picture of Sinatra with two Las Vegas chorus girls at a costume party appeared in the newspaper.

Ava's attorney set up a meeting with Frank, who flew to Los Angeles, but did not keep the appointment. On October 29, 1953, MGM officially announced that the Sinatras had reluctantly exhausted every effort to reconcile their differences and could find no mutual basis on which to continue their marriage.

Frank could not eat or sleep. He told Earl Wilson, 'If it took seventy-five years to get a divorce, there wouldn't be any other woman.'

Ava laughed, 'Frank doesn't love me. He would rather go out with some other girl, almost any other girl.'

Earl Wilson, who was the go-between, wrote in his column, 'It is rather amazing that Ava, adjudged one of the greatest sex-appeal women in Hollywood, should ever feel that Frank cares more for somebody else. Yet she feels this way keenly and frequently.'

But Ava stubbornly insisted, 'Maybe if I had been willing to share Frank with other women, we could have been happier.'

Hedda Hopper didn't help matters when she reported that Frank Sinatra was 'less than sulky with an unidentified girl in Vegas.'

Ava and Frank emphasized their career sacrifices.

Considering the risks Ava took with MGM, there was no comparison. He complained that Ava's place was with him. Instead she was going to Rome for *The Barefoot Contessa*. Friends worried about his physical and mental condition. He was on the verge of another breakdown, or worse, suicide. When Frank's weight dropped to 118 pounds, his doctor put him in the hospital for observation. Ava called to inquire about his health. Elated because they didn't argue on the phone, Sinatra checked himself out of the hospital and made arrangements to follow his wife to Italy. In the meantime he recorded several songs, one of which was suggestively titled 'Why Should I Cry Over You?'

Ava, however, was anxious to get as far away from Frank as possible. When MGM refused to loan her to United Artists for *The Barefoot Contessa*, she went over Schary's head with a memo to Nicholas Schenk, the president of Loew's, who distributed Metro's films.

Ava wrote that she was 'desperately anxious' to do the picture because it was perfect for her. More important, going abroad for several months would alleviate her personal problems. Ava stressed not being able to accumulate some money and a measure of security. Would Metro give her the opportunity to do a film of her choice? If so, she was prepared to leave for Europe immediately.

Elizabeth Taylor also wanted the part of Maria Vargas and told MGM executives, 'I want to do *Barefoot Contessa* more than any script I have ever read.'

Rita Hayworth, recently divorced from Prince Aly Khan, was the most likely candidate, but she felt the part was 'too close to home for comfort.'

When United Artists offered MGM $200,000 and 10 percent of the gross from *Contessa* for Ava's services, she was on her way to Rome.

In November 1953 Sinatra's friend Jimmy Van Heusen rushed him to Mt Sinai Hospital. Frank's doctors said he was suffering from severe emotional strain.

His recordings of 'My One and Only Love' and 'There Will Never Be Another You' were poignant enough to touch the hearts of all who had loved and lost. Conductor Nelson Riddle said, 'It was Ava who did that, who taught him how to sing a torch song. That's how he learned. She was the greatest love of his life and he lost her.'

Frank called Ava faithfully and fell deeper into a depressed state, talking incessantly about the woman he adored and how hopeless this love had become. They couldn't live together and they couldn't live apart. Ava was trying to let go, and only a complete break and hard work could clear her head. Frank was crushed when she didn't ask him to join her. For the time being she really was 'the Barefoot Contessa,' a Spanish girl destroyed by happiness. Maria Vargas began her career dancing in nightclubs and became a famous movie star who loved to go barefoot. A writer (Humphrey Bogart), who befriends Maria, watches her go from lover to lover. Her life is ended by her impotent husband, an Italian count (Rossano Brazzi).

If Sinatra was Maggio, Garbo was Camille, Heston was Moses, and Leigh was Scarlett, Gardner was the Barefoot Contessa. She would forever be identified with the role of Maria Vargas.

Ava chose to live in an apartment rather than a hotel in Rome. She found a dirty, musty place to the dismay of her publicity man David Hanna, who found Ava cleaning up the apartment with the help of her chauffeur, chef, and two maids.

She was calm during a press conference. No

personal questions were allowed and Hanna was instructed to hire an orchestra for the reception and to have the ballroom dimly lit, which was more flattering to her (young or mature, MGM actresses knew how best to present themselves).

Ava enjoyed the night life in Rome – especially Italian comedian Walter Chiari's revue. She went backstage to meet the curly-haired, handsome young man and he became a frequent guest at her Corso d'Italia apartment. But Ava was eager to spend Christmas with Luis Miguel Dominguin and friends in Madrid. Director Mankiewicz gave her the week off, but prior to leaving Rome she received a call from Frank, who said he would be in Spain for her birthday. Ava complained to Hanna, 'Damn! I was looking forward to Madrid. Why the hell does he do it?'

Hanna began to panic. 'He's not coming to Rome, I hope.'

'He says he is.'

'The press will murder you.'

'I know. It'll be a mess, but what can I do? I can't tell him not to come.'

The Christmas holidays were uneventful in Madrid, Frank had a bad cold, and when he was sick in bed, Ava slipped out to see her bullfighter. By the time the Sinatras arrived in Rome he was in a bad mood and she had caught his cold. Their New Year's Eve party was dull, according to the guest. Ava's coming down with the German measles didn't help matters. She and Frank went into seclusion for a few days before he quietly slipped out of Italy. Ava said there was no chance for a reconciliation. No sooner was Sinatra's plane airborne than Luis Miguel arrived unnoticed and checked into the Corso hotel. Humphrey Bogart, who reported for work in *Contessa* after the holidays, was Frank's friend and, therefore, sided with him. Bogie took jabs at Ava every chance he got. She shrugged them off. 'I'll never figure you broads out,' he told her. 'Half the world's female population would throw themselves at Frank's feet, and here you are flouncing around with guys who wear capes and little ballerina slippers.'

'Aren't you being just a bit nosy?' she asked.

Bogart was unimpressed with the corps of attendants that followed her to and from the movie set. Arriving for work one morning he said to Ava, 'Let me get a running start. I don't want to get trampled by your entourage. And if I waited until it passed, I wouldn't get there until Thursday.'

'I'll give you a ten-second start,' she said. 'Then you're on your own.'

Bogart joked with Ava about her Southern accent surfacing if she drank too much and nicknamed her the 'Boon Hill Gypsy.' He asked sarcastically, 'Do your bullfighter boyfriends know you're just a little hillbilly girl?'

Without pausing she replied, 'That's what attracts them, honey chile.'

Bogie's wife, Lauren Bacall, joined him in Rome and brought Ava her favorite coconut cake from Frank. 'She couldn't have cared less,' Bacall recalled. 'She wanted me to put it down on some table she indicated – not a thank you, nothing. Her reaction had only to do with Frank – she was clearly through with him, but it wasn't that way on his side.'

Ava concentrated solely on *The Barefoot Contessa* and mastered the flamenco. The most difficult sequence was a lively display of a man-woman relationship worked out as a flamenco duet. 'I practiced every night for three weeks,' she said. Her bare feet were bruised and cut, and at the end she sank into a chair while a hundred hired gypsies applauded.

When Ava's double failed to show up on a cold February day for a bathing sequence in the icy

Mediterranean, she did it herself. Mankiewicz wanted to eliminate the scene entirely, but Ava wouldn't hear of it. She emerged refreshed and radiant.

Considering Frank's visit, Rossano Brazzi's complaining about every little thing, and Bogart's obvious dislike for her, Ava maintained a sense of humor and dedication to her work. The company of Luis Miguel contributed to her healthy attitude and her decision to buy a house in Madrid.

The Barefoot Contessa received mixed reviews. Critics agreed that Joseph Mankiewicz directed a sketchy film that was as barren as the impotent Italian count. *Variety* and the *New York Times* thought there was too much emphasis on the fatal charm of Ava's character, making it difficult for her to 'make strong men swoon on one quick look.'

Edmund O'Brien, as the sweaty press agent, won an Oscar for Best Supporting Actor.

The beautiful Greek statue used in the cemetery scene of *The Barefoot Contessa* was an exact replica of Ava's face and body. At first glance Frank wanted it, and Mankiewicz complied when the movie was finished. The statue was installed in Sinatra's Hollywood backyard as a shrine. Pictures of Ava were everywhere in the house, including the bathrooms. At a card party one evening the players found Frank in the bedroom with tears in his eyes drinking a toast to Ava, staring at her favorite photo. They left him alone until they heard a crash. Frank had taken the picture of Ava and smashed it, frame and all. Then he tore up the photo. 'I never want to see her again!' he cried. 'Leave me alone.' A while later his friends found Frank trying to put the picture back together, but Ava's nose was missing. Everyone got down on their hands and knees to help him find it. The doorbell rang and when Frank answered it, a draft blew the missing piece in the air. Frank was so happy he gave his gold watch to the delivery boy.

Sinatra was suffering from depression and insomnia. His nights were spent in the dark with lighting only on Ava's pictures next to a bottle of brandy. 'I know we could have worked it out,' he said to his friends.

In March 1954 Ava bought a house in La Moraleja, Madrid's posh garden suburb, for $66,000. She was seen everywhere with Luis Miguel who, the American press reported, was not only a famous matador, but a scion of a prominent Madrid family and millionaire in his own right. He was not only a skilled bullfighter but a refined and brilliant gentleman who mingled with international society.

Still, Ava remained cool. She refused to live with Dominguin or commit herself. This was one of her most intriguing attributes – and the most defying. Sinatra could never dominate her and she remained a challenge to him. Despite the love, devotion, and sacrifices, Ava was always on a pedestal beyond his grasp. She referred to him as a 'bum' and a 'gangster' – names no one else dared use even in jest.

Dominguin was a strong contender. The splendidly built Spaniard was all that Sinatra was not. Luis had thick black hair and Frank wore a toupee. Luis was fearless in and out of the bull ring. Frank's strength was his bodyguard. Luis was an attentive and romantic companion. Frank wanted his cronies around all the time. Dominguin's close friends were Picasso and Stravinsky. Sinatra's pals were 'hoodlums.'

The elusive Ava was, regardless of the contrast, addicted to Frank. Luis eased the pain while she tried to withdraw from her obsession.

Sinatra dated a variety of girls, including Judy

Garland and Elizabeth Taylor, whose fondest wish at the time was to be the next Mrs. Frank Sinatra. Perhaps this is one reason Miss Taylor commented, 'Ava Gardner is more beautiful than I am.'

Lonely and vulnerable, Frank proposed to several women who, fortunately for all concerned, turned him down. His shrine of Ava's photographs and the statue that he showed to one and all was proof positive that he carried a blazing torch.

On the night of March 25, 1954, Sinatra claimed his Oscar for Best Supporting Actor at the Pantages Theatre in Hollywood. He kissed Nancy, Jr. and shook his son's hand before running up on stage.

Ava, nominated for Best Actress (*Mogambo*), lost to Audrey Hepburn (*Roman Holiday*). She sent a congratulatory telegram to her husband, sincerely happy for him. Though she never accepted credit for Frank's achievement in *From Here to Eternity*, members of the Academy knew the truth as they listened to Sinatra expressing his gratitude to Harry Cohn and his production staff.

Ava was relieved to be far, far away from Tinseltown. She watched Dominguin practicing with the bulls in preparation for his South American tour, after a year's absence from the ring. But in April she was hospitalized with a painful gallstone. Luis had a bed placed in her room and stayed around the clock. He paid a call on his good friend Ernest Hemingway, who was staying at Madrid's Palace Hotel, and asked the author to see Ava. Hemingway looked forward to meeting the actress who had starred in *The Killers* and *The Snows of Kilimanjaro*. When he walked into her hospital room Ava was arguing with an MGM official about the role of singer Ruth Etting in *Love Me or Leave Me*. She flatly refused to do it. 'What in Christ are you trying to do to me?' she hissed on the phone. 'I stand there mouthing words like a great goldfish while you're piping in some goddamn music?'

MGM threatened her with suspension, but she was in too much pain to worry about it. When Ava saw Hemingway she smiled. 'I'm absolutely floored you could come! I haven't anyone to talk to. Do you know the only person who sent me a telegram is Bob Mitchum?'

Hemingway squeezed her hand. 'Is it true you're planning to live in Spain?' he asked.

'Yes. I don't like New York or Paris. What do I have to go back to? I have no car, no home, nothing. Sinatra's got nothing. All I ever got out of any of my marriages was the two years Artie Shaw financed on an analyst's couch.'

'Tell you the truth, Daughter, analysts spook me, because I've yet to meet one with a sense of humor.'

'You mean you've never been in analysis?' she asked.

'Sure I have. Portable Corona Number Three. That's my analyst. I'll tell you, even though I'm not a believer in analysis, I spend a hell of a lot of time killing animals and fish so I won't kill myself. When a man is in rebellion against death as I am, he gets pleasure out of taking to himself one of the godlike attributes, that of giving in.'

'That's too deep for me, Papa.'

Hemingway looked with approval on Dominguin's choice in Ava. The author was very taken with her, but he did not pursue her. Theirs was a mutual admiration that resulted in a very close friendship. Not only did she star in another film based on Hemingway's work, but she also visited him at La Finca, his home in Cuba.

A world apart from the squabbles with Frank and MGM, Ava recuperated nicely and kept the gallstone for a souvenir. Her days were spent with Dominguin and Hemingway until she could no longer put off returning to the United States where Dore Schary,

Frank Sinatra – and Howard Hughes – were waiting patiently.

Hemingway asked Ava if she was serious about Dominguin. 'How do I know?' she shrugged. 'We've been together three months now but I speak no Spanish and he speaks very little English, so we haven't been able to communicate.'

'Don't worry,' Papa smiled, 'you've communicated very well.'

Dominguin wanted Ava to accompany him on his South American tour and she was thinking about it. The first order of business, however, was filing for divorce. Before settling in Nevada, Ava reported to MGM and in person flatly refused to do *Love Me or Leave Me*. She wasn't going to be a 'dummy' singer throughout the film and she resented playing Ruth Etting, whose singing career was made possible by a small-time hood (James Cagney would portray The Gimp). Doris Day was also reluctant to take the part. She wasn't sure that an audience would accept her as a gangster's kept woman. They did, and the film was a hit.

Ava was put on suspension by MGM, which was expected. She drove to Lake Tahoe in May and rented a lodge to establish residency for a Nevada divorce. She told Hedda Hopper, 'Sinatra and I are not going to be together again – ever.'

Once in Tahoe she contacted Howard Hughes about getting her a good attorney. Within hours his spies were everywhere – even in fishing boats on the lake near her home. Luis Miguel flew from Spain to be with Ava, who approached United Artists about a South American tour to promote *The Barefoot Contessa* which would coincide with Dominguin's bookings. The studio took the bait, but Ava would be in such demand in South America that she saw little of him.

After a week of being followed everywhere by

Hughes's spies, Luis Miguel returned to Madrid. When the bullfighter departed, the billionaire moved in, and Ava and Howard were a romantic twosome again.

It isn't known precisely when Hughes bought her a modest home in Palm Springs – near the airport for his convenience. This house would be her residence in the United States.

Except for reports that Ava and Howard were seen together in Tahoe and Reno, nobody saw or talked to her except Bappie. The press was on hand the day she was scheduled to testify in court, but she failed to show up. She could, of course, appear at a later date since she had completed her Nevada residency.

Publicity man David Hanna tried to reach Ava about the United Artists publicity tour for *The Barefoot Contessa*, but she had literally disappeared. Only one man could perform this miracle. Howard Hughes had flown her to Miami where she got a flight to Havana for a visit with Ernest Hemingway.

Newspaper accounts of Ava's decision not to pick up her divorce decree varied. Since Frank was appearing at the Sands in Las Vegas in the state of Nevada, reporters speculated they had reconciled secretly. Others claim she changed her mind entirely or backed out at the last minute to give Sinatra one more chance. Ava's press agent came forth with an explanation, but not an answer: 'She didn't have the courage to face the heavy battery of newsmen waiting for her at the courtroom.' The most believable story was that Ava was negotiating a financial settlement and had not gotten what she wanted.

To avoid reporters, Hanna met Ava in Havana, from where they proceeded to Peru and Argentina to promote *Contessa*. She looked forward to Brazil in particular, but the mob at the airport in Rio got out of hand. Trying to get through the unruly crowd, she broke the heel of her shoe. Ava took off the other shoe and the real Barefoot Contessa arrived! By accident this 'publicity stunt' made headlines all over the world. In reality Ava was furious that she didn't have better protection at the airport. Impatient and ruffled, she got into a ramshackle cab and when the driver seemed confused, she hit him over the head with her broken shoe.

A disheveled Ava arrived at the old and shabby Hotel Gloria, where United Artists had arranged accommodation. She and Hanna had a martini in her room before she called the front desk with the announcement, 'I'm checking out!' The manager told her that was impossible because the Gloria was paying for her rooms and two press receptions. That was the arrangement with United Artists. Ava threw her martini glass on the floor, called the elegant Copacabana Hotel, and left.

The next day she was involved in a scandal. The manager of the Gloria Hotel claimed he had ejected Miss Gardner because she arrived drunk, disorderly, and barefoot. A messy broken bed and smashed cocktail glasses had been photographed. The story printed in the newspaper was that Ava threw the martini – glass and all – at David Hanna. She called a press conference and told the true account of what happened. She thanked reporters graciously, but told Hanna she never wanted to see Rio again. 'Twenty years from now, David, they'll still say you're the man Ava Gardner threw a glass at. No one has gotten in touch with me about this whole thing – not Frank, my agent, no one – not one goddamn soul! And do you know why? Because they believe it.'

She canceled her publicity plans in Rio and went to New York to rest before the premiere. Luis Miguel met her at the Drake Hotel and she remained in seclusion with him for a few days. When she refused his marriage proposal again, he flew back to Spain and out of her life.

After the premiere, Ava returned to Palm Springs with Bappie and an aide provided by Howard Hughes, referred to by Ava as his 'spy.'

She came to an agreement with MGM regarding her next project, *Bhowani Junction*, to be directed by the great George Cukor. Because a suitable filming location site had not been found, Ava said she'd go on another tour to promote *Contessa*. David Hanna accompanied her to the Orient, Cairo, Athens, and Rome. She spent her thirty-first birthday and Christmas in Stockholm.

During her travels, Ava did not date anyone. She was linked only with Howard Hughes, though their actual meetings were very rarely reported. A reason he had arranged for her house in Palm Springs to be near the airport was so he could fly there at any hour, usually in the middle of the night. His 'spy' was never far away from Ava, who permitted him to swim in the pool or have a drink. He ran errands and, in general, was there to see to her every want and need, reporting her every move back to his boss.

Hughes wanted to marry Ava and give her a very generous prenuptial settlement. He offered her everything and anything. She was flattered but not interested. An interview in *Look* quoted Ava saying she had no intention of giving him up '. . . because he's never given up wanting to marry me. He makes it easy when I want things easy. You're in Palm Springs and you want to go shopping in Mexico City. All you need is to call, and within minutes there's a chauffeur outside waiting to take you to the airport where there's an airline standing by to take you to Mexico City.

'And when you get there, you're met by another chauffeured limousine and driven to the best hotel in town where there's a suite waiting for you. If you want to be quiet and left alone, he arranges it.'

Hughes offered Ava a $250,000 cash bonus if she'd make a picture for him. She refused the money and told Howard to see her agent, like everybody else.

Without a young lover courting her, Ava was exceptionally vulnerable. Journalist Joe Hyams, married to actress Elke Sommer, drove to Palm Springs for an interview with Ava. She permitted him to use a tape recorder providing it was concealed. Even a pad and pencil made her tongue-tied and nervous. As the day progressed, Ava said she wanted to have some fun, and convinced Hyams they should drive to Mexicali, across the border. On the way she insisted on stopping now and then for a drink. The handsome, dark-haired Hyams ordered Coke because he had never acquired a taste for liquor. He remained sober while Ava got frisky but annoyed that Joe continued asking questions from bar to bar in Mexicali.

Hyams was approached by a man who wanted to know if the woman at the table was Ava Gardner. The answer was, 'No, she just looks like her.' The man wasn't sure and said sarcastically, 'You're lucky to have a good physical appearance of Ava Gardner, but I hope you don't have her bad morals.'

Ava didn't blink an eye. When the man had gone, she glared at Hyams and said, 'Every place I go it's the same, thanks to the lousy things newspapermen like you write about me.' A clever and likeable journalist, Joe changed the subject tactfully. Ava talked about her childhood and how she adored her father but was haunted by the feeling she hadn't done everything she could have to make his last days more pleasant. 'In a sense that sums up my relationship with the other men in my life,' Ava said. 'I've never received as much love as I've given.'

'Did you feel guilty about your father's death?' Joe asked.

She leaned across the table and punched him in the

head. He ducked and tipped his chair over backwards in the process. 'I jerked Ava from her chair,' Hyams related, 'and started to lay her over my knee for a spanking. It was the first time I had touched her and I was surprised that she was so light and so soft and feminine.' He let her go and said sternly, 'Don't ever do that again!'

Ava was amused and clapped her hands to the Flamenco beat. 'I should have been a dancer,' she said. Hyams asked what she would rather be than an actress.

'Queen Elizabeth,' was the reply, because she had a husband and children and people loved and admired her. Ava said, 'I failed at the only things I really wanted, a husband and children. I'm terribly possessive with people . . . I want to see them, touch them.' She surrounded her husbands with so much love they sought female sympathy '. . . because "my wife loves me too much." '

They left the bar and took a walk. 'I want to stay here for the night,' Ava announced, pointing to a seedy hotel.

'Not tonight,' Hyams said. 'I'm taking you home.'

She pouted in the car with her bare feet on the dashboard. Along the way she sat up and pointed to a motel. 'I want to stay there!'

Hyams continued on his way. He was tempted, of course, but had a job to do – interview Ava Gardner, and though he'd gotten a great deal of information, there was always another day and hopefully another interview with the Barefoot Contessa. She wanted to know why they couldn't stay at the motel. 'Because,' he blurted out, 'I'll probably end up in your room and I'll do everything I can do to satisfy you, and since I know I'm nothing special as a lover I'll probably fail. By morning I'll be destroyed as a man and you'll get up bright-eyed and bushy-tailed and say, "So long, buster. I've caught your act." And that will be the end of our interviews.'

She was satisfied. Turning to him Ava smiled mischievously, 'You son of a bitch! You do know me a little, don't you?'

Joe Hyams called her a few times after that and they made the rounds of dimly lit clubs in Los Angeles. Ava knew he had a concealed tape recorder, but she liked having an escort. When she officially left the United States to live in Madrid, he was one of only four people – also including an MGM press agent, her business manager, and her hairdresser – who saw her off. When she stood on the ramp and waved goodbye, one of the small group commented, 'There goes Ava, leaving nothing behind and with nothing to look forward to.'

FOURTEEN

I Get Along Without You Very Well

Ava's self-imposed exile in Spain afforded her freedom and privacy. Her three-bedroom red-brick house outside of Madrid had no telephone. Communication with her existed only by telegram or, if prearranged, through the Hilton Hotel.

She'd had her fill of crowds, newsmen, and Hughes's spies. If Ava had any doubts about leaving the United States, a scandalous story about her in *Confidential* erased them forever. The article linked her romantically with Sammy Davis, Jr. and other 'bronze boyfriends.' Ava had posed with the black singer for *Ebony* magazine at the Drake Hotel shortly after her return from South America. Some of the less formal pictures were used by *Confidential* – Sammy sitting on the arm of a chair and Ava in the chair with her shoes off.

There had previously been a nasty innuendo in the newspaper the day after she went to the Apollo Theater in Harlem where Davis was appearing.

Sammy brought Ava onstage for a bow to plug *The Barefoot Contessa*. After the show they were seen at the Shalimar, a Seventh Avenue night spot. The gossip columnist wrote about her appearance at the Apollo and, in parentheses, 'Wonder what went on backstage?'

Confidential claimed that Ava and Sammy slipped into the Warwick Hotel, where he was staying. Davis said, 'I would have cut off my dancing feet to prevent what happened. Not only because of the injustice to Ava but because of what Frank might think.' Not long after the article was published, Sammy was in a serious automobile accident that cost him an eye. Sinatra was a daily visitor to the hospital and helped Davis through his traumatic recovery.

Ava didn't sue *Confidential* because she feared it would draw more attention to the story. MGM was swamped with insulting letters and, according to Ava, her family was critical, too. 'No wonder people say I'm bitter,' she said. 'I damned well should be!'

Ava had not seen much of Frank during 1954. When calling her long distance he always asked for 'Mrs. Sinatra.' There was a mellowness now about their tragic marriage, the hatred and the bitterness fading into an incurable sadness and regret. She referred to him as 'Frankie' or 'my old man.' The miles that separated them helped to heal the wounds. Legally married for almost six years, they had lived together on and off for only two.

Sinatra was making quality movies – *Young at Heart*, *Not as a Stranger*, *The Tender Trap*, *Guys and Dolls*, and *The Man with the Golden Arm*, for which he received an Oscar nomination. He dated many women, among them Kim Novak, Gloria Vanderbilt, Natalie Wood, Shirley MacLaine, and Jill Corey. He was quoted as saying, 'I doubt that I'll marry again.' Ava's picture and statue would not be removed for a long time to come, just as she traveled with his records, playing them late into the night.

Ava was eager to play the part of Victoria, a tormented Anglo-Indian, in the film version of John Masters' novel, *Bhowani Junction*. She hopefully anticipated working with Stewart Granger, who was cast as Colonel Savage, the British officer in the Indian Army and the most important of Victoria's three lovers in the picture. Upon their arrival in Pakistan, she and Granger were entertained by King Hussein of Jordan (no one knows what he was doing in Karachi), but it was a forgettable evening for Ava because soft drinks were served instead of liquor. After dinner the guests gathered to watch a movie. The king had chosen *From Here to Eternity*.

The location site for *Bhowani Junction* was worse than the one for *Ride, Vaquero*. Dirty garbage littered the streets, the heat and humidity were unbearable, and the Felatti Hotel, a shabby hovel, had no fans or air conditioning. Producer Pandro Berman said, 'It was horrendous, all of it. I don't know how we got through it alive.'

George Cukor shrugged off the hardships. 'All picture-making is hell,' he said. Known as a 'woman's director' of such classics as *Camille*, *The Philadelphia Story*, *Gaslight*, *Born Yesterday*, and *A Star is Born*, Cukor was brilliant, and Ava felt his very presence more than made up for the horrid working and living conditions.

There was no nightlife other than a nearby

restaurant, where Ava, British actor Bill Travers, and members of the crew spent their spare time. Occasionally she invited the group to her room for drinks and lively conversation. Ava always asked Granger, but he declined, knowing Ava wanted to seduce him. Admittedly he took plenty of cold showers to 'quiet things down.'

One night around two A.M. she burst into his room wearing a sari that clung gracefully over every curve of her body. 'I always have to go out with Bill or someone else! Why won't you take me? Don't you find me attractive?'

Granger was in bed and sat up in a sweat. 'Ava, you're probably the most attractive woman in the world, but I'm married. Remember? I'm married to Jean.'

'Oh, fuck Jean!' Ava shouted.

'I'd love to, darling, but she's not here.'

'Oh . . . all right, you faithful husband. I'll see you tomorrow.'

Every one of the cast and crew was sick at least once. Ava had sunstroke and food poisoning. Granger's stand-in, Bob Porter, disappeared and was eventually found in an overcrowded hospital ward. Granger carried him to his car with Ava and drove him back to the hotel. The doctor diagnosed Porter's condition as an infection of the membrane covering the brain and said he needed antibiotics and a nurse to watch him day and night. 'You don't have to get a nurse,' Ava said. 'I'll take care of him.' She applied cold compresses and sponged down the delirious Porter. When his fever broke, she reluctantly left him and went to bed, after three days without sleep.

Aside from trying her luck with Granger, Ava wasn't interested in men during *Bhowani Junction*. Pandro Berman said, 'I'd heard about Ava's promiscuity, but I found her amazingly chaste. Maybe she was too tired to do anything except work. People linked her with Bill Travers, who played a Eurasian in the picture, but that was ridiculous.'

Bhowani Junction was well received, but a disappointment to George Cukor after MGM edited parts of the film that dealt with the delicate subject of the Anglo-Indian. Critics gave Ava credit for her fine acting, but knowing her best scenes were on the cutting-room floor was a letdown.

On her way home from Pakistan, Ava spent a week in Rome and began dating Walter Chiari again. Known as the 'Danny Kaye of Italy,' he was one of the country's most celebrated comedians and had starred in some forty-two movies. He was the dark lean type that appealed to Ava – a kind, unassuming, and witty person. Always laughing and optimistic, Walter was good company for Ava and he accompanied her everywhere.

Ironically, Luis Miguel Dominguin married Chiari's ex-fiancée Lucia Bosé, a young Italian actress.

Christmas 1955 was Ava's first at La Bruja, which she'd named for its iron weathervane, fashioned as a witch on a broomstick. She busied herself decorating her new house, which friends described as chic and comfortable. Bappie celebrated the holidays with her sister and Frank sent Ava a Facel Vega for her thirty-third birthday. She turned the car over twice, walking away uninjured. Everyone hesitated before getting in a car if Ava was at the wheel because she was considered a fast and reckless driver.

After buying the house, Ava was nearly broke.

Whatever she earned, she spent. Saving money never occurred to her. Since she was one of the first celebrities to settle in Spain, bartenders never presented her with a check. Restaurants and night-clubs were generous, too, because business flourished once word got around that Ava Gardner frequented their establishments. She soon found out there were few places to hide 'except in the caves where the gypsies danced.' There were bullfights in Malaga and Seville, and she sought out little cafés off the main drag.

She enjoyed entertaining a small group of friends at home and cooked Mama Sinatra's spaghetti and lasagna. Spanish food did not appeal to Ava, her favorite dishes being good old-fashioned American steaks and hamburgers. She managed to master only enough Spanish to get by. Ava acquired a taste for the local drinks, anise and cognac, gin mixed with beer, and Spanish liqueurs. She remained a night person, getting out of bed in the afternoon. Lunch was around three, dinner at eleven, and supper at two in the morning. Often she closed the bars and returned to La Bruja with friends and continued partying long after dawn. Few could keep up with Ava. A neighbor dropped by one morning and wasn't sure if the party was beginning or ending until he saw bodies lying around, some passed out from too much booze and others sound asleep. Not Ava. She was dancing by herself, the phonograph blasting.

When Frank Sinatra was asked to go on location in Spain for *The Pride and the Passion*, he hesitated. The prospect of being near Ava was tantalizing. She denied feeling the same way but busied herself fixing up the guestroom, just in case. Hedda Hopper asked Frank if he planned to see Ava. 'If I do,' he replied, 'it will be in some public place. It will be a casual matter.'

The Pride and the Passion wasn't scheduled to begin until April 1956. In the meantime Ava begrudgingly agreed to do MGM's sanitized version of André Roussin's *The Little Hut* in Rome with David Niven, Stewart Granger, and Walter Chiari. Though Ava could not afford another suspension, she did not argue with Metro since Walter was getting his first break in American films. She played a showgirl shipwrecked on a desert island with three handsome men. Poor Chiari, dressed in a feather headdress and loincloth, was cast as an Italian cook. His amusing appearance was the only plausible explanation why Ava, in sarong-type outfits, avoided intimacy with all three men in the film.

The cast finished up as quickly as possible and forgot about *The Little Hut*. Granger rushed home to his pregnant wife Jean Simmons while Niven and Ava attended the wedding of their good friend 'Gracie' to Prince Rainier of Monaco on April 19. As the bride walked up the aisle Ava turned to MGM publicist Morgan Hudgins and whispered, 'Look at Grace's father. How I envy her! If only I had a father like him to lean on.' Hudgins told the story to Joe Hyams, who included Ava's sentimental comment in his *Look* article about her. She never spoke to Hyams again.

In deference to Ava and Grace, Sinatra did not attend the wedding. There were very few movie stars among the six hundred guests, who drank champagne and dined on caviar, smoked salmon, shrimp, jellied eggs, and lobster, and who shared the five-tiered wedding cake.

'She's beautiful,' Ava related to friends about the

new princess. 'How I envy her. She has a lovely husband. She's loved and admired. She's a lucky girl.'

Frank Sinatra's instruction to Stanley Kramer and United Artists were, 'If there's one reporter at the airport in Madrid I'm taking the next plane back.' His arrival in Spain to film *The Pride and the Passion* was kept quiet. He brought along beautiful twenty-four-year-old singer Peggy Connelly and checked into the Hilton Hotel. There was no mention of Sinatra until he was photographed at a society ball with his girlfriend. When Ava saw the picture she was livid and placed a call to the Hilton. Everyone in his room could hear Ava cursing him. 'You bastard! You've been here how many days and never called me?'

Sinatra's friends did not think he brought another woman to make Ava jealous. On the contrary. He hoped having a 'companion' might deter his desire to see Ava. Whatever his plans, Frank visited her at La Bruja several times. They dined publicly with friends once and had eyes only for each other. There was no reconciliation, however. A few days later they showed up at a restaurant unaware the other would be there. They nodded politely, and soon after Ava left, complaining of a headache.

When Frank arrived in Spain, he was in a good mood and cooperative on the set. His attitude soon changed. He told director Stanley Kramer, 'I have to go. No one seems able to help me – doctors, no one. I have to move. I can't stay in one place sixteen weeks. I'll kill myself!' Without permission he left Spain seven weeks early and said he'd finish his scenes in Hollywood, leaving co-stars Cary Grant and Sophia Loren to play their scenes to a dummy. Frank hoped for a miracle to happen with Ava. They both knew better, but facing the final curtain hurt more than either would admit. After his departure from Spain, Ava flew to Chiari in Rome, where she made the announcement that divorce papers had been signed in London and she would pick up the final decree in Nevada soon.

❦

Walter Chiari, unlike Dominguin, learned English quite well in Ava's company. He told newsmen he was in love and wanted to marry her. But Walter knew Ava did not feel the same way. 'I was obsessed with her,' he said. 'She was the most beautiful woman I had ever known. We were happy together, but I often felt alone in her company. I had the nagging feeling I could never possess her. The only one who possessed Ava was the adorable Ava herself.'

Though Chiari proved to be a devoted and sincere boyfriend, Ava suspected he might be using her to further his career. Their romance lasted several years because Ava dreaded being alone. Walter understood and accepted her restlessness, fits of temper, and moody impulses. Knowing she bored easily, he made himself scarce before Ava exploded. Observers thought they were good for each other and besides, even a glamorous movie queen can't rent a prince.

One of her lines in *Mogambo* was appropriate for Ava after the collapse of her marriage to Sinatra: 'No one else is going to wring me out and hang me up to dry again!'

Henry King, who directed *Snows of Kilimanjaro*, wrote to Ava about portraying Lady Brett in Hemingway's *The Sun Also Rises*. She read the screenplay and complained to 'Papa' that the movie

212

adaptation destroyed the theme of his novel. He sided with Ava, and writer Peter Viertel was given the task of rewriting the material. Ava met Peter in London during contractual negotiations for her loan-out to 20th Century-Fox by MGM. The handsome Viertel, son of Greta Garbo's dearest friend, screenwriter Salka Viertel, was Ava's escort while Chiari was working in Rome. Peter was a worldly intellectual, and not immune to beautiful women (he married actress Deborah Kerr in 1960). Friends are divided as to whether Ava was attracted to Viertel. Skeptics think she was more compatible with Dominican playboy Porfirio Rubiroso and bullfighters Curro Giron and Cumillano, whom she was also dating.

Ava was cultivating intellectual acquaintances as well. Her best friends were Betty and Ricardo Sicre, who had introduced her to Luis Miguel. Ricardo was a Catalan who had fought in the Spanish Civil War on the Loyalist side against Franco. In 1939, he fled to the United States and joined the OSS, the precursor of the CIA, and became an American citizen. His experiences as a secret agent provided him with material for a novel, *The Tap on the Left Shoulder*. He married Betty Lussier, an American OSS operative. They first met when she parachuted into German-occupied Andorra. When the war ended, Sicre returned to Barcelona, immune to Franco's vengeance, and made several fortunes, buying and selling. (He owned Spain's first Pepsi concession.)

Through Betty and Richard, Ava met one of the most versatile figures in twentieth-century literature, sixty-one-year-old Robert Graves, who invited her for a week at his home in Mallorca. At the airport she came rushing across the tarmac and embraced Graves and his wife to escape the Spanish 'wolves' on the plane who were pursuing her with amorous yelps. She had been forced to stay in the ladies' room during most of the flight. Ava asked Graves how she could begin reading and understanding poetry. He, in turn, asked her about the monstrous legendary self with which she'd been saddled. 'It isn't what I do, but what I say that gets me in trouble,' she said. Graves gave her an autographed poem, 'The Portrait,' the verse beginning:

She is wild and innocent, pledged to love
Through all disaster . . .

Graves said it was exhausting to entertain Ava – he and the others took turns sitting up all night with her. He remembered vividly 'the quality of her personality in its struggle to remain intact and uncorrupted in the sea of publicity and vulgarity in which it was unhappily suspended.'

In the never-ending search for a father figure, Ava told Graves her most intimate problems and he consoled her. Instead of feeling useless, she felt strong and worthwhile. In a letter to him she wrote, 'It's nice to know someone takes time to say good things to me.'

In 1956 Artie Shaw packed up, bag and baggage, to settle in Spain's Costa Brava. Duped into joining the Committee for the Arts, Sciences and Professions, a Communist front, he had been questioned by the House Un-American Activities Committee in Washington. Though Shaw was proved innocent of Communist ties, his phone stopped ringing and the Internal Revenue Service was reviewing his returns. Disgusted, he moved to Spain and married actress Evelyn Keyes (she was wife number eight for him and he was husband number five for her).

The Shaws had cocktails with Ava and Chiari, whom Evelyn described as 'both gorgeous, what can I tell you.' This was the second time the two actresses had been involved with the same man. Besides Shaw, it had been John Huston in the forties.

214

Ava's friend Lana Turner divorced husband number four, Lex Barker, and began dating gangster Johnny Stompanato in 1957.

Howard Hughes sold RKO Studios and married actress Jean Peters on January 12, 1957 in Tonopah, Nevada.

Two days later Humphrey Bogart died of cancer. His widow, Lauren Bacall, was consoled by her very, very close friend, Frank Sinatra, and within six months they were a steady twosome.

'I should get the hell out, get a divorce,' Mickey Rooney said in 1957.

Wife number four exclaimed, 'Again?'

In January 1957 Ava reported for work in Mexico City for *The Sun Also Rises* and was seen in the company of Peter Viertel playing tennis, swimming, and dancing the flamenco. She occupied a fifteen-room house with lovely gardens and a blue-tiled swimming pool where her co-stars Tyrone Power, Errol Flynn, and Mel Ferrer gathered to party every night. Ava was very fond of Mrs. Ferrer (Audrey Hepburn). Director Henry King said it was the happiest group he had ever worked with.

Ava played Lady Brett, in love with the impotent Jake Barnes (Tyrone Power) who is forced to watch her engaged in an affair with a young bullfighter (Robert Evans). King said the theme had nothing to do with his choosing Ava. 'She had the moving, haunting, "crying out" quality. No one else could have done it, and it was the best thing she ever did.'

The only friction was Ava's instant dislike for newcomer Bob Evans because she wanted Chiari to play the bullfighter. King could feel the tension mounting when Ava refused to invite Evans to her parties. Producer Zanuck flew to Mexico City and in front of the entire cast confirmed in no uncertain terms that Evans was not being replaced. Ava fumed until she met Alfredo Leal, Mexico's good-looking, number-one matador, hired by Fox to coach Evans in the bullring. She accepted Zanuck's decision, concentrated on her role as Lady Brett, and . . . Alfredo Leal! Evans said, 'Ava was wonderful after we got over the first hurdle. When she's in a scene she shoots off electrical sparks. Our love scene was so violent that when it ended my teeth were chattering, and she took a half-hour rest.'

Ava reflected the character of Lady Brett. She had beauty, spirit, and fame, but sadly lacked inner security. Restless and rebellious, Brett could not come to terms with herself. She wanted to settle down with the man she loved but had no conception of what this meant. Her excuse was the impotency of Jake. Ava's excuse was Mr. 'Sinada,' the last two syllables of his name transposed to the Spanish word for 'nothing.' Perhaps she was imitating Hemingway, expressing his loss of religious faith: 'Our *nada* who art in *nada. Nada* be thy name.'

Ava wasn't overjoyed when Chiari arrived in Mexico City. He thought she was having an affair with Tyrone Power, which wasn't true. In fact she didn't particularly care for her co-star. Walter might have been overly suspicious since he expected Ava to change her mind about marrying him after they spent the holidays with his family in Rome. But she was living the life of Lady Brett a hairsbreadth away from her own. One night Ava picked up a group of musicians and brought them home and called Sinatra so the mariachis could serenade him over the telephone.

Chiari had much to contend with in Mexico but

remained calm. Ava enjoyed Viertel's company, and she disappeared with the Mexican matador on her day off.

The Sun Also Rises is a Hollywood classic. Bosley Crowther told readers of the *New York Times* they would not be disappointed because not even Hemingway's pen could improve the camera's magic. About Ava's performance, Crowther wrote, 'As for Lady Brett, that tarnished beauty loved for years by so many male readers (including this one), Miss Gardner, with an occasional look of real, fleeting anguish, excellently pegs her predatory aspects. She simply doesn't, or can't, convey the lady's innate poignant air of breeding. Sorry, Miss Gardner.'

In June Ava filed divorce papers in Mexico City charging Frank with desertion. Details of the settlement were never disclosed other than her demand that he pay legal fees. He had been notified she was going to court a few days earlier and was conveniently on a cruise to the Baja California peninsula with Lauren Bacall when the news leaked out. Ava surrounded herself with friends and lovers, trying to avoid facing the reality that the last link to Sinatra had been severed. He took care of her over the years, however. A hint from Ava was his command. When she casually mentioned a piano, he sent her one. If she smashed up a car, he sent her another. When Ava was in New York, he insisted she stay in his apartment. They talked on the telephone frequently and he sent her three copies of all his records, knowing she was in the habit of scratching them.

Free to marry, Ava had no valid reason not to accept Chiari's proposal other than she wasn't interested, a fact he did not take in stride. It was now Walter who became impatient and testy, giving Ava a good excuse to retaliate. Their relationship became like all the others, bickering and making up. Resenting the past and dreading the future, she drank more than ever. Parties at La Bruja ran on for several days. One night her exhausted maid lunged at Ava with a kitchen knife. A guest got there just in time and the maid was fired.

Aside from her divorce from Frank, Ava was facing a divorce from MGM, too. In bold defiance she tried to convince everyone (and herself) that freedom from both ties was what she wanted. Yet she was very upset over Sinatra's romance with Lauren Bacall. She turned down or ignored scripts, knowing one more film was her last commitment to MGM. Director Vittorio De Sica visited her to discuss *The Naked Maja*. She greeted him in her bare feet, martini in hand. While he attempted to explain the movie's theme over the blasting record player, Ava danced with his teenage son. De Sica declined MGM's offer to direct *The Naked Maja*. 'I wouldn't do it for all the money in America!' he said. Ava, however, agreed to do the film based on the painter Goya's love for the fiery Duchess of Alba.

Ava had time before the production of *Maja* began filming. She was interested in making a film about the life of Conchita Cintron, a woman who had been a famous bullfighter in Spain. In October she visited the ranch of Angelo Peralta, the celebrated trainer of bulls, and decided to try her hand at *torea a caballo* – fighting bulls on horseback. Ava said she got in the ring on a dare and no one tried to stop her. Peralta chose a 'harmless' young bull, and gave Ava a 'harmless' lance with a rubber tip. She was in the ring only briefly before the horse reared and Ava went down.

As she was trying to get on her feet, the young bull charged and struck her on the left cheek. It appeared as though Ava was more stunned than wounded. Since there was no blood, she applied an ice pack, and stayed on for a party. But when her cheek became discolored and swollen, Ava panicked and was taken home. Weighing heavily on her mind was whether or not this was the end of her career in films.

The press reported the tragic accident and Ava Gardner's flight to London four days later. She arrived at the airport wearing dark glasses and a scarf over her head. Ava consulted a well-known British plastic surgeon, Sir Archibald McIndoe, who diagnosed the injury to her left cheek as a hematoma (blood clot). He said heat and massage treatments would have it back to normal inside a year. 'Above all,' he emphasized, 'don't let anybody touch it with a knife.'

A stunned and worried Sinatra called Ava. He was in contact with Dr. John Converse, a world-famous plastic surgeon, and insisted she meet him in New York for a consultation. It took Ava several weeks to give into Sinatra's pleas. Converse, who had done work on Gary Cooper's face and married the actor's widow, Rocky, in 1964, agreed with Sir Archibald.

Pictures of the accident were published in newspapers and magazines. Obviously Peralta had sold them for a handsome price. That she was betrayed by a friend hurt Ava, but the publicity was damaging to her reputation in Hollywood because word got out she was deformed and might not ever face the camera again. Earl Wilson headlined his column: BRAVE BULL SCARS THAT BEAUTIFUL FACE.

Terrified of being photographed, she remained in seclusion, seeing only a very few close friends. David Hanna sent her a Gesicht Sauna, an apparatus for therapeutical facial massage with steam and vapors. She had wired him in Munich because the gadget was impossible to find. By the time he saw her a few months later, Hanna could detect nothing on her left cheek. With a touch of makeup, only Ava knew the truth. The tiny, almost invisible mark was a major defect to her. She did, however, have faith in Sir Archibald's opinion and decided to go ahead with *The Naked Maja*, though no one could convince her the beautiful Ava Gardner would ever be the same again.

FIFTEEN
None But the Lonely Heart

'Miss Davis, I'm Ava Gardner, and I'm a great fan of yours.'

'Of course you are, my dear. Of course you are!' And Bette Davis swept on.

Ava cited this experience with an admission that she never knew how to react when people stared at her in public. The right way, she said, was with Bette's assurance. That Davis cared less about her looks made all the difference. Ava had no choice. She never forgot her roots in *Whistle Stop* and how she became aware of the sexual and commercial power she was capable of wielding. This bewitching quality held true off the screen as well.

Ava proved she could act, but to ignore her beauty was virtually impossible. Lacking the perfect sculptured face, the Gardner legend was shattered and no one realized this more than Ava, who became preoccupied with her cheekbone, massaging and feeling the scar, studying herself in the mirror and knowing she had only herself to blame.

She was sick with worry, seldom leaving the house, and terrified of long-lens cameras if she took one step outside. She drank to dull the pain of her neurosis, cursing friends who 'lied' about not detecting any scar and frightened that she would have no means of supporting herself if her unique image were marred.

Only thirty-six, Ava already had dark circles under her eyes. Her laughter was forced and her nervousness a springboard for a violent temper. Chiari tried to help reduce the crisis as did Hemingway, Robert Graves, and Betty Sicre. When Ava spoke about *The Naked Maja*, her eyes twitched, proof of the strain she was under.

David Hanna spent the holidays at La Bruja to discuss future films with Ava, who convinced him to work exclusively for her. 'When I'm through with MGM,' she said, 'I'll need someone to take over my business affairs.'

It was almost a year since Ava had done a movie. This lull and the injury to her face made the ordeal of filming *Maja* in Rome a grim experience for all concerned. Ava found a comfortable apartment on the Piazza di Spagna in January 1958, but principal photography did not begin for several months due to production and script problems.

Ava's moodiness intensified when she read in the newspapers that Frank was planning to marry Lauren Bacall. By the time she got him on the telephone, the wedding was off. He pretended not to know what Ava was talking about. 'Jesus,' he told her, 'I was never going to marry that pushy female.' Bacall was devastated. 'He behaved like a complete shit,' she said in her autobiography, published years later. 'He was too cowardly to tell the truth.'

Frank had indeed proposed to Bacall but unfortunately her agent informed the press in Hollywood. Sinatra was out of town and besieged by reporters. He told Bacall they'd better not be seen together for a while. *Fini*. They didn't speak to each other for six years.

Haunted by her scar, Ava argued with the lighting director and cameraman during *The Naked Maja*. An MGM press agent understood Ava's complexity because he'd worked with her over the years. He expected the worst when he arrived at Cinecittá in Rome and almost made a joke of the worldwide publicity that she was deformed. He didn't notice the scar, but he was very aware of a haggard, tired leading lady with dark circles under her eyes. Ava would have to be filmed with filters on the camera to soften her appearance. 'She had a run-down look,' he said, 'resulting from sheer terror that she was scarred for life and might be finished as a film star. She demanded a closed set and refused to work until six P.M. Ava, of course, had a reputation of partying all night, but now it was a matter of avoiding daylight to conceal a scar no bigger than a pinpoint. I think the experience of being thrown from a horse and charged by a bull was more traumatic than she wanted to admit. We never discussed that. Only the fact that her face was ruined.'

Tony Franciosa threw himself into the part of Goya. He took the role so seriously that he actually assumed the personality of the tormented and neurotic painter. His wife, Shelley Winters, said Ava ran after Tony: 'She wrung him dry, she made love to him, he lost weight.' When Shelley paid a visit to her husband on the set of *The Naked Maja* and saw a NO VISITORS sign, she was livid and barged through anyway. Guards didn't try to stop Franciosa's 'pregnant' wife. Ava told her to leave, Shelley spouted a string of four-letter

223

words, and Ava set about throwing her out personally. During the scuffle, a cushion dropped to the floor from Shelley's dress, leaving everyone stunned and speechless.

Franciosa, now divorced from Winters, said the stories about an affair with Ava were ridiculous. 'We were thrust together in an unworkable situation with a director and production team that didn't know what they were doing. That I was climbing into bed with Ava every five minutes? We acted together because we had to.'

But Shelley sticks to her version: 'Ava was chasing after Tony. He was so unsettled by her he had to have a two-week rest in Capri. She followed him and put out the story I was keeping him a prisoner. So I put out a story that I pulled out her hair so no one would use her. It was sweet revenge.'

Ava went to Capri because Walter Chiari had fled there to escape her wild tantrums. The press had another version of the Gardner-Winters fiasco. They reported that the hair-pulling, glass-smashing battle happened in a bar.

To complicate matters, Sinatra called Ava from London. She invited him to Rome but refused to take his calls after reading about his romance with a young English beauty, Lady Beatty. 'He's so smitten with the beautiful Adele,' one columnist wrote, 'he's almost forgotten about spaghetti.' The *Daily Mail* reported that Frank was planning to marry Lady Beatty. Sinatra told Earl Wilson that the publicity had embarrassed Lady Beatty and his children. Nonetheless, he was seen with her everywhere in London.

Ava changed her mind on the spur of the moment, showed up at Frank's hotel, and gave back her wedding ring. 'Give this to your English lady!' she said sarcastically. He returned to London the next day and Ava had a good cry. She hated him. He was a bastard.

But when she calmed down, he was the only man for her. She'd never get over him. Never.

❦

The Naked Maja was a disaster from the start. Franciosa said he never worked harder but got the worst reviews of his career. Ava's were only fair. She concentrated on her appearance, scrutinizing the daily rushes for any sign of a blemish on her cheek. There was a slight indentation resembling a dimple, but nothing could be done to conceal it completely, much to her distress. Photographers, anxious to soothe Ava, touched up her still pictures before publishing them.

With her personal life in disarray, an uncertain future without MGM, and the obsession of having lost her valued looks, Ava had one consolation – Stanley Kramer's *On the Beach*, a film based on the novel by Nevil Shute. She had read the book before Kramer contacted her about playing the part of a heavy-drinking Australian party girl who is one of the last survivors of an atomic war. She asked for half a million dollars. Kramer offered $400,000 plus expenses, chauffeur, and secretary in Australia. Almost in debt (and owing back taxes) Ava did not turn it down. Her salary for *The Naked Maja* had been only $90,000.

She confided her innermost thoughts to David Hanna when her last film for MGM was done. 'I wouldn't admit this to anyone else,' she said, 'but I'm terribly afraid. I never worked for any other company. I never even had another job. I have to make a lot of money in the next couple years because I'm not going to last much longer.'

❦

Back in Madrid, Ava attended the sensational comeback of Luis Miguel Dominguin in the ring. He was aware of her presence, but did not dedicate a bull to her and gallantly avoided being photographed with Ava in the background. When their eyes met, he smiled.

As for Walter Chiari, he tried to continue with his career in Italy, torn between these obligations and his love for Ava. Their relationship was warm and compatible for a few days until he did something that annoyed her. Loyal and understanding, Walter never failed to respond if she called. David Hanna had apparently taken his place as escort, confidante, and protector, though there was never a hint of anything more than a business relationship between Hanna and Gardner.

He accompanied her to England for another consultation with Sir Archibald before she began *On the Beach*, Ava offered to appear at a bazaar to raise money for the nurses' pension fund at the hospital where the doctor was in charge. She proudly arrived at the London airport without dark glasses and, for the first time in months, faced a mob of newsmen with ease. She was anxious to help Sir Archibald, who had been knighted for his outstanding work during the war for restoring the faces and bodies of the R.A.F. wounded. If Ava felt sorry for herself, it was a revelation to meet veterans who had no arms or legs.

During her visit with Sir Archibald and his wife, a simple operation on Ava's cheek was discussed. A slight incision, he explained, would relieve the pressure and allow the cheek to assume its natural form. The procedure took only a few seconds, but she was required to stay in the hospital overnight. There was some swelling and discoloration, but Sir Archibald insisted she would be her old self again. Because the operation was a well-guarded secret, Ava was able to slip out of England and into Spain unnoticed.

On New Year's Day 1959, Ava began her long flight to

Melbourne by way of San Francisco, Honolulu, Fiji, and Sydney with Bappie and Hanna. Extensive press coverage was expected in Australia since *On the Beach* was the first major motion picture filmed 'down under.' Stanley Kramer had to build a studio from the ground up. United Artists had taken over and converted an annex building of the St. James Hotel in the suburb of South Yarra for Ava and her entourage.

After a few days' rest in Hawaii she arrived in Sydney looking stunning in a black designer suit, white blouse, and gloves. In between planes on her way to Melbourne, Ava answered questions posed by friendly newsmen. When asked if she injured her face at a rowdy party, she froze. The reporter apologized, 'That was ungallant of me.' Taken aback by his courtesy, Ava smiled and said, 'Yes, it was.' She ignored questions about Chiari, but volunteered that she was 'very close' to Mickey, Artie, and Frank. When confronted about her 'late nights and high living,' Ava laughed heartily. Boarding the plane for Melbourne she was in a good frame of mind. The 'Aussie' press was a refreshing surprise for her. Fans cheered but kept their distance, many of them standing on the tops of cars and in trees for only a glance at the beautiful movie actress.

In Melbourne her living quarters offered little privacy from the hordes of fans and reporters. And there was no nightlife. The pubs closed promptly at six P.M. 'This is a picture about the end of the world,' she said, 'and it's just the place to make it!'

That statement alerted the Australian scandal press, who now waited for Ava to stub her toe. In their opinion her decision to grant several personal interviews rather than a press conference was reason enough for a headline: DON'T BE SNOOTY, AVA.

What began as a friendly relationship between her and the press turned out to be a nightmare. It was summer in Australia and the stifling heat did nothing for Ava's bad disposition. She called Sinatra frequently, agonizing over her loneliness, how the press had 'turned on her,' and how much she wanted to go home. He arranged for an April concert in Melbourne, Ava's one hope. They discussed plans to meet, knowing reporters from all over the world would be anxiously waiting for this possibility.

She got along well with co-stars Gregory Peck and Fred Astaire, and did everything expected of her during filming in heat over 110 degrees. Stanley Kramer had no complaints. 'But Ava was bored,' he said. 'I was relieved when she laughed or wanted to talk. Then she'd lapse into sheer boredom.'

She spent time with Australian tennis star Tony Trabert, whom she'd met on the plane from San Francisco, and accepted his invitation to attend a match he was playing at the Velodrome against Merv Rose. Following Trabert's victory, he left with Ava in her Bentley provided by United Artists. The press tried to link Ava with the married Trabert, but it was an unfounded rumor. She soon lost interest in tennis, anyway.

Waiting for Frank to finalize arrangements for his concerts in Australia seemed like an eternity to Ava. In a moment of weakness she called Chiari. At his own expense he flew to Melbourne to be with her Exhausted, he arrived to find Ava sarcastic and aloof. Chiari followed her around like a devoted puppy, getting very little attention in return. When he arranged to do a variety show in Melbourne to defray expenses, Ava accused him of exploiting their affair. He tried to cancel the show, but was barred from leaving Australia and forced to fulfil his obligation. Ava refused to attend his performance and flew to Sydney. Her nerves raw and her temper short, she was hounded by fans and the press. Having dinner one

evening, she signed autographs, trying to be cooperative until a reporter from the Sydney *Sun* attempted to
interview her without asking permission. She threw a
champagne glass at him. It shattered against his chest.
Newspaper headlines the following morning read:
AVA BUBBLES OVER!

Chiari's variety show was a hit. He was seen about
town with an attractive young dancer, Dawn Keller,
and left Australia with an announcement to the press
that his romance with Miss Gardner was finished.

Ava in turn had a wild party that culminated with a
pair of horses being led upstairs to her suite for some
champagne.

The main event, however, was Sinatra's arrival in
Australia. Hanna strongly suggested Ava meet Frank
at the airport to satisfy the press. She refused and
slipped into the stadium for his second concert. The
carefully planned reunion went along smoothly until
she jumped into a car, puffing nervously on a cigarette,
with reporters giving chase to Frank's hotel. A press
car was forced off the road by Sinatra's group.
Surrounded by newsmen everywhere, Ava stayed
with Frank for only half an hour. The next day he flew
to Sydney for a concert.

Ava completed *On the Beach* and stopped off in
Hollywood, Palm Springs, Miami, Haiti, New York,
and finally Madrid. She had hoped to see Frank, and if
she did, it was a well-guarded meeting. The tables had
turned. Ten years ago it was a lonely, moody, and
depressed Sinatra grieving over Ava, who was at the
peak of her career. Now he was busy making movies
and campaigning for John F. Kennedy's presidential
nomination while Ava roamed aimlessly, hoping to fit
into Frank's hectic life. His friends felt she was still
very much in love with Sinatra and broken-hearted
over their divorce.

In Spain Ava dated a variety of men. One was a U.S.

Air Force doctor, who tried his best to have a sober courtship. He was blond, tall, and ten years younger, captivated but not mesmerized. She liked the fact that he wouldn't put up with her nonsense. Ava spent quiet evenings with him at La Bruja, but occasionally went out drinking and dancing alone, ending up at his door in the middle for the night. He listened to her problems over coffee until she was able to drive home. Watching her self-destruct became too painful and he bowed out. For a while Ava was seen with handsome Spaniards or dining with officers from the United States Air Force base at Torrejon, drifting, talking about 'her old man,' attending the bullfights, and brooding over the future. When she heard from old friend producer-director Nunnally Johnson about *The Angel Wore Red*, Ava seemed relieved to be working again. In the movie she portrayed a prostitute in love with a priest (Dirk Bogarde) during the Spanish Civil War. Ava suggested Frank play the embittered priest, but he had prior film commitments.

She arrived in Rome on November 2, 1959 with her entourage and thirty pieces of luggage – first class all the way. Johnson had known Ava ever since her starlet days at MGM, and loved her dearly, but he had not been exposed to the difficult, stubborn and self-conscious Ava who traveled à la Joan Crawford and was fawned over on the set by her staff à la Norma Shearer. 'She would always be a hillbilly and I told her so,' Johnson laughed. 'I thought Ava might have slowed down a bit, but she stayed up all night, took a shower and reported for work, line perfect. She could drink twenty-four hours a day. I never saw anything like it. Ava always told me she couldn't act and I'd tell her she gave a pretty good imitation. She was very, very conscious about the injury to her face. I didn't notice it, frankly, but she was obsessed with the scar. "All I have going is my looks," she said sadly. "When my beauty goes, I'm through." '

Secretaries, male and female, did not remain with Ava for any great length of time. She expected them to escort her to dinner, to continue on all night, and to tend to business matters or be with her at the studio. One male secretary said, 'I never knew what to expect. She was two people. One was the glamorous star and the other was a frightened orphan who had no roots, no home, and no family. I got the impression she was pushed into being an actress and didn't know what it was all about. Her marriage to Rooney was similar but she loved him very much and thought they'd have kids and settle down. She married him to be a housewife. I heard Ava tell a friend that she'd missed out in life. She was crying when she said it. I worked for her a short time and only saw her happy when she was talking to Frank Sinatra on the telephone or thought he was coming to Spain for a visit.'

Nunnally Johnson took Ava's moods in his stride. If she was late and he began filming without her, she went home. Another time she simply got bored with a scene and left the studio. The following day she went through it smoothly. Ava and Walter Chiari renewed their friendship in Rome but they saw very little of each other.

She invited Johnson to spend the holidays at La Bruja with her and Bappie. The best present Ava received for her Christmas Eve birthday was acclaim for *On the Beach*. Bosley Crowther, critic for the *New York Times*, finally gave her a good review: 'Surprisingly good, beyond conformance, are Fred Astaire in the straight role of the scientist, and Ava Gardner as the worldly woman who finds serenity in love.' *Newsweek*'s comment made one hesitate: 'Miss Gardner has never looked worse or

231

been more effective.' That some critics considered her 'typecast' was both annoying and amusing to her.

The Angel Wore Red, unfortunately, was so bad it was withdrawn from theaters in the U.S. and had only a short run in Europe. The disappointment was one reason why Ava did not make another movie for two years. She turned down *Sweet Bird of Youth* and *The Graduate* 'and a lot more good ones.'

There is a line from *The Sun Also Rises* that describes Ava during this period of her life: 'You're an expatriate. You've lost touch with the soil. You drink yourself to death. You've become obsessed by sex. You spend all your time talking and not working. You hang around cafés.'

Ava's heart was in Jake's reply, 'It sounds like a swell life.'

She did not have to read *Variety* or the *Hollywood Reporter* to keep up with Sinatra. An article in *American Weekly* entitled 'The Reign of King Frankie' read, 'Not since the late '30s when L.B. Mayer ruled from his Metro throne has anyone had such power.' *Good Housekeeping* wrote that Sinatra was a law unto himself, 'the most feared man in Hollywood.' Film Exhibitors of America voted Frank and Elizabeth Taylor the 'Top Box Office Stars of 1960.' *McCalls* labeled Sinatra one of the 'Most Attractive Men in the World.'

Columnist Dorothy Kilgallen considered Frank's choice of girlfriends less than desirable: 'A few women like Ava and Lana were public idols themselves and priceless examples of feminine beauty. The others belong to the classification mostly described as tawdry.'

As she did with everyone and everything in her life, Ava was getting bored living in the country at La Bruja and found a duplex apartment on the top floor of 8 Calle Dr. Arce in Madrid. While she decorated her new place, Ava moved into the Hotel Richmond on a noisy corner in the center of town. She said people took her for granted after five years and paid little attention to her, but taxi drivers, bellhops, waiters, and bartenders related stories about her wild antics.

This writer was staying at the Castellana Hilton in Madrid in the mid-sixties. Sitting in the empty cocktail lounge, pale and shaky, I told the bartender about the bullfights, how I lasted only a few minutes and fled in tears. Hands trembling, I said, 'Most women react this way, I suppose.' He nodded sympathetically, but spoke about Ava Gardner's passion for the sport. 'Many bulls are dedicated to her at Las Ventos,' he said.

I should never have asked what that meant.

'The matador's cape is displayed on the railing in front of her,' he explained. 'After the kill, he presents her with the bull's ears.'

I cringed and asked for another dry Rob Roy. The bartender apologized for the story, but said it was the custom and Ava thrived on it. 'She loves the night and is uninhibited. I'm told she was seen in only a bra and panties in the Plaza Argentina and went after someone in a nightclub with a broken bottle. Supposedly she took a hammer to her boyfriend's car after a big fight.'

'Do you think the stories are true?'

'Yes, but maybe exaggerated.'

The bartender said she hung out at the air force base at Torrejon playing the slot machines and joking with the officers. 'I don't know much about her private life,' he said. 'Firsthand, I do know she drinks too much, but she was asked to leave a bar only one time, and people are still talking about it.'

He said that Ava and a friend went to a German restaurant for dinner. She ordered a dry martini. When it was served she shouted, '*Falsificado!*' She poured the drink on the floor and shouted, 'That's Spanish gin, and they're passing it off as genuine English!'

The waiter presented her with an unopened bottle,

broke the seal, and mixed another drink at her table. Without tasting it, Ava again poured the cocktail on the floor. The waiter calmly suggested she switch to vodka 'because we do not make it in Spain.' She nodded and was served a vodka martini. 'I hope this will please you, Miss Gardner,' the waiter bowed. Without looking up at him she took hold of his belt, pulled it forward and poured the drink inside his pants. With that, she proceeded to leave the restaurant, but before her exit the manager said she would never be allowed in the restaurant again.

I caught a glimpse of Ava Gardner only once. It was at a flamenco club in Madrid. The name escapes me, but it was not for tourists. She was with a group of people, some American and some Spanish. She was dressed casually and wore no makeup. Whatever has been written about her fading beauty seemed to me an exaggeration. She was a rose in a bed of thorns and weeds. The waiter refused to admit she was Ava Gardner so I asked, 'If she *were* Ava Gardner, would she dance the flamenco later?' He walked away. My friend, the bartender, said most likely she chose a partner and danced until the club closed, and then invited the entire troupe home for a party.

Ava's downstairs neighbor was the exiled Argentian dictator Juan Peron, who complained about the noise he had to endure at all hours. She said he went out on his balcony and made speeches to himself. Apparently they were effective. 'Would you believe they took him back?' she laughed when Peron moved out.

Ava denied to friends that she was an alcoholic. 'Anyone who has my appetite can't possibly be one,' she exclaimed. She could stop drinking without ill effects, as she had often done while filming. During *On the Beach*, she went on the wagon for several weeks. Ava took up golf for a while but was never interested in outdoor exercise.

Her 'health kicks,' which were few and far between, usually resulted after the death of a good friend. Tyrone Power died suddenly of a heart attack in 1958, and though Ava wasn't close to him, the fact that he was only forty-two was a blow. And she was saddened when Clark Gable died of a heart attack in November 1960. But the greatest shock was Ernest Hemingway's suicide in July 1961. That Papa put a double-barreled shotgun in his mouth and pulled the trigger depressed Ava for a long time.

Unpredictably, Ava agreed to interviews and then changed her mind at the last minute. 'I can't imagine why anybody would want to have an interview with me,' she said. 'I'm such a dull subject.' Italian journalist Oriana Fallaci did not give up and Ava finally invited the reporter 'for a drink.' Signora Fallaci described Ava's eyes as large, frightened, hard with suspicion, underslung by bluish bags of flesh, her cheeks asymmetrical. 'Her real wounds are her eyes,' Fallaci wrote. 'Her breasts, in a red-flowered cheong-san, assail you arrogantly, all this maternal abundance corrected by two muscular highly nervous arms. She shook my hand without warmth and without seeking my eyes.'

Ava told Fallaci she hated America and was tired of Spain. London was wonderful because after a few photographs at the airport, reporters left her alone. 'I love the climate and the people,' she said.

Fallaci asked, 'But there's no sun in London. It rains all the time.'

'What does the sun mean to me?' Ava laughed. 'I never see the sun. I sleep during the daylight. The night is company. It clarifies my mind. I love the rain in

London. The thin, fine rain . . . It gives me tranquility for a time. It appeases me.'

In the winter of 1962, Ava flew to New York for a round of parties. Walter Chiari, who was appearing in a play on Broadway, was seen with her on the nightclub circuit. Occasionally, she was seen dining peacefully alone. One evening she couldn't get a cab and was standing by herself on the street at four in the morning when a garbage truck came along. 'Hey, Ava!' one of the men shouted. 'Want a lift?'

'Sure do,' she said and they hoisted her up. When they got to the hotel she invited the sanitation men in for a few drinks. Fifteen minutes later the night manager called her, 'Miss Gardner, I wonder if you'd mind asking your friends to move their . . . uh, vehicle from the front entrance.'

Earl Wilson reported that 'Frank Sinatra and Ava Gardner went on the town with the Porfirio Rubirosos, the George Axelrods, Mrs. Mike Romanoff, and others . . .' A photographer who asked for a picture of Frank and Ava was told, 'No, we're only part of a group.' The *New York Post* reporter persisted and Frank allegedly spouted, 'It's terrible – you creeps with cameras. That doesn't make you anything more than a parasite or whore. Why don't you do something worthwhile?'

Ava flew to Sinatra's opening at the Sands in Las Vegas. Knowing he would be at the airport, she spent most of the time primping in the powder room, according to a newsman on the same plane. Nervous and excited, she left her coat on board, returned to get it, and missed Frank. When Ava got to the hotel she found out the first Mrs. Sinatra and daughter Nancy had decided to attend the show also. Ava turned around and caught the next plane back to New York and on to Madrid. Her next chance to see Frank perform in Las Vegas was also canceled at the last minute when he invited Marilyn Monroe as his guest of honor.

Louella Parsons, informed of Ava's trip to Las Vegas and her sudden departure, wrote, 'Ava Gardner is one of the more tragic figures in recent Hollywood history.'

In January 1962 Frank gave dancer Juliet Prowse an engagement ring after an 'I go my way and he goes his' courtship that no one took seriously. When he proposed she said, 'I'll think it over.' Frank liked that. Dorothy Kilgallen, Sinatra's arch enemy, claimed it was a publicity stunt to promote Miss Prowse's career as a dancer.

Juliet told reporters, 'Frank doesn't want me to work. But I do.'

Frank said, 'She's not going to work. I'd rather not have it.'

A month later the wedding was off due to 'conflicts in career interests.' Miss Prowse's price at Las Vegas jumped from $500 to $17,500 a week.

Columnist Sidney Skolsky said Frank should get married. Referring to the 'Rat Pack' that was breaking up, he wrote, 'On any night when the laughs get sleepy and there's no more booze and there are no more hours, Dean Martin goes home to his wife, Peter Lawford goes home to his and Sammy Davis to his. But Frank just goes home. What a sad, lonely little man.'

The Rat Pack dissolved when Lawford, married to a Kennedy, was told to 'break his ties to Hollywood.' Sinatra was snubbed by the President-elect because of his reported Mafia connections. Frank went on a charity tour trying to prove his benevolence, but John Kennedy chose to stay at Bing Crosby's Palm Springs home rather than Sinatra's. Frank began having recurring bouts of his psychosomatic ailment, laryngitis, when his link to the White House was broken.

SIXTEEN

Back to Work

Philip Yordan, who was responsible for Ava's first big break in *Whistle Stop*, was living in Spain and ran into her at parties once in a while. He was writing a screenplay, *55 Days at Peking*, for Allied Artists in 1962 and thought Ava would be perfect for the part of the Russian countess caught in the Boxer Rebellion in China. Charlton Heston did not agree. He had cast approval and wanted Melina Mercouri in the role. Above all, he did not want Ava Gardner because she didn't look like a Russian countess. When he arrived in Spain to begin work on the picture, the battle continued, but the European movie distributors wanted Ava, and Heston gave in. He said the only reason he consented to do *55 Days* was as a favor to Philip Yordan, who needed the money. 'As for Ava,' he said, 'she wasn't the most disciplined or dedicated actress I ever worked with. None of us should have made that piece of crap in the first place.'

Ava leaned on producer Samuel Bronston, who had

so many obstacles to surmount that he suffered a heart attack. Though he survived, Bronston never worked again. His biographers claim it was *55 Days* that ruined him, physically and professionally. The $7 million disaster involved 3,500 extras and 46 stunt men. Ava remained in her dressing room, drinking and sulking – terrified of the crowd scenes and feeling inferior to Dame Flora Robson and other members of the cast. 'I killed Ava off early in the script,' Yordan said. 'She was snide, hard, corrupt, impossible, and still incapable of reading lines.' Ava's double appeared in endless over-the-shoulder shots. Heston begged her to join him on the set, but she hid and drank.

55 Days at Peking is better off forgotten. Critics considered Ava's performance 'coarse and clumsy.' The money was more important to her than good reviews.

In a candid 1963 interview for *The Ladies Home Journal* she said, 'Being a film star is still a big damn bore. I do it for the money, that's all. After all these years I don't know a damn thing about movies. I was never an actress. But I can't write or paint or anything. I had dinner with director George Cukor not long ago, and he and his friends were going on about the business and what was happening, and do you know, I didn't understand a damn thing they were talking about. As for acting, I know nothing about it.'

Seven Days in May, about a plot by the military against the President of the United States, appealed to Ava. The small but important part of the discarded mistress of General Scott (Burt Lancaster) brought her back to Hollywood. She had faith in director John Frankenheimer and writer Rod Serling. She was not disappointed. Ava blamed her dreadful appearance on the screen to an unsympathetic cameraman, but Bosley Crowther, critic for the *New York Times*, called Ava's performance 'superb.'

She was forty and seemed to have aged considerably in the past two years. Unlike her Metro sisters, Ava did not consider a face-lift because she knew the problem was too much partying and excessive drinking. Beneath the dark circles under her eyes, the puffiness and hard exterior was still the magnificent contessa, a beautiful, mature, and proud woman. A friend said, 'It was Ava's soul that aged, not her face.'

George Cukor told author Charles Higham, 'She's a real movie queen. When she walks across a sound stage she creates a sense of excitement, she stirs the pulses. It's as though she were "born to the cloth." She has that feeling of command, that control, that mark her down as an authentic star. Ava's a gent.'

In August 1963 director John Huston and producer Ray Stark flew to Madrid for the specific purpose of convincing Ava Gardner to play Maxine in *The Night of the Iguana*, a Tennessee Williams classic. Since Huston and Ava were old pals he knew her temperament only too well. He warned Stark their mission might take several days and long nights of gentle persuasion, sprinkled with casual chitchat about the film.

The Night of the Iguana revolved around the Reverend Lawrence Shannon, an Episcopal clergyman, who had been locked out of his church after a scandal involving a young girl. He is reduced to serving as a guide to a group of schoolteachers on a cut-rate tour of Mexico. When their bus breaks down, Shannon's group is stranded at a broken-down hotel.

Huston and Stark went to see Richard Burton in Switzerland about playing Shannon. He signed for $500,000. Deborah Kerr agreed to portray Hannah Jelkes, an itinerant artist, for $250,000. Most actresses would have jumped at the chance to work with Burton and Kerr. With Ava, it was the opposite, and the intuitive Huston knew she would feel inferior. His phone calls prior to the visit were witty and fun. Ava loved his humor and admired his creative ability and the sensitivity that lay hidden under a gruff and often ruthless exterior. Their close relationship years ago had been a passing fancy, one of many for both of them. Now legally separated from his fourth wife, Huston at fifty-seven was still charming, roguish, blunt, and appealing. His intense brown eyes were underlined with deep pouches. Tall and thin, his hunched-over posture gave one the feeling he was leaning forward to listen or observe more intently during a conversation. He was an imposing man, a rebel, and a dedicated drinker.

When Huston arrived at 8 Calle Dr. Arce, Ava mixed the cocktails while he sprawled his lanky body over the couch as if he'd seen her only yesterday. He did not press the issue about her playing the floozy hotelkeeper in *Iguana*. She liked the idea of working in Mexico, but dismissed the part of Maxine that Bette Davis had portrayed so brilliantly on the stage. Huston ignored Ava's disinterest. He knew she was going to do it; she did, too – but wanted to be courted.

'So Ray Stark and I stayed on in Madrid another week and played the game,' Huston said. 'I should say we stayed for the dance. The first night we went out I left the scene around four A.M. Ray stayed on with Ava. This continued for three or four days through most of the night spots and flamenco dance groups in Madrid. Ray became more haggard and gray faced. Ava blossomed. When we left, poor Ray was a shattered wreck, but Ava had agreed to do the picture.'

Huston got her signature on the $400,000 contract, knowing his difficulties with her had only begun. Their phone conversations were consumed with Ava's fears and doubts. He poured on the praise, emphasized his faith in her, and finally, exasperated, exclaimed, 'Goddamn it, Ava, not one more word about backing out!'

The tangled web of relationships among the principals of *Iguana* was something of a challenge to Huston. He and Ava were amused that his ex-wife Evelyn Keyes was married to her ex-husband Artie Shaw. Most interesting was Richard Burton being accompanied by Elizabeth Taylor, who was still married to Eddie Fisher; and Michael Wilding, Elizabeth's ex-husband, arriving to handle the job of publicity for Burton. Peter Viertel, Deborah Kerr's second husband, was Ava's former boyfriend. Then there was the reputation of Burton's flings with his leading ladies and Ava's with her leading men. Could Elizabeth hold on to Richard whom she had recently captivated as Cleopatra to his Marc Antony?

Huston presented gold-plated derringers to Sue Lyon, Deborah, Ava, Elizabeth, and Richard. Each gun came with four golden bullets engraved with the names of the other recipients. 'I told them they could always use the guns if the competition grew too fierce. I was lucky to have selected blanks,' Huston said.

The international press flocked to Puerto Vallarta, Mexico, and wrote about every little detail. They noted that an overweight Elizabeth Taylor arrived with forty bikinis. One day she wore a sheer overblouse with no bra and Burton gulped down some tequila with a beer chaser and said, 'She's trying to seduce me again.' Ava, who was very fond of Elizabeth, told her, 'Richard is the man I should have married. If you hadn't got him I certainly would have tried to get him. He's got a sense of humor and he's a real man!'

Ava didn't want to possess Burton, but she was curious about his sexual prowess. Perhaps she flirted with him on the set to tease Elizabeth, but he was in a sweat, wanting but not daring to take a chance. Ava was quoted as saying, 'Some people say Liz and I are whores, but we are saints; we do not hide our loves hypocritically, and when we love we are loyal and faithful to our men.'

Each member of the cast had his own house. Ava said she had one lousy air conditioner. 'Look at it,' she said. 'Look where they installed it! In the wall between the kitchen and the living room. It blows cold air in the kitchen and hot air in the living room.'

The only accessibility to the filming location on the island of Mismaloya was by water. Everyone had to be ferried across from Puerto Vallarta. Ava waterskied to and from work behind her own speedboat.

Heavy rains often interrupted filming, leaving the cast and crew with nothing to do but play gin rummy and drink. Correspondent Jim Bacon said Richard Burton had twenty-three tequilas at one sitting. 'I know,' Bacon said, 'because I paid the bill. There was something about Puerto Vallarta that caused everyone to drop inhibitions. One of the crew members suddenly kicked off her shoes, smoked opium, and shacked up with one of the natives. Ava Gardner took up with a twenty-one-year old beach boy who mistreated her in public, much to the amazement of the tourists. John Huston took up drinking an illegal native brew called *raicilla* that was 180 proof and went down like Drano.'

Ava actually amused herself with several beach boys, who followed her everywhere, but when she had to do a scene where Maxine makes love to two beach boys in *Iguana*, she froze. John Huston stripped down to his undershorts and showed her how he wanted the sequence done in the water. It was a funny sight watching the director with legs like a stork, running around like a dizzy teenager. He and Ava had a few drinks and she got through the scene with no problem.

She needed Huston's attention and companionship throughout *Iguana*, but he had no control over her where the press was concerned. When a photographer hung around the set after getting all the pictures he wanted, Ava kicked him in the stomach and chased him away. The incident was so irritating, she blew her lines in a scene with Burton. Instead of saying, 'In a pig's eye!' Ava blurted, 'In a pig's ass!' Burton knew she was terrified of playing Maxine. 'But once she got into the part, her intuition took over,' he said. 'Ava really knew that sad, defeated woman at "the end of the world," as it were, and at the end of her tether. Like Maxine, Ava was what they used to call in mystery thrillers, "a woman with a past." '

There were sad memories from *Iguana*. Three-quarters of the way through, two assistant directors, Tommy Shaw and Terry Morse, were sitting on their cottage balcony and it gave way. They fell twenty feet like rag dolls to the ground below. Shaw, who was in serious condition with a broken back, was accompanied by Huston on a fishing boat to Vallarta. Morse walked away, but no one in the cast will forget the screams when the two men fell. This tragic accident and the assassination of President Kennedy put a damper on the last few weeks of filming.

Ava did not attend the Thanksgiving Day dinner for the cast, but went to the end-of-shooting party.

The Night of the Iguana New York premiere six months later was a black-tie gala. The audience paid $100 a seat to attend the opening at Philharmonic Hall followed by a champagne banquet on the second-floor balcony. Ava was stunning in a pale blue strapless grown and a white lace greatcoat. After his evening performance on Broadway in *Hamlet*, Richard Burton arrived with his bride, Elizabeth Taylor. The newly-weds might have been the center of attention, but the consensus from the audience and critics of *Iguana* was that Ava Gardner stole the picture, with possibly the most inspired performance of her career. 'I was determined to do my best,' she said. 'I even made myself look awful. They'll say, "Ava's lost her looks." '

The New Yorker wrote that she was 'splendid.' *Life* thought she ran away with the picture, and *Newsweek* commented, '. . . a great woman to play a great woman.' But keen competition from *My Fair Lady*, *Mary Poppins*, and *Zorba the Greek* kept *Iguana* off the list of Oscar nominations, other than one for Dorothy Jeakins, who won for costume design in a black and white film.

Ava received criticism from *Show* magazine about her attitude in Puerto Vallarta: 'She was her customary self, as amiable as an adder . . . She gave a photographer a look Medusa might have envied . . . Both Elizabeth Taylor and Ava are as spoiled as Medieval queens. They expect men to fall at their feet, and they are accustomed to being catered to and having everything done for them.'

In December 1963 a moody and depressed Ava returned to Madrid for the holidays and her forty-first birthday. She hoped *Iguana* would pave the way for future character roles. Her personal life was a maze of drinking and dancing. That Bappie's new husband was required to work in Europe a good deal of the time was of some consolation to Ava, who maintained the house in Los Angeles for her sister and stayed there whenever she was required to work in Hollywood.

What Ava could not overlook much longer was Spain's growing popularity with tourists. It was not a haven from newsmen who kept their distance, but got their red hot stories anyway. She was linked with numerous bullfighters, and it's true her door was always open to them. Some were intimate companions, others simply fun to be with. One of her neighbors said in bad English, 'All times they come.'

Confidential wrote, 'Two o'clock in the morning, a gray Cadillac convertible races over the La Coruna highway north to Madrid. The driver is a woman whose auburn-red hair flies in the dry, warm wind. Next to her sits a beautiful young Spaniard with broad shoulders and narrow hips.'

Ava was reported dancing in the street in London's Covent Garden flower and vegetable market, where the bars were still open at five in the morning. In a white fur coat, she kicked off her sandals and livened up the local trade.

One night she strode onto a thick plate-glass nightclub floor, lit from below by multicolored lights, and danced the flamenco for half an hour. She whirled and stamped so magnificently that the glass floor broke in half.

Redbook ran an article about Ava in the mid-sixties. 'She is haughty and demanding, playing flamenco records endlessly, marshalling her forces – her secretaries, drivers, wardrobe women – to perform all the tasks that need to be done every day. She will quibble over a small bill, count the eggs in the cupboard, check over her silver for fear a gypsy visitor has stolen it. But she will cheerfully pay for a servant's operation or buy her sister a new car.'

Ava fired a male secretary, accusing him of stealing one golf ball. He said, 'I don't think theft had anything to do with it. The time had come for me to leave. That's all.'

Admittedly she was neurotic, but, 'Isn't everybody?'

Referred to in Europe as the 'Goddess of Love,' Ava was amused by the label. In a rare interview, she said it was Mickey Rooney who helped her try to overcome an inferiority complex that had always surrounded her. 'I remember wondering what he could have seen in me,' Ava said. 'He was the first guy I'd met that I didn't figure was laughing at me.'

Ava was either blunt or said nothing. 'Maybe I shouldn't have started wearing shoes. Makes it that much more comfortable when I put my foot in my mouth.' She said little about Sinatra other than repeating that success went to his head. 'When we were separated for either professional or personal reasons, he used to call just to hang up on me,' she laughed with a twinkle in her eye.

What did she think of a newspaper article about the 'beautiful and seductive Ava Gardner, who has rocked men back on their heels from Zanesville to Zanzibar leaving fans and friends wondering what makes Ava run – what makes her tick so furiously.'

'I wasn't meant to act,' she replied. 'I was meant to have babies.'

The men who knew Ava – if any could be said to know her well in this tempestuous stage of her life – would not talk about her.

Ava's popularity as a film star was now attributed to her frenzied search for happiness and peace of mind. All she did in response was to mimic the rest of the world looking on at her amorous adventures – by raising an eyebrow.

John Huston tackled the job of convincing Ava to play Sarah, the barren wife of Abraham, in *The Bible*. The epic, based on several books of the Old Testament, would be filmed in various locations: Rome, Sicily, Sardinia, and North Africa. Huston had to coax Ava bit by bit, showing her the beauty, suffering, and patience in the character of Sarah – the quiet acceptance with which she made Abraham take another woman to sire a son. For Ava, who had never borne a child, the role had deep meaning. Huston's promise to coach and guide her through the interpretation of every line gave Ava the courage to go through with it. Not only was Huston directing and narrating the movie, he was portraying Noah.

When Ava arrived in Rome reporters were there to greet her. She said there was 'nobody special' in her life at the present time, but the paparazzi staked out her rented villa on the Via Appia Antica, and were not disappointed. In the role of Sarah's husband Abraham was George C. Scott, a fine and dedicated actor who fell in love with Ava instantly – and intensely.

The thrice-married Scott, five years younger than Ava, rose to Broadway prominence with *The Andersonville Trial* and scored big in films as the assistant prosecutor in *Anatomy of a Murder*. His role as the hard-hearted gambler in *The Hustler* won him an Academy Award nomination in 1962, but he eliminated himself from consideration.

A production assistant working on *The Bible* said, 'Ava was very attracted to George, but not in love. She was a remarkable woman. I went to her dressing room about dialogue changes and she said, "We'll discuss it later. Let's go to bed first." That's what we did. Then we went over the script.'

Scott became a regular visitor to Ava's villa. His wife, actress Colleen Dewhurst, who was appearing in the Broadway production of Eugene O'Neill's *Desire Under the Elms*, was not available for comment.

John Huston wrote in his memoirs, 'Scott fell in love with Ava. He was insanely jealous, extremely demanding of her time and attention, and he became violent when they were not forthcoming. This intensity turned her off, and pretty soon she started avoiding him. Scott is an on-and-off drinker, and he was on at the time. Although it didn't interfere with the shooting, it did make life rather difficult on occasion.'

The cast and crew of *The Bible* witnessed Scott's fierce possession of Ava. She was having a cocktail with one of her co-stars, Peter O'Toole, when Scott, in a jealous rage, drunk and unruly, found them. Huston jumped on Scott's back and carried him around the room bumping into everything because his arms were wrapped around George's head. Eventually Huston calmed Scott down.

Ava was, nonetheless, very taken with the ex-marine turned actor. He defended her against the press, using force if necessary, and he could drink Ava under the table. When she gave him an argument, he pushed her fully clothed into a swimming pool. They both had a rebellious nature, and contempt for the rules of show business. (Scott later caused a stir in 1970 when he refused an Oscar for Best Actor in *Patton*.)

Ava's turbulent affair with George affected their working together on occasion. John Huston minded his business until Ava called him one morning after a bitter quarrel with George. 'I'm afraid what might happen on the set,' she said. 'It could be embarrassing.' In turn, Scott refused to work with Ava if their relationship wasn't going smoothly. A concerned Huston insisted Ava take time off whenever possible to relieve the tension.

Frank Sinatra was filming *Von Ryan's Express* in Italy and staying outside Rome in an eighteen-room villa. On the grounds were ten fountains, stables, indoor and outdoor swimming pools, a landing strip for helicopters, and a ten-foot wall that surrounded the villa estate. Ava took refuge there for a few days. Still trying to rekindle a flame that was dim but still burning, they spent time alone together. Sinatra knew about Scott and thought Ava should have a bodyguard, but she laughed it off. Frank's close friend Edie Goetz, daughter of L.B. Mayer, said, 'Frank wanted to try again, but Ava was not in the right frame of mind. Maybe she was thinking about George Scott. Their romance was a hot item in all the newspapers. It was her heavy drinking that annoyed Frank. She didn't let up and he hated to watch her self-destruct. Too bad, because Mia Farrow had her eye on Frank.'

Ava infuriated Scott further by taking a yachting trip with the Sicres and Adlai Stevenson around the Aeolian Islands. When they docked at Messina in Sicily, Ava seemed to be enjoying herself, swimming and taking long walks with Stevenson. But without warning she announced her plans to fly back to Rome immediately.

Though Scott was seething during her absence, he was overwhelmed with passion when Ava returned. They were devoted to each other, until she made it clear to him that nobody owned her and she was free to come and go as she pleased. When he tried to change her mind, Ava punched him in the stomach so hard that she fractured her collarbone and had to wear a neck brace. Scott wasn't fazed.

Huston went out of his way to complete Ava's scenes in *The Bible*. She packed hurriedly and fled to London. Though Scott hadn't finished his work in the film, he followed her to the Savoy Hotel, broke the door down to her suite, threw out Ava's agent, and went after her. Hysterical, she tried to get away. According to John Huston, Scott struck her, nearly breaking her jaw. Black and blue, Ava finally managed to escape and hid in the servants' quarters.

Scott was arrested by police and spent the night in jail. At Bow Street Magistrate's Court, he pleaded guilty to 'drunk and disorderly' conduct, and was fined ten shillings ($1.40). He returned to Rome but continued to telephone Ava, who refused his calls, according to Huston. The press, however, reported that the couple dined together on several occasions. Scott kept tabs on Ava. One observer said he followed her 'clear across the map' while others insist their meetings were planned.

Huston said that Scott repeated the Savoy incident at a Hollywood hotel. Sinatra hired two bodyguards to protect her. He told *Photoplay* in 1965, 'If there's one guy I can't tolerate, it's a guy who mistreats women. They are real bullies and what they need is a real working over by a man of their own size.' Scott wasn't cut down to size, but his clothes were. When he returned to his hotel room one night he found that all his shirts and sweaters and suits had been cut off at the shoulders.

John Huston said, 'George was depressed over Ava for a long time. He disappeared for a while – to sort things out, I guess. That's what love did to the man.'

Ava helped out Mickey Rooney financially when he filed for bankruptcy in 1962. She gave him a monthly allowance until he got back on his feet. The day after his divorce from Elaine Mannken was final in 1952, he married Miss Muscle Beach of Santa Monica, Barbara Ann Thomasen, fifteen years his junior. Four months later, the first of their four children, Kelly Ann, was born. Ten years later Rooney was bankrupt, saying he had made and spent £12 million during his career, but now he owed almost $400,000. He filed for divorce from Barbara and named a young Yugoslavian actor, Milos Milocevic, as correspondent. A reconciliation ensued, with Barbara promising not to see the young actor again. But on February 1, 1966, while Rooney was ill in hospital suffering from a fever he had contracted in Manila while filming *Ambush Bay*, Milocevic shot Barbara to death in Rooney's Brentwood home, and then took his own life with the same gun. Nine months later, Rooney married Margaret Lang, a friend of his deceased wife, but the union lasted only a few months. In May 1969 he married for the seventh time, to a secretary, Carolyn Hockett.

In the early seventies, he sought custody of his four children by his deceased wife. In a Santa Monica court he said he had curbed his bad temper through Christ. 'I'm a member of the Science of Mind Church,' Mickey testified. 'I now live a Christian life.'

Artie Shaw and Evelyn Keyes moved back to the United States in 1961 and settled in Connecticut. Artie had written two books, *The Trouble with Cinderella*, a 1952 autobiography that did not mention his wives, and in 1965, *I Love You, I Hate You, Drop Dead*, composed of three short novels about marital disaster.

Artie commented on his personal life, 'Evelyn and I had a one-to-one monogamous relationship. After five years, that no longer sufficed, so we fumbled our way into "open marriage." Neither of us wanted a divorce, so we moved aside to live as we pleased. I like her very much and she likes me, but we've found it impossible to live together.'

Ava called Artie frequently. 'He was a clarinetist,' she said, 'but he gave himself the air of a cultured man without having any real culture. He learned a few pages of Dostoyevski by heart and recited them at breakfast.' Ava might have joked about his trying to educate her, but she turned to Shaw whenever she had the urge to talk. He had a cool philosophy and pulled no punches, and that's what Ava needed.

Frank was seeing nineteen-year-old actress Mia Farrow, who was younger than two of his children. In 1965 he told *Life* magazine, 'I don't say marriage is impossible, but if I would marry, it would have to be somebody out of show business, or somebody who will get out of show business. I feel I'm a fairly good provider. All I ask is that my wife looks after me, and I'll see that she is looked after.'

Mia was playing Alison Mackenzie in the popular TV series, 'Peyton Place.' Her mother is actress Maureen O'Sullivan (Tarzan's Jane), divorced from director John Farrow. According to Frank's friend, Edie Goetz, 'Mia knew what she wanted. She was a determined young lady and wanted to marry Frank. He invited a group of us to his Palm Springs house one weekend and I remember seeing Ava's pictures everywhere – over his bed, in the bathroom, living room, and kitchen. Mia was oblivious to them.'

No one took the May-December romance seriously. Sinatra's pals said he was getting over the trauma of turning fifty by running around with a little girl thirty years younger. 'She's a good kid and I'm lonely,' Frank, said.

In 1965 Ava told her great friend Nunnally Johnson, 'I'm broke.'

'How can that be?' he asked, knowing she was earning $400,000 a picture.

'I relied on the wrong people in the States,' she complained. 'I was double-crossed and I need money.'

'You're exaggerating, Ava.'

'No, I'm not. Matter of fact, I'm in debt.' She said taxes in Spain were outrageous. 'Besides, I'm bored here,' Ava exclaimed. 'The same old thing. I'd like to live in London, but I need money.'

Johnson did not take her literally. 'I'm sure Ava meant that she couldn't retire. Morgan Maree, her business manager, was the best and invested Ava's money no differently than he did for Bob Hope, Bing Crosby, Barbara Stanwyck, and God knows how many other big, money-making stars. Ava was and is a survivor. I heard about the Scott incident at the Savoy. She was a hysterical mess. But the next morning she looked serene and beautiful, absolutely magnificent, just as if nothing happened.'

Ava moved out of the apartment in Madrid, rented a chalet in the Colonia Ramira de Maetzu area for a few months, and finally into a suite at the Castellana Hilton where this writer was vacationing. I was writing about another MGM star at the time and it never entered my mind to try arranging a chat with Ava Gardner about my book. The friendly bartender suggested it, but said he'd rather face a bull than Ava. He did the next best thing, however, and introduced me to a good-looking matador who had been in Ava's company often. He spoke little English, but a bar is a good place to find translators. Ava was, according to him, uninhibited. All woman! 'She lived in a house, La Bruja, the witch, and that's what she is,' he said. 'Without trying, Ava casts a spell that drives men mad. Making love to this woman is like a dose of magic potion that stays in the blood forever. No man can forget her.' He tried to explain the torment of being ignored by her when she lost interest. Love and pride had nothing to do with it. She was a magnet. Men were helplessly drawn to her. 'For Spaniards this is not dangerous,' he shrugged, 'only very frustrating.' He said one bullfighter nearly got killed because his mind was on Ava. The bartender laughed, 'More than one . . .'

The young matador said Ava attended almost every important bullfight in Spain, sitting in the front row '*barrera*' below the President's box. 'The matadors must come to ask the President's permission to fight,' he said. 'Afterward Ava goes to *tientos*, parties organized on wealthy bull-breeding ranches where young bulls are brought out to be tested. Distinguished guests eat, drink, and dance until the small hours.'

I asked if Ava was hurt at such a ranch and he nodded. 'But if the guests wish to play with the young bulls, they do not ride horseback.' Then he looked at the bartender with the eyes of a bloodhound, droopy and sad. It was I who shrugged this time. 'Will you see Ava again?' I asked. His answer was translated into, 'It is not for me to say.'

Ava had another life other than matadors and dancing the flamenco. She attended parties in London, flew to New York for a change of pace, and valued her friendships with Robert Graves, Noel Coward, Tennessee Williams, the Gregory Pecks, Sue Carol (Mrs. Alan) Ladd, George Cukor, John Huston, MGM hairdresser Sydney Guilaroff, and Princess Grace. Following the George Scott publicity, she stayed out of the spotlight for a while. There were no particular men in her life, but she fought with photographers if they tried to take her picture.

After a series of gynecological problems Ava checked into the Chelsea Hospital for Women in London for several days in January 1966.

*

Sinatra's decision to marry Mia Farrow caught his friends off guard. He gave Bill and Edie Goetz only forty-eight hours' notice that they were to be best man and matron of honor at the Sands in Las Vegas. Only minutes before the ceremony on July 19, 1966, Sinatra told his valet to get Ava on the telephone. Edie Goetz recalled, 'Frank did not want her to hear about it from anyone else. If it took hours to reach Ava, he wasn't going through with the ceremony. She was his greatest love.'

Ava's comment to the press about the nuptials was, 'Ha! I always knew Frank would end up in bed with a little boy.'

Mia pursued her career with enthusiasm, an actress first and a wife second. Sinatra made it known in the industry he did not want her to work, but the little ninety-eight-pound Mia convinced producers otherwise.

Along with his marriage troubles, Sinatra was having problems at the Sands. Howard Hughes bought the hotel in 1967 after purchasing the Silver Slipper, the Frontier, the Desert Inn, and the Castaways. Frank's animosity towards Hughes began over Ava in the mid-forties when the poor crooner could not compete with the expensive gifts and vacations the millionaire lavished on her. Frank also remembered with hatred being followed by Hughes's spies in 1950. He wanted to forget that Hughes gave him a job on Ava's behalf when no one else in Hollywood would hire him.

When Hughes refused to accept Frank's phone calls ('Frank who?') regarding his contract with the Sands, Sinatra backed out of his Labor Day appearance pleading illness, got drunk, and was refused credit in the casino. He shouted to the crowd that Hughes should share the profits with him because, 'I made the Sands what it is!'

Sinatra signed with Caesar's Palace, but returned to the Sands for a showdown with Carl Cohen, executive vice-president in charge of the casino. Frank started a fistfight and lost a few teeth. Cohen walked away without a scratch. The district attorney said, 'You don't go around a hotel screaming four-letter words and breaking windows. He [Sinatra] did a disservice to this community by that kind of behavior.'

Working behind the scenes, Hughes made Frank look silly by refusing to press charges.

In the fall of 1967 Frank served Mia with divorce papers. When her pleas for another chance failed, she traveled to India to meditate with her guru.

Johnny Carson said in his TV monologue, 'Hear about the trouble at Frank Sinatra's house? Mia Farrow dropped her Silly Putty in Frank's Poligrip!'

SEVENTEEN

Alone

Ava went back to work as the Austrian Queen Mother of Omar Sharif in the costume epic *Mayerling,* a remake of the 1935 film. Ava wanted to do the picture because her good friend James Mason would co-star as her husband. Working at the Studios de Boulogne in Paris did not appeal to her, but Omar Sharif did. Ten years younger than Ava and recently divorced, Sharif had the exotic allure of a refined Latin lover, with his curly black hair, moustache, and liquid eyes. Rumors persisted about their close relationship. Sharif was her type, and what Ava wanted, Ava got. Omar's leading ladies were usually attracted to the Egyptian-born actor, who was cultured, charming, and obliging. There was more enthusiasm over the Gardner-Sharif romance than the film. Ava had no comment other than, 'I'm too young to play his mother in the picture.'

The $5-million *Mayerling* was panned by critics. Ava was striking as the Empress, though her role called for little else than sitting regally in the background. She would never regain confidence as a reigning beauty. The tiny scar on her face made growing older more painful. She allowed this inferiority complex to hold her back from fighting for better roles, which were scarce to begin with in the sixties. Joan Crawford and Bette Davis were reduced to doing horror films, and when Ava was approached she replied bitterly, 'I'm not a freak! I'm just a miserable lonely woman who should never have been a film star.'

Barbara Stanwyck, Loretta Young, Donna Reed, and Ann Sothern had their own popular TV series. After divorcing several millionaires, the beautiful Hedy Lamarr was arrested for shoplifting in 1966 and found not guilty. Judy Garland's TV show was bumped for *Bonanza*. She floundered until her death, from an accidental overdose of barbiturates, in 1969. Lana Turner made an occasional film, tried the stage and TV. She said, 'I'm not working because I need the money. I'm doing it because I need activity.' After *Madame X* in 1966, critic Pauline Kael said, 'Miss Turner is not Madame X, she's Brand X; she's not an actress, she's a commodity.'

L.B. Mayer died in 1957. His last words were to Howard Strickling – 'Don't let them worry you. Nothing matters.' In the same year an influential motion picture newspaper, *Showman's Trade Review*, published their list of all-time great stars – Joan Crawford, Greta Garbo, Bette Davis, Mary Pickford, Clark Gable, Ava Gardner, and Marlene Dietrich, who said, 'There is a haste and lack of dignity to film stardom.'

But the truly envied ladies of the screen were Merle Oberon, Rosalind Russell, Greer Garson, and Claudette Colbert, who married wealthy men. They were admired and respected by their peers in the motion picture business and international society. These actresses proved what every mother tells her daughter, 'It's just as easy to fall in love with a rich man as a poor one.'

Though there was no mention of alimony when Ava divorced Frank Sinatra, he continued to look after her. Early in 1968 while doing a movie in Miami Beach, he came down with pneumonia and ran a temperature of 104. Mia came to visit him at the Fontainebleu, but did not stay. Frank called Ava, who flew to his side complete with maid, secretary, and thirty pieces of luggage. It was while she was visiting Sinatra that a piano in his suite was pushed out of a window during a party. The incident made headlines. 'That was too much for me to take,' Ava said, packing her thirty suitcases. 'I got the hell out!'

Frank and Mia were divorced. She asked for no alimony, only her jewelry, clothes and ... stuffed animals.

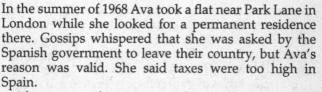

In the summer of 1968 Ava took a flat near Park Lane in London while she looked for a permanent residence there. Gossips whispered that she was asked by the Spanish government to leave their country, but Ava's reason was valid. She said taxes were too high in Spain.

After a year of resting, traveling, and making final preparations to leave Madrid, Ava filmed *Devil's Widow* as a favor to her friend, Roddy MCDowell, the former child actor, who was directing the movie about a rich widow and leader of a strange cult. When the film was finished in December 1969, Commonwealth United studios collapsed. *Devil's Widow* was edited, released, and forgotten. McDowell thought the movie was ahead of its time and that Ava was exceptionally good as the evil widow. But after Commonwealth recut the picture, it bore no resemblance to what Roddy had directed.

In 1970 Ava Gardner was living in England and staying out of the public eye. She no longer danced in the streets of London or dated young bullfighters. Nor did the press bear down on her. She was seen walking her dog early in the morning. When her pet dogs Rags and Corgi died, Ava bought another corgi named Morgan whom she adored and called long distance just to hear him bark over the telephone.

There were many requests for magazine interviews and Ava granted them occasionally. The questions were the same: Was she trying to destroy herself? Is it true she engaged in drunken orgies? Does she want to marry again? Was she actually 'thrown out' of Spain?

'I haven't taken an overdose of sleeping pills,' Ava spoke up rather proudly. 'I haven't been in jail, and I don't go running to a psychiatrist every two minutes. That's something of an accomplishment these days.' As for marriage, she said, 'I was mad about Artie, just as I was about Mickey and Frank. I guess you think that mad love can cure anything. Well, it can't. You have to have more in common for marriage to work. I married three exciting men, all very talented, and fascinating to the ladies, and, I might add, vice versa. But it's not all entirely my fault, when you consider that my three husbands have had a collection of twenty wives!'

Ava had a series of gynecological problems in the late sixties and was hospitalized for minor surgery, but the details were (and are) not known. She cut down on drinking and confined her social life to small dinner parties with visiting Hollywood chums and new acquaintances living in London.

Content as she was, John Huston convinced Ava to make a brief appearance as the beautiful theatrical actress Lillie Langtry in a Paul Newman western, *The Life and Times of Judge Roy Bean*, on location in Arizona. Ava is seen at the end of the movie on a visit to

Langtry, Texas, named after her by the late Judge Bean who admired Lillie from afar.

John Huston hired an old jockey-friend to play a little crippled miner, one of two people left in the western town. 'Anyone except Billy Pearson would be banished or murdered for some of the things he's done,' Huston said. 'Instead he's cherished. The best example of this was during *The Life and Times of Judge Roy Bean*.'

Ava's scene with Pearson was beautifully staged. The train pulls into the station and there is a glimpse of this perfect beauty through the train window. Billy Pearson is at the bottom of the steps to help her down. He puts up his hand. She takes it and they walk up the street toward the museum with the camera preceding them. It went perfectly. The old train had stopped precisely where it should have. Ava was her most graceful and elegant self. Suddenly Billy looked up at Ava and said, 'How'd you like an old man to go down on you, Miss Langtry?' She walked a few steps and then broke into gales of laughter.

'Only a character like Billy could have gotten away with that!' Huston grinned. 'I was just delighted that Ava showed up at all for only three days' work in Tucson, Arizona. We gave her a welcome dinner the first night and she looked absolutely great!'

Knowing George C. Scott was filming *Rage* nearby, Huston had guards posted to prevent him from bothering Ava on the set and at the hotel. She found out and secretly arranged to see Scott. 'George and I kept ducking the guards,' Ava told columnist Earl Wilson, who wrote, 'She wasn't exactly on Huston's side – and maybe didn't want to be protected. When Huston found out, he was furious.'

Ava spent her $50,000 for *Judge Bean* to go waterskiing in Acapulco. 'It more than paid for the trip,' she said, 'so what the hell.'

There were visits to Madrid to see friends, too, but Ava told one, 'I can't tell you what a thrill I used to get coming back to this city. Now I can't wait to leave again.'

In London, Ava found an apartment in a quaint old townhouse overlooking a private square in Knightsbridge, near Hyde Park. The furnishings were elegant but unpretentious, reflecting her life in Spain. The few reporters permitted into the antique-filled drawing room saw no evidence that a movie queen was living there.

In 1973, Ava returned to Hollywood for Universal's box office bonanza, *Earthquake*. The title tells it all. Cast as Lorne Greene's daughter and Charlton Heston's wife, Ava fights to save her marriage and survive an earthquake in Los Angeles. She manages to do both. In a life and death situation at the end, Heston saves her instead of his mistress. It had been ten years since the disastrous *55 Days at Peking* when Gardner and Heston clashed. His anger at her drunkenness, sarcasm, and unprofessionalism was justified, but during *Earthquake* she was sober, mature, and cooperative.

Ava stayed with Bappie on Rinconia Drive, shopped, and attended one party for charity. Nunnally Johnson was living in Howard Hughes's house. When Ava walked in she looked around and said, 'Christ! What memories. What fights! And yet . . . Howard was one of the kindest and most generous men I've ever known.'

She went to an intimate dinner given by George Cukor, who told her about his forthcoming trip to Russia for *The Blue Bird* with Elizabeth Taylor, recently divorced from Richard Burton. 'George said they didn't have much money in their budget,' Ava said, 'so I told him I'd work for free. Well, it was hell! It probably hastened his death. It was very, very difficult. One day we were doing a scene and George suddenly turned nasty. He was a wonderful man but could be extremely rude. When I was done, I left without saying goodbye. We didn't speak for a long time. Then I saw one of his old movies with Katharine Hepburn and Spencer Tracy, *Pat and Mike*. I sent him a telegram – "They don't make 'em like that anymore." And he wrote me a telegram back, "They don't make 'em like you anymore, Ava." George once told a reporter that I was a gentleman. I like that.'

Elizabeth Taylor, who was doing *The Blue Bird* for only a percentage of the profits, had the flu and a severe case of amoebic dysentery. She shared a bathroom with Ava, which was definitely not star accommodations for either actress. Despite everyone's illness in Russia, Ava's refusal to drink the water saved her from the same fate.

The Blue Bird failed dismally at the box office. *Cue* magazine wrote, 'If you have any naughty children you want to punish, take them to *The Blue Bird* and make them sit all the way through it.'

In a Grimms' fairy-tale setting, the two children of a woodcutter seek the bluebird of happiness in the past, the future, and the Land of Luxury, but eventually discover it in their own backyard. In the film Ava was 'Luxury.' Elizabeth played four parts – Mother, Maternal Love, Witch, and Light. Through it all she suffered from constant colds and flue, but regained her strength, finished *The Blue Bird*, and got Richard Burton back. Six weeks later they remarried.

Ava did a series of mediocre pictures in the late seventies: *Permission to Kill*, a boring spy melodrama, with Dirk Bogarde and Timothy Dalton; *City on Fire*, a shoddy disaster movie, with Henry Fonda and Barry Newman; and *The Sentinel*, about a haunted house that turns out to be the gateway to hell, with John Carradine, Jose Ferrer, Arthur Kennedy, and Burgess Meredith. *Newsweek* wrote that *The Sentinel* was a perfect film for those who like to slow down and look at traffic accidents. Ava cared less about reviews – 'I do it for the dough, honey!'

When she joined Sophia Loren, Burt Lancaster, and Richard Harris in Italy for *The Cassandra Crossing* in 1976, Sinatra feared for her safety from terrorists. He arranged for a limousine, driver, and bodyguard for Ava's protection.

On July 11 of the same year, Sinatra married forty-six-year-old Barbara Marx in Rancho Mirage, California. Author Kitty Kelley described Barbara as 'a blonde Ava Gardner without the layers of sensuousness – and without Ava's fiery temperament.'

After her first divorce, Barbara took her young son to Las Vegas and became a showgirl at the Riviera Hotel, where she met Zeppo Marx, youngest of the famous Marx brothers but twenty years older than Barbara. They were married in 1959 and moved to Palm Springs, where they became friendly with Sinatra. After thirteen years, the Marx marriage fell apart when Barbara fell in love with Frank, who refused to discuss marriage. Barbara pressed the issue and he broke off the relationship. But when she saw pictures of Sinatra with widow Jackie Kennedy Onassis, Barbara went back to Frank and he gave her a $360,000 diamond engagement ring. One major drawback to the marriage was Dolly, who disliked Barbara and refused to speak to her. Frank did not tell Mama about the wedding, but Dolly found out and telephoned her son from New

Jersey with a battery of curses.

Ava's statement to the press about the marriage was dignified and sincere: 'I'm glad he has found happiness with Barbara. Even though we were divorced long ago, I've always counted on Frank to advise me in business affairs. He's always been so generous with his time and interest. I'm sure his new wife won't object if I continue to call on him in the future.'

Six months later Dolly was killed in a plane crash on a flight from Palm Springs to Las Vegas. Devastated by his mother's death, Frank turned to religion for consolation. In 1978 he had his marriage to Nancy annulled. After Barbara converted to Catholicism, they were remarried by a priest. Marriages to Ava and Mia, outside the Church, were not recognized.

In the early seventies, Ava said it would be very difficult for her to adjust to marriage: 'When you're used to living on your own, you get selfish. I am very happy as I am.' She was tired of the hunt and bored with the catch.

Her frequent escorts were entertainer Bobby Short, MGM British representative Paul Mills, and actor Charles Gray, whose balcony faced hers. In his 1983 biography of Ava, Roland Flamini wrote, 'There was the black singer Freddie Davis, aged thirty. The year was 1974 and Ava was fifty-two. For Freddie's sake she even went on the wagon, more or less, checking into a well-known English health farm, Grayshott Hall, to dry out. "I'm not drinking anymore because I'm in love with Freddie," she told friends. "There was a time when I drank a lot, but I've drastically reduced the whiskey now." '

But Ava made peace with the bottle on her own, winding down her hectic social pace to fit into a more refined way of life in London. Maturity helped her separate happiness from contentment. Twenty years ago she had envied Grace Kelly's Camelot wedding to a prince, but Princess Grace's life was nowhere near a fairy tale. She wanted very much to resume acting.

When Grace announced her plans to make an Alfred Hitchcock movie, the people of Monaco objected so strongly that she gave in to their protests. She thought life in Monaco would be more rewarding than show business, but in an interview ten years later Grace was asked if she were happy. 'I don't expect to be,' she replied and went on to explain the illusion of happiness compared to contentment. A lonely lady, she dedicated herself to embroidery, painting, charities, and her children. When the eldest, twenty-one-year-old Caroline fell in love with Philippe Junot, Grace forbade them to marry. But her daughter threatened to 'live in sin' with the European playboy. 'Perhaps it's for the best,' Grace told Rainier. 'This way she'll have a successful second marriage.'

The wedding took place on June 29, 1978, preceded by a ball for eight hundred guests, attended by European royalty and Grace's Hollywood friends, Cary Grant, Frank and Barbara Sinatra, Gregory Peck, David Niven, and Ava Gardner. Frank sang 'My Way' to the bride and groom. As predicted by Grace, the marriage lasted only two years.

On September 14, 1982, Princess Grace was fatally injured in an automobile accident. She was fifty-three.

Ava said Her Serene Highness was a great lady and good fun. 'After a couple of dry martinis she was just another one of the girls dishing the dirt. In Africa she was so cute. A few glasses of champagne made her little nose turn red. She never forgot my birthday after

Mogambo. We got a bottle of champagne from some bootlegger, and she and Clark and John Ford and I had a party in the tent, for her birthday and then for mine. After that, no matter where in the world I was, every year a birthday present would arrive from Grace. She never forgot, and every year at Christmas she sent a handwritten card, not left for a secretary to do. We were never exactly bosom buddies, but very good friends.'

Nunnally Johnson died in 1977, and George Cukor in 1983. Howard Hughes and Jean Peters were divorced in 1970. He took up residence in London, moving into the Inn on the Park. Howard sent flowers to Ava on her fiftieth birthday and their friendship was renewed. A year later he went into final seclusion in the Bahamas and died on April 5, 1976.

It was only a matter of time before Ava accepted offers to appear on television. The public hadn't seen much of their favorite movie stars in a few years, preferring to watch TV instead. The power of television was foreign to Ava. 'It's getting to be the same in London,' she said in the early eighties. 'Everyone seems to be mad about shows like "Dynasty." I had arranged for a friend to see Frank's concert, and at the last minute she called it off, said she didn't feel well. That wasn't it. She wanted to stay home and watch "Dynasty"!'

Ava's agent convinced her to appear in seven episodes of 'Knots Landing' for $50,000 a show. The press responded with headlines of warmth, sincerity, and enthusiasm: THE GODDESS ON THE LITTLE SCREEN – THE GRAND LADY SWEEPS KNOTS LANDING OFF ITS FEET – TIME LEAVES LITTLE TRACE ON FILM'S LOVE GODDESS – WORLD'S MOST BEAUTIFUL ANIMAL ON TV.

In an article entitled, 'Gable to J.R. with Ava Gardner,' she said, 'Oh, television. It's awfully small, isn't it? Tatty. Except for J.R., he's not that small. I love "Dallas" and since it's Friday maybe I can find a lobster, bring it back to the room, and watch the program. I met J.R. last week and I was just as excited as I was the first time I met Clark Gable.'

In the *New York Daily News* (February 28, 1985), Kay Gardella wrote about Ava's appearance in 'Knots Landing':

> As a member of her loyal legions of fans, I awaited Ava Gardner's arrival on TV with keen anticipation. Please, I prayed to the cameras, be kind. Don't erase my memory of this sultry star, who did for brunettes on the screen what Grace Kelly did for blondes. A real beauty with an animal magnetism, she was the sexiest female in the movies, bar none.
>
> The cameraman heard my prayer. She's first seen standing with her back to the camera, in shadow. She's Ruth Galveston, wife of billionaire Paul Galveston, a man she married on his deathbed. She's still stately, well-dressed, wearing clothes that hide an extra pound or two. And although she's much older, the earmarks of having been a great beauty are still there – the almond eyes, arched eyebrows, and the perfectly shaped face, which looks like it's been allowed to age at its own pace, without the benefit of facelifts.

Ironically, the actor portraying Ava's husband Paul Galveston who dies in the first episode ... Howard Duff.

A reporter for *The New York Times* wrote:

The Barefoot Contessa wore rubber thongs. She walked over the cream carpet at the Waldorf Towers, which was the same shade of cream as her calves, in a pair of tight watermelon-pink toreador slacks. Above the slacks was a cherry-colored sweatshirt with a sequined letter 'A' over one breast, and above the red sweatshirt was a hot-pink scarf, above which was the face of Ava Gardner.

Miss Gardner's face will be appearing in two television projects in the next month, the first two she has ever done. The first is 'Knots Landing.' The second is 'A.D.,' a colossally produced mini-series about early Christian zealots.

With her green eyes and shaken-out auburn coif, Miss Gardner did not look so very different from the way she looked in *The Barefoot Contessa*. She sat with a bottle of spring water and chain-smoked. About 7:30 Miss Gardner exchanged the water for a Scotch. She said Mr. Sinatra is a great artist. 'He has a thing in his voice,' she explained. 'I've only heard it in three people: Maria Callas, Frank, and Judy Garland. A quality that makes me want to cry. These three people make me cry for happiness.'

Miss Gardner said that 'Knots Landing' made her 'a buck,' but thought she looked bad. 'I'm not terribly vain, but I don't like to look like a monster. And TV is too fast. It's a lovely thing for people of my age to watch, but it's for young people to make.'

As for her role in 'A.D.,' Ava made a face. 'I play a dreadful, horrible creature,' she sighed. 'I knock off my husband Claudius [Richard Kiley], and get bumped off by Nero [Anthony Andrews].'

In a Hollywood restaurant Ava was politely approached by a reporter for the *Los Angeles Times* and instead of throwing her drink at him, agreed to a brief chat. Before he sat down she said, 'I'd rather be misquoted than sit in front of a damn tape recorder.' Ava sat in the booth chewing gum, drinking and smoking, seemingly unaware that everyone in the restaurant was staring at her. She confessed to being a nervous actress who had to chew a mint to keep her mouth from drying up. 'Sometimes in scenes it looks as if I've got a loose tooth rolling around,' she laughed.

The reporter asked Ava if it was difficult chewing gum, drinking, and chain-smoking at the same time. 'Yes,' she said, continuing to do it with ease.

Did she have any beauty secrets? 'Soap and water at night. Cold water in the morning,' she replied, touching her face. 'I've certainly never taken the care of myself that I should have. On the contrary. I've done a lot of late nights without enough sleep and all that. But I've had fun. Whatever wrinkles are there, I've enjoyed getting them.' She appeared bored '. . . because I love London. The other day I was walking somewhere and it began pouring rain. I thought I should have taken all those movies offered me when I was in my thirties and forties – then I could have been driving a Rolls-Royce.' Changing moods again, Ava barked about 'Knots Landing': 'Nobody's going to offer me another job after this, I promise you. I look like hell among those babies.' The reporter didn't think she looked like hell at all. He wrote that she was very striking.

Critics said that Ava Gardner was the best thing in the sprawling 'A.D.' The consensus was that her claim that she was only working for money might be true, but she was too good too often. She opted for a four-hour TV version of 'The Long Hot Summer', William Faulkner's short story, with Jason Robards, Don Johnson, and Cybill Shepherd.

When Ava agreed to another miniseries entitled 'D'Ardenelle' with Omar Sharif and Sarah Miles, Liz Smith in the *Daily News* wrote in her column that, 'We never get enough of Ava Gardner these days. But at least we get something of a glamorous star who used to sizzle at MGM.'

❧

For Ava 1985 was a busy year. She would be eligible for her MGM pension in two years. 'Then I can stop working altogether,' she said. 'I might do one more picture before then, but I haven't made up my mind.'

She was glad to get back to England and her dog, Morgan. Ava wasn't seen again in public until the memorial service in London for her dear friend Robert Graves on January 22, 1986. He had died the month before at the age of 90. She stood in the windswept, pouring rain until someone came to the rescue with an umbrella.

❧

In 1981 a hometown admirer of Ava Gardner decided Smithfield, North Carolina, should pay tribute to their famous daughter. Tom Banks bought the old teacherage where Ava lived with her mother. 'That's where Ava played in the dirt and climbed the water tower in the back,' he recalled. Banks displayed his memorabilia – posters from all of Ava's movies, costumes she wore in twenty films, scripts, hundreds of photographs, and twenty-six oil portraits – in the old building that is now called the Ava Gardner Museum.

Ava was so touched she welcomed Banks and his wife whenever they were in London. 'Bappie has been to the museum,' he said. 'Their brother Melvin, a former state legislator, died in 1981. A sister Inez died a month later. And Elsie, the second-oldest sister, died in 1986. We miss old Elsie. She was a frequent visitor to the museum.'

The teacherage containing the museum stands between Best's Store and the brick shell of Brogden School, which burned down on New Year's Eve 1985.

Joe Hyams came the closest to finding out the root of Ava's lack of security and direction during their jaunt to Mexicali. She told him, 'I worshipped and adored my father and was much closer to him than my mother. In a sense that sums up my relationships with the other men in my life. I've never received as much love as I've given.' Because her conversation was 'sprinkled with psychological jargon,' Hyams concluded the death of Ava's father and growing up without his love and guidance were the key to her vulnerability. When he asked her about this she lunged across the table at him.

There is a pattern, however, and not necessarily coincidental, that Jean Harlow, Joan Crawford, Marilyn Monroe, Lana Turner, Clara Bow, and Judy

Garland grew up without the guidance of a father. These women had everything else – glamour, beauty, sex appeal, fame, and desirability.

Ava was the only member of the family to inherit her father's green eyes, his dimpled chin, volatile temper, and passionate appetites. He died as she was blossoming into womanhood – at a time when she needed a strong and self-confident male image. She never knew what it was like to be loved and hugged by a man who wanted only her happiness, with nothing in return.

Ava's comment about how lucky Grace Kelly was to have a father to lean on was another clue. It was a beautiful observation in the midst of a commoner marrying a prince.

Joe Hyams did a thorough job researching the article about Ava. His wife, Elke Sommer, thought he was *too* perceptive, and the editor for *Look* magazine felt the story destroyed Ava's glamorous image. 'I had not meant to be cruel,' Hyams said, 'but I portrayed what I found – a restless, tormented woman, who raced recklessly through life seeking happiness in a love she would never be able to find.'

Despite the heartbreak and tumultuous romances, however, Ava will always have a substitute father to look after her. Without Frank Sinatra, she might not have been as staunch a survivor.

On October 6, 1986, Ava was flown from London to Saint John's Hospital in Santa Monica, California, suffering from a persistent virus that developed into pneumonia. During her illness Ava had a minor stroke.

While she was being treated in a Los Angeles hospital, Sinatra was admitted to the Eisenhower Medical Center in Rancho Mirage, a suburb of Palm Springs, for an acute attack of diverticulitis. On November 9, doctors removed an abscess from his large intestine during a two-hour operation. He was in a great deal of pain, but no cancer was found in the twelve inches of large intestine removed.

Five months previously Sinatra had two benign polyps removed from his colon and a small patch of skin cancer cut out from underneath his left eye.

Cindy Adams wrote in her column that Kitty Kelley's unauthorized biography about Frank, released in late 1986, was as painful to him – mentally and emotionally – as the operation. One of Sinatra's friends told Adams, 'If someone wrote a book about me that had this kind of killing stuff, it would cause me stress, too.'

Ava was still confined at Saint John's when Frank was discharged from the hospital on November 17. He made sure she did not want for anything. Money was no object. In March Ava was back in London. A picture of her sitting on a park bench doing therapeutic exercises with her nurse appeared in the newspapers. The photo was unkind – arms raised over her head, a pained but determined expression on her face.

Ava's respiratory problems persisted and she returned to Saint John's Hospital in January 1988. Sinatra spent $50,000 to have her flown from London to California in an air ambulance. He kept in touch every day by telephone. Her expenses were enormous, and reliable sources said Frank spent over £1 million on Ava's recovery. A Hollywood columnist wrote, 'Sinatra still affectionately calls Ava a "broad" – and when he sent a huge floral arrangement to her, the note was signed "Chi-Chi," her old pet name for him.'

In May she was back home with her beloved Morgan, strolling through London's damp springtime streets. 'Everything is okay,' she said. 'I'm not ready to be written off yet.'

Ava Gardner, the reluctant goddess, bore the distinction of being MGM's final mold of a screen legend, but it was not only her extraordinary beauty that made her one of the great movie stars. Her image, which was quickly developed, was that of the independent-minded, worldly wise, and sexually knowledgeable good-bad dame who fascinates men and worries women. She was the girl from the wrong side of the tracks who crossed over carrying her shoes and not asking for anyone's help.

Epilogue

Ava Gardner died of pneumonia in London on January 25, 1990 at the age of sixty-seven. For the few years preceding her death she was plagued by ill health, and she remained a recluse until the end. Those who loved and admired Ava will remember her as a vibrant woman who lived life with the zest and passion that novelists attempt to emulate in fiction.

Even the film goers of today who might not have been around in Ava's glory days will discover – through video rentals and revival theaters – the appeal of the actress's most memorable characters – the electrifying Maria Vargas in *The Barefoot Contessa*, the saucy Honey Bear in *Mogambo*, or the hard-bitten Maxine in *The Night of the Iguana*.

She could not be possessed by anyone during her turbulent lifetime, but Ava Gardner belongs to us on film . . . now and forever.

The Films of Ava Gardner

Ava Gardner's Screen Appearances as an Extra at Metro-Goldwyn-Mayer

1942: *We Were Dancing; Joe Smith American; Sunday Punch; Calling Mr Gillespie; This Time for Keeps; Kid Glove Killer; Pilot No. 5*

1943: *Hitler's Madman; Reunion in France; Du Barry Was a Lady; Young Ideas; Lost Angel; Ghosts on the Loose* (Monogram Pictures)

1944: *Spring Fever; Music for Millions*

Films in Which Ava Gardner Played Significant Roles

Three Men in White
(MGM, 1944)
Director: Willis Goldbeck
Cast: Lionel Barrymore, Van Johnson, Marilyn Maxwell, Ava Gardner

Ava tried to vamp Van Johnson, an intern applicant for the job of Doctor Gillespie's assistant.

Maisie Goes to Reno
(MGM, 1944)
Director: Harry Beaumont
Cast: Ann Southern, John Hodiak, Tom Drake, Ava Gardner

Ava plays the millionairess wife of Tom Drake.

She Went to the Races
(MGM, 1945)
Director: Willis Goldbeck
Cast: James Craig, Edmund Gwenn, Ava Gardner

In this comedy, a scheming Ava gets involved with a group of professors who have a foolproof system of picking horserace winners.

Whistle Stop
(United Artists, 1946)
Director: Leonide Moguy
Cast: George Raft, Ava Gardner, Tom Conway, Victor McLaglen

A city girl returns to her small-town home and finds herself torn between a nightclub proprietor and an indolent charmer. From a novel by Maritta M. Wolff.

The Killers
(Universal, 1946)
Director: Robert Siodmak
Cast: Burt Lancaster, Edmond O'Brien, Ava Gardner, Albert Dekker

In a small sleazy town a gangster waits for two assassins to kill him, and we later find out why. Ava plays a gang moll. From a short story by Ernest Hemingway.

The Hucksters
(MGM, 1947)

Director: Jack Conway
Cast: Clark Gable, Deborah Kerr, Ava Gardner, Sidney Greenstreet, Adolph Menjou, Keenan Wynn, Edward Arnold

Back from the war, an advertising executive finds it difficult to put up with his clients' tantrums. Ava plays a good-time girl who falls in love with Gable, but is rejected in favor of prim and proper Kerr. From a novel by Frederic Wakeman.

Singapore
(Universal, 1947)

Director: John Brahm
Cast: Fred MacMurray, Ava Gardner, Roland Culver

Ava is a tragic war victim who has lost her memory in a bombing raid in Singapore. When special agent MacMurray returns postwar, she resumes her affair with him.

One Touch of Venus
(Universal, 1948)

Director: William A. Seiter
Cast: Ava Gardner, Robert Walker, Eve Arden, Dick Haymes, Olga San Juan, Tom Conway

In a fashionable department store, a statue of Venus (Ava) comes to life and falls in love with a window dresser. From a play by S.J. Perelman.

The Great Sinner
(MGM, 1949)

Director: Robert Siodmak
Cast: Gregory Peck, Walter Huston, Ava Gardner, Agnes Moorehead, Ethel Barrymore, Melvyn Douglas, Frank Morgan

A serious young writer becomes a compulsive gambler. Ava plays the daughter of an inveterate card player who attempts to reform Peck.

East Side, West Side
(MGM, 1949)

Director: Mervyn LeRoy
Cast: James Mason, Barbara Stanwyck, Van Heflin, Ava Gardner, Gale Sondergaard, Cyd Charisse, Nancy Davis, William Conrad

A New York businessman is torn between his wife and another woman, Ava. From a novel by Marcia Davenport.

The Bribe
(MGM, 1949)

Director: Robert Z. Leonard
Cast: Robert Taylor, Ava Gardner, Charles Laughton, Vincent Price, John Hodiak

A U.S. agent tracks down a group of criminals in Central America. Ava, married to Hodiak, becomes involved in counter-espionage and with another man.

My Forbidden Past
(RKO, 1951)

Director: Robert Stevenson
Cast: Ava Gardner, Melvyn Douglas, Robert Mitchum, Janis Carter, Lucille Watson

A New Orleans beauty (Ava) seeks vengeance when

her cousin prevents her marriage to the man she loves.
From a novel by Polan Banks.

Pandora and the Flying Dutchman
(MGM, 1951)

Director: Albert Lewin
Cast: James Mason, Ava Gardner, Harold Warrender,
Nigel Patrick, Mario Cabre

A cold but beautiful Ava, an American woman in
Spain, falls for a mystery man, who turns out to be a
ghostly sea captain. To be with him she dies.

Showboat
(MGM, 1951)

Director: George Sidney
Cast: Kathryn Grayson, Howard Keel, Ava Gardner,
William Warfield, Joe E. Brown, Robert Sterling,
Marge and Gower Champion, Agnes
Moorehead

Lives and loves of the people on an old Mississippi
showboat. Ava portrays a tragic mulatto.

Lone Star
(MGM, 1952)

Director: Vincent Sherman
Cast: Clark Gable, Ava Gardner, Lionel Barrymore,
Broderick Crawford, Ed Begley, Beulah Bondi

Ava plays a tempestuous Texas newspaperwoman in
this story of Andrew Jackson and Texas's fight against
the Union.

The Snows of Kilimanjaro
(20th Century-Fox, 1952)

Director: Henry King
Cast: Gregory Peck, Susan Hayward, Ava Gardner,
    Hildegarde Neff

A wounded hunter reflects on his life. Ava plays the woman he loved and lost and finds again as he lies dying during the Spanish Civil War. From a short story by Ernest Hemingway.

Ride, Vaquero
(MGM, 1953)

Director: John Farrow
Cast: Robert Taylor, Ava Gardner, Howard Keel,
    Anthony Quinn

Ava is married to rancher Keel but menaced by bandit Taylor in this western set in nineteenth-century Utah.

Mogambo
(MGM, 1953)

Director: John Ford
Cast: Clark Gable, Ava Gardner, Grace Kelly, Donald
    Sinden

The headquarters of a Kenyan white hunter (Gable) is invaded by an American showgirl (Ava, as Honey Bear) and a British couple. A remake of 1932's Red Dust with Clark Gable and Jean Harlow.

Knights of the Round Table
(MGM, 1953)

Director: Richard Thorpe
Cast: Robert Taylor, Mel Ferrer, Ava Gardner, Anne
    Crawford, Stanley Baker

Lancelot, banished from King Arthur's court for loving Guinevere (Ava), returns to defeat the evil Mordred.

The Barefoot Contessa
(United Artists, 1954)
Director: Joseph Mankiewicz
Cast: Humphrey Bogart, Ava Gardner, Edmond
O'Brien, Marius Goring, Rossano Brazzi

A glamorous barefoot dancer in a Spanish cabaret, Ava
is turned into a Hollywood star: a Cinderella story that
ends in tragedy when the prince turns out to be
impotent.

Bhowani Junction
(MGM, 1956)
Director: George Cukor
Cast: Ava Gardner, Stewart Granger, Francis
Matthews, Bill Travers

The adventures of an Anglo-Indian girl (Ava) during the
last days of British India. From a novel by John Masters.

The Little Hut
(MGM, 1957)
Director: Mark Robson
Cast: Stewart Granger, David Niven, Ava Gardner,
Walter Chiari

Ava plays a showgirl stranded on a tropical island with
three handsome men. From a play by Andre Roussin.

The Sun Also Rises
(20th Century-Fox, 1957)
Director: Henry King
Cast: Tyrone Power, Ava Gardner, Errol Flynn, Eddie
Albert, Mel Ferrer, Robert Evans, Juliette Greco

Ava plays Lady Brett, an unhappy woman in love with
the impotent Jake Barnes (Power), as their odd group
of friends roam aimlessly around Europe. From a novel
by Ernest Hemingway.

The Naked Maja
(MGM, 1959)

Director: Henry Koster
Cast: Ava Gardner, Anthony Franciosa, Amedeo Nazzari, Gino Cervi

Ava is the violent Duchess of Alba, patroness and lover of painter Goya (Franciosa).

On the Beach
(United Artists, 1959)

Director: Stanley Kramer
Cast: Gregory Peck, Ava Gardner, Fred Astaire, Anthony Perkins

About the end of the world following an atomic holocaust, Ava is a sad Australian party girl in love with scientist Peck. From a novel by Nevil Shute.

The Angel Wore Red
(MGM, 1960)

Director: Nunnally Johnson
Cast: Ava Gardner, Dirk Bogarde, Joseph Cotten, Vittorio De Sica

Ava plays a prostitute in love with a priest during the Spanish Civil War.

55 Days at Peking
(Allied Artists, 1963)

Director: Nicholas Ray
Cast: Charlton Heston, Ava Gardner, David Niven, Flora Robson, Paul Lukas, John Ireland

Ava is a Russian countess in this story of the Boxer Rebellion in China.

Seven Days in May
(Paramount, 1964)
Director: John Frankenheimer
Cast: Ava Gardner, Burt Lancaster, Kirk Douglas, Frederic March, Martin Balsam

Ava, a Washington society hostess, helps in disrupting a fascist anti-presidential plot. From a novel by Fletcher Knebel and Charles W. Bailey II.

The Night of the Iguana
(MGM, 1964)
Director: John Huston
Cast: Richard Burton, Deborah Kerr, Ava Gardner, Sue Lyon, Grayson Hall, Cyril Delevanti

Burton, a defrocked clergyman, becomes a tour guide in Mexico. Ava plays Maxine, a hotelkeeper who befriends him. From the play by Tennessee Williams.

The Bible
(20th Century-Fox, 1966)
Director: John Huston
Cast: John Huston, George C. Scott, Ava Gardner, Peter O'Toole, Stephen Boyd

The Old Testament from Adam to Isaac. Ava is Sarah, the barren wife of Abraham.

Mayerling
(MGM, 1968)
Director: Terence Young
Cast: Ava Gardner, Omar Sharif, Catherine Deneuve, James Mason

Ava is the Empress of Austria in this tragic story of her son's suicide pact with his mistress in 1889. From a novel by Claude Anet.

The Devil's Widow (also known as *Tam-Lin*)
(Commonwealth United, 1971)
Director: Roddy McDowall
Cast: Ava Gardner, Ian MacShane, Stephanie Beacham, Richard Wattis, Cyril Cusack

Ava, a sinister, beautiful, middle-aged widow, has a diabolic influence on the bright young people she gathers around her.

The Life and Times of Judge Roy Bean
(United Artists, 1972)
Director: John Huston
Cast: Paul Newman, Ava Gardner, Jacqueline Bisset, Tab Hunter, Stacy Keach, Roddy McDowall, Anthony Perkins

A fantasia on the famous outlaw judge who names a Western town after an actress he worshipped for years. Ava plays his idol, Lillie Langtry.

Earthquake
(Universal, 1974)
Director: Mark Robson
Cast: Charlton Heston, Ava Gardner, Lorne Greene, Barry Sullivan, George Kennedy, Genevieve Bujold, Walter Matthau

Various personal stories intertwine during a Los Angeles earthquake. Ava is cast as Heston's wife, who fights for her husband's love and her life during the quake.

The Blue Bird
(20th Century-Fox, 1976)
Director: George Cukor
Cast: Elizabeth Taylor, Ava Gardner, Cicely Tyson, Jane Fonda, Harry Andrews

In a Grimms' fairy-tale setting, the two children of a poor woodcutter seek the bluebird of happiness in the past, the future, and the Land of Luxury – personified by Ava. From a play by Maurice Maeterlinck.

Permission to Kill
(Warner Brothers, 1975)
Director: Cyril Frankel
Cast: Ava Gardner, Dirk Bogarde, Bekim Fehmiu, Timothy Dalton

British agents try to stop a Communist returning home from the West. From a novel by Robin Estridge.

The Sentinel
(Universal, 1976)
Director: Michael Winner
Cast: Ava Gardner, Jose Ferrer, Arthur Kennedy, Burgess Meredith, John Carradine

A haunted house turns out to be the gateway to hell.

The Cassandra Crossing
(AGF/CCC/International Cine, 1976)
Director: George Pan Cosmatos
Cast: Sophia Loren, Richard Harris, Ava Gardner, Burt Lancaster, Martin Sheen, Lee Strasberg

A terrorist carries a plague virus on a transcontinental train.

City on Fire
(Astral-Bellevue-Pathe, 1979)
Director: Alvin Rakoff
Cast: Ava Gardner, Henry Fonda, Susan Clark, Barry Newman, Shelley Winters, James Franciscus

A slum fire threatens an entire city.

The Kidnapping of the President
(Sefel Pictures, 1980)
Director: George Mendeluk
Cast: William Shatner, Hal Holbrook, Ava Gardner,
Van Johnson

Third-world terrorists devise a plot to bring America to its knees by kidnapping the president.

Priest of Love
(Filmways Pictures Inc.-Enterprise Pictures Ltd., 1981)
Director: Christopher Miles
Cast: Ian McKellan, Janet Suzman, Sir John Gielgud,
Ava Gardner

The last years of D.H. Lawrence, when his books were banned and he was seeking a warmer climate to help his TB.

Ava Gardner's Television Appearances

'Knot's Landing' (CBS), 1985, special guest star

'A.D.' (NBC), mini-series, 1985

'The Long Hot Summer' (NBC), 1985

'Maggie' (CBS), 1986

Selected Bibliography

Books

Bacall, Lauren, *By Myself* (Knopf, 1979).

Bacon, James, *Hollywood is a Four-Letter Town* (Regnery, 1976).

Bradford, Sarah, *Princess Grace* (Stein & Day, 1984).

Conttrell, John, and Fergus Caskin, *Richard Burton* (Prentice-Hall, 1972).

Daniell, John, *Ava Gardner* (St Martin's Press, 1982).

Eells, George, *Robert Mitchum* (Franklin Watts, 1984).

Flamini, Roland, *Ava* (Coward, McCann and Geoghegan, 1983).

Graham, Sheila, *Confessions of a Hollywood Columnist* (William Morrow, 1969).

Hanna, David, *Ava* (Putnam, 1960).

Higham, Charles, *Ava* (Delacorte, 1974).

Higham, Charles, *Bette* (Macmillan, 1981).

Huston, John, *An Open Book* (Knopf, 1980).

Hyams, Joe, *Mislaid in Hollywood* (Wyden, 1973).

Kelley, Kitty, *His Way* (Bantam, 1986).

Keyes, Evelyn, *Scarlet O'Hara's Younger Sister* (Lyle Stuart, 1977).

Kobal, John, *People Will Talk* (Knopf, 1986).

Linet, Beverly, *Star-Crossed: The Story of Robert Walker and Jennifer Jones* (Putnam, 1986).

Parish, James Robert, *MGM Stock Company* (Arlington House, 1973).

Pastos, Spero, *Pin-Up: The Tragedy of Betty Grable* (Putnam, 1986).

Pero, Taylor, and Jeff Rovin, *Always Lana* (Bantam, 1982)

Rooney, Mickey, *I.E. Autobiography* (G.P. Putnam, 1965).

Seymour-Smith, Martin, *Robert Graves* (Henry Holt & Co., 1982).

Shaw, Arnold, *Sinatra* (Holt, Rinehart & Winston, 1968).

Spada, James, *Grace* (Dolphin Doubleday, 1987).

Torme, Mel, *It Wasn't All Velvet* (Viking, 1988).

Turner, Lana, *Lana* (Dutton, 1982).

Wayne, Jane Ellen, *Gable's Women* (Prentice-Hall, 1987).

Wayne, Jane Ellen, *Robert Taylor* (St Martin's, 1989).

Winters, Shelley, *Shelley* (William Morrow & Co., 1980).

Other Sources

Dr Thomas M. Banks, founder, The Ava Gardner Museum, Smithfield, North Carolina

Library of Performing Arts, Lincoln Center, New York City

Pat Wilks-Battle, *The New York Post* (clippings from national and international newspaper files)

Index

293